The Pickled Pantry

BIG HARVEST DILL PICKLES

HERBED JARDINIÉRE

KIMCHI

TOMATILLO SALSA

ITALIAN TOMATO RELISH

GINGER PEAR CHUTNEY

SAUERKRAUT

THE Pickled Pantry

Andrea Chesman

Illustrations by Lisa Congdon

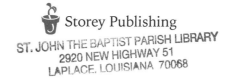

Storey Publishing

To Sam, the pickle palate master, whose boundless enthusiasm kept me going

*The mission of Storey Publishing is to serve our customers by
publishing practical information that encourages
personal independence in harmony with the environment.*

Edited by Margaret Sutherland and Pam Thompson
Art direction and book design by Mary Winkelman Velgos
Text production by Vicky Vaughn Shea/Ponderosa Pine Design
Indexed by Andrea Chesman

Illustrations by © Lisa Congdon/Lilla Rogers Studio
Photography by © Addie Holland 17, © David Shankbone/Wikimedia Commons 245,
    © John Polak 214, © Rick's Picks LLC 78, © Robert Waterhouse 24, © Sebastian Collett 38,
    © Xan Price 138, © Yvonne Tchida 220, and © Zac Wolf 128

Storey Publishing
210 MASS MoCA Way
North Adams, MA 01247
www.storey.com

Printed in the United States by Versa
10 9 8 7 6 5 4 3 2 1

Library of Congress Cataloging-in-Publication Data

Chesman, Andrea.
  The pickled pantry / by Andrea Chesman.
      p. cm.
  Includes index.
  ISBN 978-1-60342-562-9 (pbk. : alk. paper)
  1. Pickles. I. Title.
TX805.C437 2012
641.6'162—dc23
                          2012004608

contents

Introduction

People come to pickling for so many reasons. Some people are motivated by sheer love of eating all things sour. Others are practical do-it-yourselfers who pickle to preserve excess produce or to extend their options for eating local year-round. Still others are preserving tradition. I came to pickling for a combination of those reasons.

I made my first batch of pickles a long time ago. I was a recent college graduate with my first garden, a small patch in a community garden. What a thrilling experience it was. I put a seed in the ground, and it grew!

Naturally I wanted to pack all that freshly harvested goodness into jars to preserve it for the coming winter. I asked my grandmother how she made her pickles. My grandmother was not a woman enthralled by the domestic arts, nor was she overly chatty. She told me to put cucumbers and dill in a crock, cover them with water, then add enough salt so "it's just before you gag."

Did I mention my grandmother had an indomitable will and a cast-iron stomach? I followed her instructions to the letter, adding only enough salt so it was just before I gagged. Within days, I had a slimy, foul-smelling brew. Apparently, our gag reflexes did not match. It was years before I tried pickling again.

Many gardens later, I had the opportunity to collect pickle recipes and gather them together for a book. It began with a "pickle barter party." Because so many traditional recipes yielded seven or nine jars of pickles (a boiling-water-bath canner load), I thought it would be a great idea to swap jars of home-canned pickles the same way people swap cookies at

Christmastime. My friends were all fellow back-to-the-landers, and preserving food by canning, pickling, and freezing was part of the lifestyle. Today's urban food swaps accomplish much the same thing.

For the book *Pickles & Relishes: 150 Recipes from Apples to Zucchini*, I tested hundreds of different types of pickles. Each batch of pickles was tasted and evaluated by a group of colleagues at Garden Way Publishing (which later became Storey Publishing, the publisher of this book). Throughout the better part of a year, I brought a jar of pickles to work each day to be sampled and evaluated at lunch by pickle aficionados. We called it the "pickle du jour program."

What I learned as I tasted my way through batch after batch of pickles is that preferences vary widely. For some people, no pickle is too sweet; others hate garlic. But inevitably, there is a perfect pickle for every taste. It just requires collecting and inventing many, many recipes.

Over the years, I've watched many trends in pickle making. In the 1970s, many people rediscovered pickle making as they moved "back to the land" and reclaimed many traditional skills: home brewing, wool spinning, bread baking, and, of course, pickle making.

Then came the health food years, when many people, including myself, worried about salt and sugar in pickles. I had a few "no salt" pickle recipes in my first book that I don't think about revisiting. Interest in making pickles waned as the global super-market enticed Americans to eat fresh foods regardless of the season. In the 1980s, few saw the need to preserve food as long as the supermarket was able to supply fresh veg-etables year-round. A couple of times I was asked to teach a pickling course, but the courses failed to attract many students.

A lot of pickling knowl-edge wasn't so much lost as it was buried, skipping a genera-tion or two.

Recently a perfect storm of food safety scares plus an economic downturn has led many people to reconsider gardening and preserving. A desire to eat local foods in season and reduce the carbon footprint of the food we eat has made pickle making par-ticularly attractive. As people have delved into local foods, a whole artisanal food movement around fermented foods — making wine, cheese, beer, and lacto-fermented vegetables and fruit (i.e., pickles) — has evolved. Some pickle devo-tees are attracted to claims regarding the health benefits of fermented foods, while others are enthusiastic about reviving traditional foodways. And, of course, pickles taste good!

Pickles are foods preserved with either salt or vinegar. Both the salt and vinegar act to inhibit the growth of spoilage bacteria. Pickles may contain enough acid to keep well in a refrigerator without heat processing, or they may be canned (i.e., processed in a boiling-water bath). Some pickles can be frozen.

When pickles are preserved in salt, they may be called crock pickles, salt pickles, brined pickles, fermented pickles, or lacto-fermented pickles. Whatever you call them, these are, I think, the most wonderful pickles, preserved by methods that have changed little over the centuries. Pickles that are preserved with vinegar are called fresh-pack pickles or vinegar pickles, because the vegetables are packed fresh into a vinegar solution. Bread and butter pickles are a traditional favorite among the many fresh-pack pickles. Most fresh-pack pickles are processed in a boiling water bath for long keeping.

This book explores all the options for making pickles: in a crock, in a jar, with salt, with vinegar, for the freezer, as a relish or chutney. It also includes some special recipes that make use of the pickles, such as Korean Bulgogi Tacos with Kimchi, (page 284), all-American Sweet Pickle Macaroni Salad (page 251), and Roasted and Braised Duck with Sauerkraut and Root Vegetables (page 274).

Before the advent of the global supermarket, when people ate with the seasons, pickles served to punch up the flavors of a meal. The same root vegetables or hearty cabbage-family greens were served meal after meal after meal. Most home cooks had one ethnic style of food in their repertoire, and menus were repeated often. Pickles added much-needed spice. Pickles can fulfill that same role once again. There's no point in making pickles if you aren't going to enjoy them.

People unfamiliar with preserving often think it involves a lot of slaving over a hot stove. In the old days, when you had to fire up the woodstove to get the canner heated, it was a hot job. But a good exhaust fan does wonders for removing steam from a kitchen. Power burners on newer-model stoves reduce the length of time needed to bring the canning water up to temperature. Food processors, dishwashers, and other handy tools ease the labor considerably. We can even bring music into the kitchen to keep our feet moving!

Another myth is that most fermented pickles take a long time to cure, and the dangers of spoilage are great. In fact, many brined pickles ferment for just a day or two and are then refrigerated to slow down fermentation and prevent molds from growing. It is a much easier process than most people think.

Let's get started.

PRODUCE MATH

This chart may help you gauge quantities, but remember the numbers are all approximate. Shape, degree of ripeness, variety, and shape of container will affect the weight of your produce in relation to volume. Tomatoes, in particular, vary depending on degree of ripeness and variety (plum tomatoes have less juice than beefsteak types).

PRODUCE	WEIGHT	APPROXIMATE QUANTITY	YIELD
Apples	1 pound	6 medium	3 cups chopped
Beets	1 pound	4 to 5 medium	2 to 3 cups cubed
Bell peppers	1 pound	2 to 3 medium to large	2 to 3 cups diced
Cabbage	1 pound	1 small head	3½ cups shredded
	2 pounds	1 medium head	7 to 8 cups shredded
Carrots	1 pound	4 large	2½ cups sliced or diced
Cauliflower	1½ pounds	1 medium head	4 cups florets
Corn		16 to 20 ears	8 cups kernels
Cucumbers	1 pound	3 pickling	2½ to 3 cups sliced
	6 pounds	100 tiny	1 gallon
Green beans	1 pound	3 to 4 cups	2⅔ to 3½ cups chopped
Okra	1 pound	20 medium	4 cups
Onions	1 pound	3 large	2 to 2½ cups diced
Peaches	1 pound	3 to 5 medium	2 to 2½ cups peeled and sliced
Pears	1 pound	4 medium	2½ cups peeled and sliced
Plums, prune	1 pound	12 to 20	2 cups sliced
Rhubarb	1 pound	4 to 8 stalks	4 cups diced
Summer squash and zucchini	1 pound	2 small	4 cups sliced
Tomatoes	1 pound	3 medium globe 8 small plum 25 to 30 cherry	2 cups cubed 3 cups quartered or cut in wedges

Chapter 1

All About Pickling

Pickling happens all over the world, and with all sorts of ingredients. It is a process that preserves food by increasing its acidity and making an inhospitable environment for the microbes responsible for spoilage. Some pickles are fermented, a process in which anaerobic bacteria are encouraged to convert naturally occurring sugars in the food to lactic acid. The lactic acid is what flavors authentic kosher dills, sauerkraut, and kimchi. It is also responsible for preserving the vegetables. Other pickles, especially traditional American and British pickles, are infused with vinegar and canned or refrigerated for long-term storage.

If you are an old hand at pickling and canning, feel free to skip ahead to the recipes. If you have questions about ingredients, equipment, or heat processing, read on.

Ingredients

You can pickle just about every fruit and vegetable — and eggs, fish, and meats. So let's start with the main ingredient.

The difference between a good pickle and a great pickle is often the freshness of the ingredients you use.

Select young, even slightly immature fresh fruits and vegetables. The less-than-perfect fruits and vegetables that you harvest or buy can be used in cooked relishes, but not when you are making whole or sliced pickles.

Chill your produce as quickly and thoroughly as possible. This is particularly important with cucumbers and zucchini if you want a crisp pickle — and who doesn't? Your fruits and vegetables will make crisper pickles if they are harvested early in the day, before they have been wilted by the heat of the sun. Then it is important to get that produce pickled or chilled as soon as possible.

Ideally, you should make your produce into pickles as soon as you harvest. But that isn't always possible. If you are a gardener, you know that allowing a cucumber or squash to stay one extra day on the vine may result in an overgrown monster. And, if you are a CSA member, you know that your pickup is on Saturdays (or whenever) and you can't go to the farm anytime it fits your pickling schedule.

So what do you do when the refrigerator is full? My refrigerator is full even before the harvest season begins. My family jokes that I inherited my refrigerator-management skills from my mother, whose refrigerator contained archival records of meals served long ago. But, in my defense (and yours, perhaps?), it is inevitable that if you make pickles, you will end up with refrigerator shelves bursting with half-filled jars of pickles. If you find pickles piling up in your refrigerator, consider the recipes in chapter 7 as a means to use up your overflow.

But back to the problem at hand: chilling the produce. I find it convenient to store fresh vegetables in a large picnic cooler layered with ice made by freezing water in sealable plastic bags. The bags are heavy-duty and designed for the freezer; they can be reused. If you go this route, just remember that water expands as it freezes, so don't fill a bag more than two-thirds full, and squeeze out as much air as possible.

When a recipe calls for soaking the vegetables in ice water, you can use the freezer bags or ice cubes. If the recipe doesn't call for soaking, don't do it. Vegetables and fruits can become waterlogged and lose crispness. In fact, don't even wash your produce until you are ready to pickle. If you must refrigerate or store your produce over ice, store it unwashed.

If you don't grow your own produce for pickling, try to buy directly from local farmers — at roadside stands, at farmers' markets, or through a CSA.

CONTINUED ON PAGE 14

CRISP IS THE HOLY GRAIL OF PICKLE MAKING

The reality is that crispness is the holy grail of pickles, and heat is the enemy of crispness. The crisp in a pickle is derived from pectin in the cell walls. Heat breaks down pectin, as do the actions of certain bacteria. So if only crisp pickles will do, focus on salt-brined and refrigerator pickles. If long-term preservation is the goal, then here are some tips for mitigating the effects of the heat of the boiling water bath.

- Use freshly harvested vegetables that have been kept chilled.
- Pickling cucumbers make a better pickle than salad cucumbers. Salad cucumbers take up water to grow big. As for the pickling cucumber, smaller is better.
- Remove the blossom end from each cucumber. The blossom harbors enzymes that can cause softening.
- Instead of the boiling water bath, consider using low-temperature pasteurization. It is a fussy method, and takes longer, but it does create a slightly crisper pickle. Cucumber pickles can be processed for 30 minutes at temperatures between 180°F and 185°F. According to the USDA, this method is safe only if you are certain that the water temperature remains above 180°F during the entire 30 minutes. If it drops below 180°F at any time, you need to start the timing all over again.
- Use Pickle Crisp Granules (see page 22).

CUCUMBER VARIETIES

Although you can pickle any cucumber, some varieties are better for pickles than others. Basically, you want a thin cucumber with a good ratio of crunchy skin to softer middle. Pickling cucumbers have thinner skin and crisper, crunchier flesh than most slicers. This means "pickling" cucumbers are better than "slicing" cucumbers for pickles. Among pickling varieties, there are plenty of choices and all are good for eating in salads as well as pickling. I no longer grow slicing or salad varieties.

American Pickling Cucumbers. Kirby is the best known of the American pickling varieties, but there are others that share characteristics with Kirby cukes. Most are mature at 3 to 5 inches in length and are blocky in shape. These are the cucumbers of choice for kosher dills.

European Pickling Cucumbers. These can be harvested small (at 2 to 3 inches in length) for gherkins. The skins are smoother than those of American picklers.

Middle Eastern Cucumbers. Also called Persian or Beit Alpha cucumbers, these cucumbers make excellent pickles when harvested at ¾ inch in diameter and 5 to 6 inches in length. They have few seeds and thin, bumpy dark green skin. They are tender and crunchy, with a delicate, very pleasant, mildly sweet flavor. If allowed to grow large, however, the seeds become bitter.

Japanese Cucumbers. The ridged Japanese cucumber is dark green and slender with tiny bumps. Thin-skinned with small seeds, Japanese cucumbers have a crisp texture and a clear sweet flavor. Trellises are recommended for straight fruit, which can be 11 to 12 inches long.

The produce will be fresher. If you buy your produce from the supermarket, beware of waxed fruits and vegetables. Supermarket suppliers coat some produce with a thin film of wax to prevent moisture loss and add a glossy shine. Pickling brine cannot penetrate the waxy coating, and it is impossible to remove the wax without using scalding hot water, which will cook the produce. Cucumbers, bell peppers, apples, grapes, and plums are most commonly waxed.

I SAY "CUCUMBER," YOU SAY "PICKLE."

Even though we pickle a great number of vegetables and fruits in the United States, when we say "pickle," we usually mean a pickled cucumber. So, in a diner, if a sandwich comes with "chips and a pickle," that pickle is invariably a dilled pickle spear. This is due to the profound impact Jewish and German deli cuisine has had on the food culture of the United States. But the default pickle in the United Kingdom is a pickled onion.

A Special Note about Cucumbers

The variety of cucumbers available to gardeners is vast. In the not-so-distant past, a gardener had a choice of pickling cucumbers (also called Kirby cucumbers) or slicing cucumbers (also called salad cucumbers or regular cucumbers). Today we have European and American pickling cucumbers (European cucumbers have a smoother skin than American pickling cukes and are perfect for harvesting tiny to make gherkins or cornichons) and European greenhouse cucumbers, Middle Eastern (also called Persian or Beit Alpha) cucumbers, and Japanese (or Asian or long-fruited) cucumbers. Armenian cucumbers are a different species altogether, but there's no reason not to pickle them.

For pickling whole cukes, a short pickling cucumber is best. Otherwise, for eating fresh and pickling slices, I really prefer Asian cucumbers for flavor, for productivity, and for quality retention on the vine. They do grow long — around 12 inches long — which is why you don't want them for pickling whole, and the fruit will curl and coil if not trellised. The big size can be a plus, though, because they don't hide under the cucumber leaves like pickling cukes do.

Many people turn to making cucumber pickles when they become overwhelmed by the quantity of cukes they are harvesting. There's no reason not to pickle a standard slicing cucumber, but the skins can be tough and the seeds large. I think they are best suited for recipes that call for the cucumbers to be peeled, seeded, and cut into chunks, or in relish recipes.

Salt

Salt is one of the most important ingredients in pickles. In fermented pickles, the salt is the preservative. In vinegar-brined pickles, it is part of the flavoring. Many vinegar-brined pickle recipes have a short brine with salt water. The salt draws excess water from the vegetables, resulting in a crisper pickle with more concentrated vegetable flavor.

As a preserving agent, salt creates a hostile environment for the microorganisms that spoil foods. When you make fermented pickles (i.e., salt-brined pickles), the fermentation process is a fight between the good microbes that can turn your vegetable into a sour delight and the bad microbes that can turn your vegetable into rotted slime. The salt undermines the bad microbes to give the good microbes a chance to turn the naturally occurring sugars in the vegetable into lactic acid. Then the lactic acid also acts as a preservative.

Old-time recipes often called for a brine "strong enough to float an egg." This is a 10 percent solution made by dissolving 1½ cups of salt in 1 gallon of liquid, a very strong salt solution. Food cured in a 10 percent brine must be "freshened," or desalted, in several changes of water before it is edible. With modern-day refrigeration, preserving with this level of salt is no longer necessary (but it's a good survival skill to keep in the back of your mind). Most of the fermented pickles in this book use a brine of about 2.5 to 6 percent.

Most cookbooks recommend using pickling salt or canning salt (they are one and the same) for pickles because they contain no additives to keep the salt from clumping. The additives will not alter the effectiveness of the brine, but they may darken the pickles or make the brine cloudy. Using pickling salt, then, is an aesthetic decision, rather than a safety decision.

There are specialty food stores devoted to salt, but most of the differences people taste among salts are too subtle to be tasted in a complex pickle. Chemically there is little difference between edible salts. All are at least 97.5 percent sodium chloride.

Table salt is mined from underground salt deposits and includes a small portion of calcium silicate, an anti-caking agent added to prevent clumping. It possesses very fine crystals and a sharp taste.

Sea salt is harvested from evaporated seawater and receives little or no processing, and so it may contain other minerals that flavor or color the salt. If you do use sea salt in your pickles, be sure the texture is the same as table salt or figure out the difference in weight and apply it to the recipes. Recently, fine sea salt, with no additives, has become available in the supermarket in the same easy-pour cylinders as table salt. If you switch over to this type of salt, you can use it for all your pickling needs.

Kosher salt takes its name from its use in the koshering process, where it is applied to draw blood out of the meat. It contains no preservatives and can be derived from either seawater or underground sources. You can use kosher salt in pickles, but the volume measures in this cookbook will be off. The standard substitution for kosher salt is that 1 teaspoon table salt is equivalent to 1⅛ to 1½ teaspoons kosher salt. Because the size of the salt flake varies among brands

CONTINUED ON PAGE 18

15

BLUE-RIBBON PICKLES

Traditionally, award-winning pickles were found at the county fair every summer, and their recipes were found in community cookbooks across the nation. That kind of competition still goes on, but for the new generation of artisanal pickle producers, there are the Good Food Awards.

Organized by the Seedling Project, the GFA were created through a collaboration of food producers, farmers, food journalists, and independent grocers to honor food that is "tasty, authentic, and responsibly produced."

In its inaugural year, the GFAs received 780 submissions and recognized 80 winners in seven categories: beer, charcuterie, cheese, chocolate, coffee, preserves, and, of course, pickles. A combination of master tasters and enthusiastic amateurs judged and scored the products in blind tastings. The 71 winners were honored in a special ceremony hosted by Alice Waters in San Francisco, and the pickle award was given by fermentation guru Sandor Katz (see page 38). If you live in an area where any of these first-prize winners are located, check them out:

- **Savory Brussels Sprout Relish** from Ann's Raspberry Farm (Fredericktown, OH)
- **Edamame Kimchee** from Artisanal Soy (Washington, DC)
- **Arame & Ginger Sauerkraut Salad** from Ceres Community Project (Sebastopol, CA)
- **Spicy Oregano Purple Carrots** from Cultured (Berkeley, CA)
- **Spicy Green Tomato** from Farmer's Daughter (Carrboro, NC)
- **Yin Yang Carrots** from Firefly Kitchens (Seattle, WA)
- **McClure's Brine** from McClure's Pickles (Detroit, MI)
- **Pickled Corno di Toro Peppers** from Olympic Provisions (Portland, OR)
- **Organic Garlic Dill Pickles** from Real Pickles (Greenfield, MA)
- **Peppered Okra** from Sour Puss Pickles (Brooklyn, NY)
- **Purple Sauerkraut** from Spirit Creek Farm (Bayfield, WI)
- **Spiced Baby Carrots** from Tender Greens (San Diego, CA)

The Real Folks behind Real Pickles

A couple of travelers down the locavore highway, Dan Rosenberg and Addie Rose Holland, are the real folks behind award-winning Real Pickles' Garlic Dills.

Rosenberg started the Greenfield, Massachusetts, business in 2001 after learning about the craft of pickle making while attending a workshop at a Northeast Organic Farming Association (NOFA) conference in 1999. Fresh out of college, Rosenberg apprenticed at an organic vegetable farm and was excited about the benefits of locally grown food. He started pickling cabbage, turnips, greens, and other vegetables as a way to keep eating local through the winter.

Two years and countless batches of pickles later, Rosenberg realized that making pickles on a commercial scale could support local farmers and produce a healthy product that would enable people to enjoy local vegetables through the winter. Real Pickles was born. "My biggest reason for starting the business was to promote regional local food systems. I wanted to create more supply to help people eat locally in the winter," he says. A few years later, Addie Rose Holland joined as his life and business partner.

Addie Rose Holland + Dan Rosenberg

Real Pickles are all made by fermentation. "We make about ten different products: a few dills, a couple of sauerkrauts, beets, carrots. All the vegetables are from local farms."

Sourcing locally in New England means that all the production happens in the warm weather. The vegetables are fermented in 55-gallon barrels. "The cukes go into a saltwater brine. For the sauerkraut, we just pack the cabbage with salt in a barrel." Once the pickles are fully fermented, they go into refrigeration to stop the fermentation process.

Although the pickles are available only in the Northeast, they proved so popular that Real Pickles outgrew its original space in a community incubator kitchen. "Two years ago we bought a hundred-year-old industrial factory in Greenfield." This way they can keep up with the demand in the three hundred or so places, mostly natural food stores, in which the pickles are stocked.

To learn more about Real Pickles, go to www.realpickles.com.

of kosher salt, I can't provide a precise equivalent. The only way to figure out how much kosher salt (or flaked sea salt) to use is to weigh it out and do the math yourself. Figure that 1 tablespoon of pickling salt weighs 17 grams.

Pickling salt (also called **canning salt**) is inexpensive and comes with minimal packaging. I transfer the salt from the box to a glass jar and keep it handy for measuring out what I need. It has the same texture as table salt and can be used for all your regular cooking needs. I use flaked sea salt at the table and to finish dishes, but I don't taste any differences in the salt when it is in solution (in a brine, in a soup).

Vinegars

Here is one of the few exceptions to the rule that homemade is best. To be sure the vinegar acts as a preservative, you need one that is 5 percent acetic acid, or 50-grain strength. While it is possible to determine the acidity of homemade vinegar, I can't vouch for the accuracy of any of the methods floating around the Internet, so I recommend you use commercial vinegars.

Distilled white vinegar. In the United States, white vinegar is generally made from corn, potatoes, or wood, though it can also be made from wheat, beets, and apples. The common Heinz brand is

---

Mixed Pickling Spices

Makes about 4 cups

Ingredients

- 1 cup mustard seeds
- ½ cup allspice berries
- ½ cup crushed bay leaves
- ½ cup black peppercorns
- ½ cup crushed cinnamon sticks
- ½ cup whole cloves
- ½ cup coriander seeds
- ½ cup fennel seeds
- 6 crushed dried red peppers

Here is my formula for making mixed pickling spices. Use mine, make up your own — there are no hard and fast rules — or buy it at the grocery store. The problem with the grocery-store mixed pickling spices is the jars are small and relatively expensive. By making your own, you can make as much as you need for one season. Adjust this recipe to get you through your canning season without running out and without having too much extra. This recipe assumes a pretty active pickling season.

1 Mix all the spices in a bowl and transfer to a glass jar.

2 Seal tightly and store in a cool, dark place.

made from corn. Celiacs will be happy to know that the Celiac Disease Foundation has found that the distilling process makes this vinegar gluten-free, whatever its grain source. This sharp-tasting vinegar is popular to use for pickling, because it is clear and doesn't color the pickle. This is particularly important when you are making cauliflower or Jerusalem artichoke pickles.

Cider vinegar. Commercial cider vinegar made from apples has a more nuanced, slightly fruity flavor when compared to white vinegar. It is amber in color and is generally the preferred vinegar in sweet pickles and chutneys. (Unfiltered artisanal cider vinegars taste better still, but they rarely express the grain strength on the label and so should not be used for pickling.)

Malt vinegar. With many pickles of British origin, this is the vinegar of choice. It is made from cereal grains, has a delicate, almost sweet flavor, and will darken the pickles somewhat. Since it's often made from barley malt and not distilled, this vinegar is not gluten-free.

Wine vinegars. Commercially made red wine, white wine, and balsamic vinegars are used in many European pickles, and you can use them as well. Be sure the vinegar has a strength of 5 percent acidity.

Rice vinegar. Also known as rice wine vinegar, this is the one wine vinegar that should be used with caution. It is usually diluted to a strength of 4.3 percent acidity, so the USDA does not consider it safe to use for canned pickles. You can, however, use it in fresh pickles that are stored in the refrigerator or freezer. Its lower acidity is often a plus in terms of flavor. Buy unseasoned rice vinegar (if it doesn't say "seasoned," it is unseasoned).

As long as the vinegars have the proper level of acidity, they can be used interchangeably, and that includes flavored vinegars. Never reduce the amount of vinegar called for in a recipe for a canned pickle. If the brine tastes too sharp or too sour, increase the sweetener.

Sweeteners

White sugar, brown sugar, honey, maple syrup — they all have their place in sweetening vinegar-brined pickles.

Granulated white sugar. In many ways, white sugar is the sweetener of choice. It sweetens without adding extra flavor and does not affect the color of the finished product.

Brown sugar. Brown sugar is particularly suited to many sweet pickles, relishes, and chutneys. When measuring brown sugar, be sure to pack each cup firmly. Brown sugar will darken the brine. You can use light and dark brown sugars interchangeably.

Honey or maple syrup. Use these sweeteners cautiously because they will make a darker pickle and can overpower its flavor and make a cloudy brine. If you want to substitute honey or maple syrup, use ¾ cup for every 1 cup of sugar. Honey in any form should not be given to children under one year old.

Other sweeteners. There is no reason not to use alternative sweeteners, such as agave syrup, stevia, or even Splenda. But none of the recipes here have been tested with those products.

Water

The water you use to make pickles should taste good. If you can drink it, you can use it

How to Make a Spice Bag

1 Cut a 6-inch square of muslin fabric. Alternatively, cut a 6-inch by 12-inch piece of cheesecloth and fold it in half to make a 6-inch square.

2 Place your spices in a heap in the center of the cloth.

3 Gather up the edges of the cloth and tie the square into a pouch with clean cotton kitchen string or twine.

for vinegar-brined pickles. On the other hand, if it contains too much in the way of off-tasting minerals or chlorine, then you might want to use bottled water.

Definitely don't use chlorinated water in salt-brined pickles. The chlorine may kill off the beneficial microbes. If you are on city water, there is chlorine in the water. Boiling the water for at least 2 minutes will vaporize the chlorine.

Let the water cool before using it in a brine. Or better still, use spring water.

Hard water can, but doesn't always, interfere with fermentation. If you suspect that hard water is interfering with your process, boil the water for 15 minutes and let stand, covered, for 24 hours. Skim off any scum and pour off the clean water, leaving behind any sediment.

You may notice a mineral residue building up in your canner. To clean the canner, fill it with water, add 1 cup white distilled vinegar, and let it sit overnight. Then scrub away the residue. If more drastic action is needed, boil full-strength white distilled vinegar in the pot for a few minutes, let cool, and rinse with plain water.

Spices and Herbs

There are some traditional herbs and spices when it comes to pickles: dill, mustard seeds, celery seeds, turmeric, pepper, cloves, and mixed pickling spices. Mints, oregano, basil, fennel, caraway seeds, and tarragon also have their place.

It is very important to use fresh herbs and spices; once they age, they take on a dusty attic flavor. It is a good idea to date your herb and spice jars when you open them (or when you store your own freshly dried or freshly bought dried herbs) and throw them out one year after opening. If you buy herbs and spices, consider buying in bulk from natural food stores or ethnic food stores where the stock turns over rapidly. And don't store your herbs and spices in the cupboard over the stove — or on a tray right next to the stove — because heat destroys both flavor and color.

To obtain a clear pickling solution, use whole spices and herbs only; ground spices and herbs will make the liquid cloudy. If you are substituting ground spices for whole, use about one-quarter as much. In some recipes, a spice bag (see How to Make a Spice Bag, opposite) is called for. Make the bag out of cheesecloth or muslin and remove it before pouring the brine into the jars. Discard the spices and either discard or wash and reuse the bag.

If you don't want to make a cloth spice bag, try using a stainless steel tea ball instead. The tea ball is much easier to clean, and it can be washed with other cooking utensils. Alternatively, you can strain out the spices before pouring the pickling liquid into the canning jars.

Dill. Having a sure supply of fresh dill throughout the cucumber pickling season is among the top challenges facing a gardener-cook. Figure that your dill plants will go to seed about 8 weeks from seeding. Cucumber plants generally start yielding about 7 weeks from transplanting. It should work out — but it often doesn't because the cucumbers keep yielding while the dill goes to seed rapidly. As a gardener, you may want to seed new plants every two weeks to ensure a good supply. And do be aware of the variety, if you can. Some dill varieties are better for foliage, and some for seed. The plant, once established, can take a lot of benign neglect, but pinch off the growing tip to ensure a bushier, less leggy plant.

If the weather is particularly hot, the plants will go to seed very quickly. You can use seeds, the whole dill heads, or

sprigs of fresh dill. I generally figure that 1 dill head is the equivalent of 1 tablespoon dill seeds or 6 sprigs fresh dill. If I want to be sure there is plenty of dill flavor, I use both seeds and fresh sprigs. I have used dried dill in a pinch. It tends to cling to the pickle, which is less than ideal, but better than nothing. I figure 1 teaspoon of dried dill is equivalent to 2 sprigs of fresh dill.

Because dill goes to seed so easily and quickly, I usually have dill "volunteers" all over the garden each spring. I just let them grow to assure an adequate supply.

Garlic. Garlic sometimes turns blue in an acid brine. This is normal and nothing to worry about. I use a lot of garlic in my recipes. If you aren't a fan, you can omit it.

Crisping Agents

When it comes to crisping — or firming — ingredients, I am an enthusiastic promoter of a new ingredient: Pickle Crisp Granules. Scrupulous attention to keeping your fresh produce well chilled, pickling soon after harvest, and carefully following the times in the recipes will also aid in creating firm pickles. But let's be honest here. Heat softens and cooks pickles. If a truly crisp pickle is important to you, don't preserve in a boiling water bath. Make your pickles in small batches and store in the refrigerator.

Pickle Crisp Granules. Made of calcium chloride, a naturally occurring salt, Pickle Crisp does what lime used to do, but without the fuss. You just add a rounded ⅛ teaspoon of the Pickle Crisp Granules to a pint of pickles (a rounded ¼ teaspoon to a quart) right before sealing the jar and processing in a boiling water bath. The difference in crispness is noticeable if you make a batch of pickles in which one jar has the Pickle Crisp added

and one does not. I especially recommend using it for all pickles made with cucumbers and zucchini, but you can use it for any vinegar-brined, fresh-pack pickle. If you forget to use it, no big deal. But I do recommend using it. You will probably need to order it online because it just isn't popular enough to be stocked in stores. It is made by Jarden Home Products, which owns the Ball canning line. As of this writing (fall 2011), it is available online (so don't believe everything you read on the Internet).

Old-fashioned recipes often used solutions of **lime** (or slaked lime) to firm up pickles. After soaking the fruit or vegetable pieces in the lime solution, you had to rinse and soak them repeatedly in fresh water to remove the excess lime. These recipes required several days to accomplish.

Alum is another ingredient called for in old-fashioned recipes to help make pickles crisp. Although approved for pickling by the USDA, it is toxic in large quantities (more than an ounce). (The USDA has also established "safe" levels of pesticides in our vegetables. Need I say more?)

Horseradish. Horseradish is supposed to contain enzymes that help firm pickles, but I haven't noticed a difference in the pickles I've experimented with. Horseradish does add a sinus-clearing mustardy flavor, so use sparingly.

Grape and other leaves. Leaves of various types, including grape, oak, currant, and cherry, supposedly contain tannins that have a firming effect on fermented pickles. Again, I haven't noticed the difference so I rarely bother. Note that these are advised only for pickles that aren't canned. The enzymes these leaves contain are deactivated by heat.

Pickling Equipment

It is a mistake to think you need to invest in all sorts of equipment to make pickles. Many of us have a tendency to buy the book, buy the expensive equipment, and then never get around to making something with the equipment. Here's a look at the equipment you will need, and the equipment that might be useful.

Of course, you need a normally stocked kitchen, with pots and pans, sharp knives and cutting boards, and a couple of big-capacity bowls and colanders. Everything must be nonreactive with acids, which is the case with most modern-day pots and pans. Don't use uncoated aluminum cookware because the aluminum reacts with acids and can produce off flavors. Cast iron should be avoided for the same reason. Anodized aluminum and enamel-clad cast iron are both fine to use, as long as the surfaces are intact.

Boiling-Water-Bath Canners

Boiling-water-bath canners are used to preserve pickles for long-term storage. They aren't necessary for fermented pickles — or any pickle for that matter. They are needed only if you don't have cool storage space. And let's be clear, heat processing does soften pickles. On the other hand, canned relishes and sauces are incredibly convenient to have on hand, and plenty of pickles are just fine after the canner — particularly sliced cucumber pickles and other fruits and vegetables.

Boiling-water-bath canners are inexpensive, lightweight pots (they start at about $30) made of aluminum or porcelain-covered steel. They have removable perforated racks or wire baskets and fitted lids. They are designed to be deep enough so that at least 1 inch of briskly boiling water will be over the tops of jars during processing.

CONTINUED ON PAGE 26

23

The Joy of Pickling

"Failure is a part of life. That's why gardening is so important. It teaches important lessons about life." Linda Ziedrich is hardly a failure when it comes to gardening or making pickles, but it is something she thinks about.

"I always overplant. You never know if you are going to have a drought or bad weather. I am always trying to do things a little better. My daughter built me three raised beds this year, and we filled them with store-bought dirt. It's ridiculous, but my soil is heavy clay. Sometimes I have standing water in the garden in June."

As for making pickles, she doesn't have many failures, and she thinks people worry about failure too much. The author of *The Joy of Pickling*, Ziedrich says, "Pickles are inherently safe because they are preserved in an acid environment. If something goes wrong, it is obvious."

Still, her inbox is frequently filled with questions about pickling from anxious readers. They keep her on her toes, and they keep her making pickles, even though her household has shrunk,

Linda Ziedrich

with her children mostly grown and on their own.

"I can't stop. People email me a lot, sometimes even call, to ask questions. I have to remember specific recipes, ones I might not have made in a few years. So I have to keep making them."

She's not complaining, really. Pickling is part of her heritage. She grew up in a household where gardening and preserving the surplus were just what you did. "There's a romance to canning right now, and it is a little amusing to me because I guess I'm an old-timer. My mother canned, I can. It's just what you do when you have more than you need. It's a way of life. But for many years, people didn't do any canning and young people today never saw canning done at home. For them it's a novelty."

Is it a novelty that will turn into a way of life again?

"With us running out of oil, I can't see us continuing the trend of *not* cooking and preparing our own food. I think people want more local food, they want to have more connection to the food they eat. So, yes, I think people will continue to make pickles."

Ziedrich credits Sandor Katz, a.k.a. Sandorkraut (see page 38), for creating a "fermentation craze." "He is the fermentation guru," she observes. "He has AIDS, and even though he has been on the cocktail for years, he credits his diet of fermented foods as part of his success. Fermented foods are really part of the health-food movement."

When Ziedrich was researching her book, she found a study that looked into the health effects of a diet rich in kimchi, the fermented pickle that is ubiquitous in Korea. She said the researchers found that the bacteria living in kimchi generated vitamin C, and that the enzymes in kimchi helped make food more digestible.

But the bottom line, she says, is that the flavor of fermented foods is richer and more variable.

One trend Ziedrich sees that she doesn't consider helpful is the paranoia over safety. "There is a lot of misinformation on some websites, and it is really tiresome. Pickling is not canning. You can can pickles, but that generally is an extra preservation method on top of the pickling. The canning isn't really necessary."

She should know: She has a garage floor that is covered with crocks of vegetables at various stages of pickling. She will eat some, her son will eat plenty, and she will give away a lot of it. And then it will be summer again, and time to make more pickles.

You can learn more about Linda Ziedrich at www.lindaziedrich.com, where she writes about food and family life from her homestead near Scio, Oregon.

Boiling-water-bath canners work well. The racks enable you to handle all the jars at once, setting them securely into the pot and lifting them out easily at the end of processing. The light weight of the pot means the water heats quickly.

You can substitute a deep stockpot as long as you can fill it so that there is 1 inch of water above the jars. But then you have to jerry-rig a device to keep the jars off the bottom of the pot. Some people use metal screw bands and set the jars on the screw bands. Others use cake racks. I find the screw bands torturous to use because boiling water can disturb them before the jars are set on them. A jar that is knocked over during the canning process because of its unsteady perch on a cake rack or screw band is much more likely to break than a jar held securely in a rack.

Jars and Lids

I use the same mason jars and lids for fermenting my pickles as I do for canning them. They are readily available at most hardware stores, are inexpensive (compared with Weck jars), and are approved of by all the authorities.

Mason jars come in various sizes, with half-pints being the smallest ones I use for some relishes and chutneys. Most pickles go into pint or quart jars. I use 2-quart canning jars for fermenting pickles. At the pint size and larger, the jars come as either regular or widemouthed; the widemouthed jars are much easier to fill when you arranging large pieces of vegetables, as with whole cucumbers.

Two-piece lids are used with mason jars. A flat lid covers the mouth of the jar and is used only once for heat-processing. A screw band secures the lid; it is reusable. A drawback of the standard lid is that it is coated with plastic that contains BPA. An alternative is the lid sold under the Tattler brand. The reusable BPA-free plastic Tattler lids are designed to be used with a rubber ring, which is also reusable. A metal screw band secures the lid. A drawback of the Tattler lids? They are expensive. But at least they are a one-time-only purchase. I have used Tattler lids, and they work for me.

Many people are enamored with Weck jars, which are glass jars manufactured in Europe with glass lids, rubber rings, and two clips that secure the lids. I don't have any experience with them. They are also more expensive than the American-made mason jars.

Pickling Crocks and Jars for Fermented Pickles

There are lots of products on the market to entice picklers — beautiful stoneware crocks, European canning jars with glass lids, glass jars with airlocks, Harsch crocks with water-sealing lids. All of them are fine to use, and I don't recommend one over another.

I do almost all of my pickling in widemouthed glass mason jars. They are easy to use, easy to clean, easy to replace if they break, and good for both boiling-water-bath canning and on-the-counter fermenting.

Kitchen Scales

It's a darn shame that Fanny Farmer put her extraordinary culinary know-how to standardizing American volume measures rather than exhorting Americans to cook by weight. Using weights for produce is sometimes necessary to ensure you are using the proper proportions of produce to salt or produce to vinegar. There's just no getting around it.

Many of the recipes call for a certain weight of vegetables. If you don't have a kitchen scale, you can (1) weigh the produce at the store, (2) weigh yourself with and without an armload of produce on the bathroom scale and do the math, or (3) use the chart of Produce Math on page 9 to approximate. And good luck! Pickling is easier with a kitchen scale.

The best ones for picklers have at least an 11-pound capacity and a tare feature that allows you to weigh the produce in a bowl without worrying about subtracting the weight of the bowl.

Odds and Ends

There are items that prove to be immeasurably useful for pickling or canning, though you may have first encountered them for a different purpose. A **food processor** with at least an 11- to 14-cup capacity makes life so much easier that I think it is essential. Here are some of my other favorites.

Canning funnel. This is one of those tools that is so handy it is impossible to imagine canning without it. And in my house, it gets used all the time — to pour bulk items into storage containers — as well as when I am canning. Without a canning funnel, brine poured into a jar of pickles can splash right out. It keeps the rims of the jar clean.

Jar lifter. A jar lifter isn't essential and doesn't have multiple uses, but it is inexpensive and quite handy for moving hot jars.

Bubble releasing tool. My bubble releasing tool is a wooden chopstick. Other people use a narrow spatula or a plastic knife. You just need a long tool to run along the inside of a filled jar to release air bubbles.

Assorted tamping tools. When packing greens into crocks or jars, you need something to press down on the layers. A flat-topped potato masher works pretty well with crocks. When packing into jars, I use a small Asian rolling pin, the type that is essential for making dumplings. Basically it is just a 1-inch dowel cut about 6 inches long.

Dish towels. Most kitchens are stocked with dish towels already. Just a reminder that they are essential for canning — for setting empty hot clean jars on (top down), for wiping clean the rims of filled jars before setting on the lids, and for setting processed jars on (top up).

MANDOLINES

I have a love-hate relationship with mandolines. I do use one — especially for making matchstick shapes — but I hesitate to recommend buying one because I think they are dangerous. I have used both the expensive steel ones and the less-expensive plastic ones. If you are going to use one, you have to really commit to stop slicing before you get to the end of the vegetable. I always cut myself when I start thinking, "Oh, just a few more slices. . . ." Better to compost those vegetable nubbins than to sacrifice skin.

Fresh-pack pickles are ones that are preserved with vinegar. After being combined with the vinegar and seasonings, they may be refrigerated or they may be canned in a boiling-water bath. Here are the steps to follow if you are making fresh-pack pickles. The general canning procedure is the same for all pickles.

Organize Yourself

- Read the recipe first. This is the step many people forget. With pickles, it is critical. Why go to all the bother of preparing the vegetables and pulling the canner from the pantry only to read that the vegetables have to stand in a salt brine overnight, and you won't have time to finish the recipe in the morning?
- Lay out all the equipment and ingredients you need.

Prepare the Vegetables and Fruits

- Wash the vegetables and fruits well. Scrub gently with a vegetable brush and wash under running water or in several changes of water. Lift the fruits and vegetables out of the water; don't let the dirty water run out of the sink and redeposit dirt on the produce. Be sure to slice off the blossom end of the cucumbers, which contain enzymes that can soften the pickles.
- Drain the produce in a colander.
- Slice, dice, grate, or chop the produce according to the recipe.
- If the recipe calls for salting the vegetables and chilling in ice water, do so. Don't even consider skipping this step. The salt draws water from the vegetable, and the result is a much, much crisper pickle. The amount of time this step takes isn't an exact science. I generally recommend 2 to 6 hours, but if you are pressed for time and the vegetables are very thinly sliced, 1 hour may be sufficient. Taste one of the salted slices. If it is too salty, give it a rinse. But the pickles should be a little salty; an undersalted fresh-pack pickle will taste flat and sour.

Prepare the Jars and Preheat the Canner

- While the vegetables are sitting in their salt bath, wash the canning jars, lids, and screw bands in hot, soapy water, and rinse well

BOILING-WATER-BATH CANNING

ALTITUDE IN FEET	INCREASE PROCESSING TIME BY:
1,001–3,000	5 minutes
3,001–6,000	10 minutes
6,001–8,000	15 minutes
8,001–10,000	20 minutes

HEADSPACE FOR CANNED PICKLES

Leaving the proper amount of headspace guarantees that your jars will seal properly. Fill too full and it is likely that the contents of the jar will boil out of the jar, leaving a residue on the lid and preventing it from sealing. Leave too much headspace and it is possible that a good vacuum seal will be unable to form. That said, if I have a half-full jar I will go ahead and can it. If it seals, fine. If it doesn't seal, I'll store it in the fridge, which is what I would have done anyway.

in scalding water. Unrinsed detergents may leave undesirable flavors or color on the food. Scale or hard-water films can be removed by soaking the jars for several hours in a solution of 1 cup vinegar (5 percent acidity) per gallon of water. Filling the jars with hot water and covering them with more hot water in a large pot will protect them from airborne molds and yeast while they wait to be filled. Alternatively, set them upside-down on a clean kitchen towel, if you have the counter space. Prepare the lids according to the manufacturer's directions; the instructions vary by brand.

• If your recipe calls for sterilized jars, put them right side up on the rack in the boiling-water-bath canner and fill the canner and jars with hot (not boiling) water to 1 inch above the tops of the jars. Bring the water to a boil and boil for 10 minutes. (Above 1,000 feet, add an additional 1 minute for every 1,000 feet of altitude.) Leave the jars in the water until you are ready to pack them. The USDA recommends that you sterilize jars if you are heat-processing pickles for less than 10 minutes.

• If you are not sterilizing jars, fill the canner half full with water and bring the water to a boil.

• Heat additional water in a tea kettle.

Prepare the Pickling Solution

• Combine the ingredients to make the pickling solution, according to the recipe directions. You can vary the amount of spices, but do not alter the quantities of vegetables, fruits, or vinegar. If the brine tastes too sour, add some additional sweetener.

• Cook the pickling solution as the recipe directs.

Pack the Jars

• If you are packing thinly sliced cucumbers or zucchini, or a chutney, relish, or salsa, set the canning funnel in an empty hot prepared jar and pack the chutney or vegetables into the jar. If you are packing whole cucumbers, green beans, or other large pieces of fruit or vegetables, you may find it easier to hold the jar so it is tipped at a 45-degree angle and pack the jar by hand, using a wooden spoon or chopstick to help arrange as needed, and shaking the jar occasionally to settle the contents. Do not pack so tightly that the produce is squished; the pickling solution should be able to circulate freely for even pickling. On the other hand, packing too loosely will result in the fruits or vegetables floating in the jar, which doesn't look attractive.

• As you pack, leave the amount of headspace indicated in the recipe. Headspace is the gap left between the food (or pickling solution) and the rim of the jar. With pickles (as opposed to sauces or relishes), the solids are packed first. Then slowly pour in the pickling solution through the canning funnel.

• Remove trapped air bubbles by running a chopstick or other utensil between the food and the side of the jar. This step is critical; omitting it could result in the jars not sealing, if you are processing.

• Add more pickling solution if necessary to achieve the proper amount of headspace.

• Wipe the rim of the jars with a clean, damp cloth to remove any brine or food particles. Again, this is a critical step; omitting it could result in the jars not sealing.

• Cover the jars with the lids and tighten according to the manufacturer's directions. If no directions are given, tighten screw bands on traditional flat metal lids until fingertip tight. Tighten Tattler lids fingertip tight and then turn back about ¼ inch to allow the jars to vent while processing (very important!).

Process

• Set the jars in the preheated canner. The water in the boiling-water-bath canner should be hot, but not boiling, to prevent the jars from breaking. Add boiling water to the canner from the kettle to bring the water level to 1 to 2 inches above the tops of the jars.

• Over high heat, bring the water to the processing temperature. Generally this means bring the water to boiling. The exception to this is low-temperature pasteurization (see next page).

• Process for the length of time indicated in the recipe, adjusting for altitude if necessary, and starting the

31

timing when the water comes to a boil.

Cool and Store

• When the processing time is up, remove the jars and set them on a towel or wooden rack away from drafts. Leave space between the jars so air can circulate. If you are using Tattler lids, immediately tighten the metal band.

• Allow the jars to cool undisturbed for 12 to 24 hours.

• Test the seals. The center of the lid on the traditional two-piece metal lid and screw band should be depressed. Remove the screw band. If you push on the center of the lid it should not pop back. If you remove the screw band and lift a sealed jar by the lid, it should hold.

• To test Tattler lids, remove the screw bands and lift the jars by the lids. The lids should hold.

• Wipe the jars clean. Label with a date and recipe name. Store the sealed jars in a cool, dark place. Store unsealed jars in the refrigerator and use within a couple of months.

• Most pickles should be stored unopened for at least 6 weeks to allow them to develop their full flavor.

Low-Temperature Pasteurization

Because USDA guidelines for safe canning practices have gotten more and more stringent, food scientists have developed low-temperature pasteurization as a way to safely can pickled cucumbers. It does result in a slightly crisper pickle, but it is a method that requires careful attention and is more time consuming. You will need a candy thermometer to monitor the water temperature. This technique is not recommended for other vegetable pickles.

Here's how to do it:

1 Place the filled jars in a canner filled halfway with warm (120° to 140°F) water.

2 Add hot water to a level 1 inch above the jars.

3 Heat and regulate the water temperature to maintain a 180° to 185°F water temperature for 30 minutes. Begin

timing when the water reaches 180°F. Check frequently with a candy or jelly thermometer to be certain that the water temperature is at least 180°F during the entire 30 minutes.

4 Remove the jars from the water and cool and store as with regular boiling water bath canning.

The drawbacks to this method are: (1) if the temperature goes below 180°F, you have to bring the water temperature back up and start timing all over again; (2) if the temperature goes above 185°F, the pickles are likely to soften and you've lost the advantage of the low-temperature method; (3) it takes more time and more attention. The temperature must be monitored frequently, and the flame under the pot carefully adjusted. I don't think most electric burners are capable of making timely adjustments of the heat for this method.

As the industrial revolution was causing a sea change in the 1800s, Justin Smith Morrill of Vermont was instrumental in getting Congress to set aside land and funding for land-grant universities. These universities were charged with giving young people practical knowledge in the fields of agriculture and engineering. Part of the mission of these land-grant institutions was to "extend" the research and knowledge of these fields into the farming and homesteading practices of rural Americans via the Extension Service.

Part of the Extension Service focused on nutrition and food preparation. The Extension Service today provides master classes on preservation and writes the rules about canning safety. The rules have gotten progressively stricter over the years. For example, in my 1983 pickling book, many pickles were canned for just 5 minutes. Today most of the processing times are 10 minutes or more. What changed? Who died?

Well, no one died. But food science research has proven that longer times are necessary to eliminate any chance of food spoilage organisms surviving the boiling water bath. Of course, in order to test that theory, the food had to be inoculated with deadly bacteria. If you instead thoroughly wash your hands, utensils, jars, lids, and produce, you are unlikely to be dealing with deadly bacteria in the first place. Still, if I am going to use a boiling water bath, I might as well follow the times suggested by food scientists.

As for a lot of the other "rules," much is common sense. If you reuse jars that are not intended for canning (old mayonnaise or pasta sauce jars, for example), it is likely you will have some breakage in the canner. No one will die, but dealing with a full jar of food and broken glass in a full pot of hot water is a miserable chore. Been there, done that; now I stick to mason jars. Likewise, you may get away with reusing old lids, but once you have a batch of jars that don't seal after they've been canned, or a batch that becomes unsealed in storage, you'll probably agree that new lids (or lids designed to be reusable) are best.

Sometimes the USDA and I part ways. The USDA advises that *all* salt-brined pickles be heat-processed for long keeping, and I just haven't found that necessary. Refrigeration works for me, and I'm willing to risk any problems that might arise. They also recommend brining dills in ½ cup salt to 8 cups water, a brine strength of 6.9 percent. That's too salty for my palate. Yes, I do have batches that go funky over time, but the spoilage is obvious, and I just throw it on the compost heap.

The bottom line is that the USDA and the Extension Service have plenty of online and published resources for home picklers. If you want a guarantee that every single recipe has been tested for safety by food scientists, stick with theirs.

Chapter 2

Fermented Pickles

L et the fun begin. No other type of pickle inspires as much passion as salt-brined pickles, fermented pickles, lacto-fermented pickles — call them whatever you want. No other pickling process involves more alchemy. Something about the sour-salty flavor of these pickles turns ordinary people into addicts.

At the top of the chart when it comes to potentially addictive pickles is kimchi. I've gone weeks where it was kimchi every day, everywhere. As a result there are recipes in chapter 7 for Kimchi Fried Rice (page 260), Kimchi Noodle Bowl (page 262), Kimchi Fish Stew (page 268), Kimchi Chicken Stir-Fry (page 272), and Korean Bulgogi Tacos with Kimchi (page 284). Type the words "kimchi addict" in your favorite search engine, and you will see lots more kimchi combinations. Kimchi hot dogs anyone?

Part of the fun of this chapter is that the recipes draw from all over the world and from very ancient food preservation techniques. People have been fermenting vegetables since ancient times, along with fermenting honey (to make mead), grapes and other fruits (to make wine), and cereal grains (to make beer). For me, part of the pleasure of fermented foods has to do with learning about these ancient practices, and part has to do with making a product that is a little different each time. I can take batch after batch of identical bread and butter pickles out of the water bath canner, but every batch of sauerkraut, dill pickles, or kimchi is a little different from the previous batch.

Please read All About Fermented Pickles (page 36) before you get started with the recipes. If you want to go deeper into fermented foods, I highly recommend reading the book *Wild Fermentation* by Sandor Katz (see page 38).

The batches in this chapter are small. Until you have experience under your belt, it is wise to keep the batches small to avoid waste if something goes wrong. Even more importantly, unless you eat tons of pickles, large quantities of fermented foods will linger in your refrigerator. Refrigeration slows fermentation but does not halt it. The pickles will become more sour and softer over time. I much prefer working in small batches, making a variety of pickles, and not having jars linger in the back of the refrigerator. If you like, multiply the recipe by the amount of produce you have to work with. The size of your crock should not be a limiting factor because you can divide a big batch among canning jars.

The recipes in this chapter are arranged more or less alphabetically by main ingredient. I had to start with cucumbers because my attraction to pickling — and most everyone else's I know — begins with the kosher dill cucumber pickle, perhaps the finest pickle ever.

All About Fermented Pickles

Back in the good old days, a nickel bought a pickle and just about every general store had a pickle barrel by the counter. You could reach right in — no latex gloves required — and extract a pickle. Farmhouses had still-rooms where pickles and beers and wines were brewed. General stores and stillrooms may be all mostly in the past, but fermented foods live on. These days fermented foods, particularly pickles, are enjoying a strong revival. Indeed, festivals can be found all over the country in celebration of fermented foods.

Making fermented pickles is both easier and more complicated than making fresh-pack pickles. It is easier because naturally occurring bacteria do most of the work, and it doesn't involve slaving over a hot stove. It is more complicated because you have to rely on your own common sense.

When it comes to making brined or fermented pickles, there are three basic rules.

1. Be especially careful about cleanliness.

2. Keep the vegetables submerged in the brine.

3. Taste frequently. You decide when your fermented pickles are ready for the refrigerator.

About Cleanliness

Obviously it is important to wash your vegetables. The bacteria that cause botulism can be found in the soil. It should also be obvious that if your produce is damaged or moldy, it is already harboring microbes that could destroy your pickles. Throw it out!

It is also important to clean your fermenting crock and utensils. Some dishwashers have a sterilizing cycle, which makes sterilizing everything pretty easy. You can also boil water-filled glass canning jars in a boiling water bath for 10 minutes. Finally, you can use a wine-making sanitizing solution to sanitize your equipment (follow the manufacturer's directions for use). At the very least, all your equipment should be rinsed with boiling water before use.

Make sure your hands and all your cutting surfaces are also clean. Cleanliness will make a difference!

About the Brine

In many recipes, the brine is a combination of the salt you add to the vegetables and the water that is drawn from the cell walls. Typically, the fresh vegetables are chopped or grated in preparation for fermentation; this creates a lot of surface area for the salt to act upon. The veggies are then salted and left to stand for a while. Through the process of osmosis, the salt pulls water out of the cell walls. Pounding or tamping down the vegetables breaks down cell walls to allow even more liquid to escape from the cells.

Some vegetables — such as whole cucumbers, green beans, and green tomatoes — aren't suited to this treatment. In those cases, the brine must be made up of water and salt.

Brine Strength

Old-style recipes used a 10 percent salt solution, meaning that 10 percent of the weight of the solution was comprised of salt. With this concentration of salt, spoilage microbes are unlikely to survive. On the other hand, a pickle fermented in such a strong brine must be freshened (rinsed) in several changes of water before it is even edible. Brining in a 10 percent solution is a survival method. We have refrigeration to help us preserve our pickles, so a weaker brine is desirable for most of us.

Most of the recipes in this chapter use a brine in the 2.5 to 6 percent range. The USDA standard is 3 tablespoons of salt per 5 pounds of vegetables. More salt will slow the fermentation process; less will speed it up. If you use less salt, your pickles will be vulnerable to spoilage.

Keeping the Vegetables Submerged

You want the vegetables to be held under 1 to 2 inches of brine. There are various ways to accomplish this. If you have a crock, you can fill it with the vegetables and a generous amount of brine, then set a plate on top of the vegetables to hold them under the brine. Fill a food-safe plastic bag with more brine and set it in the crock so it completely covers the plate and brine, excluding air. (Use brine rather than water in the bag in case the bag leaks into the crock.)

I prefer to work in small batches and with canning jars, rather than crocks. I fill the jars to the very top with brine, then place the lids and screw bands (barely tightened) on the jars. I set the jars on saucers to catch overflowing brine. And they do overflow once the fermentation starts. But with the lid in place, I know that air is mostly excluded. I top off with additional brine as needed. Since I switched from crock fermenting to canning jar fermenting, I haven't had any batches of pickles go bad.

Since fermenting pickles are so chemically active, I am happy to avoid using plastic bags, though they do an excellent job of excluding air. I have also switched from using the Ball- and Kerr-brand canning lids to reusable Tattler BPA-free lids. (See page 26 for a fuller discussion of the lids.) Pickl-It sells European-style glass jars with locking glass lids (as does Weck). The Pickl-It jars also come with airlocks

CONTINUED ON PAGE 40

BRINE STRENGTH

Brine strength is the percentage of salt by weight in a given volume of water. For every 4 cups of water:

AMOUNT OF SALT	BRINE CONCENTRATION
1½ tablespoons pickling or fine sea salt	2.7 percent
2 tablespoons	3.5 percent
3 tablespoons	5.4 percent
4 tablespoons	6.9 percent

Wild Fermentation Man

When you meet someone who goes by the nickname Sandorkraut, you can be pretty sure he is going to be a lover of sauerkraut, and Sandorkraut, or rather Sandor Ellix Katz, is just that.

The beating heart of the so-called lacto-fermentation movement, Katz is the author of *Wild Fermentation: The Flavor, Nutrition, and Craft of Live-Culture Foods* (and a second book, *The Revolution Will Not Be Microwaved*). The lacto-fermentation movement is part health-food movement, part food-preservation movement, and part political movement. It belongs to those pickle makers who believe that fermented pickles, like sauerkraut and brine-cured dill pickles, are the very best pickles to make because fermented foods contain enzymes that promote health and have a more nuanced flavor than vinegar-cured pickles. And these pickle-makers believe that fermentation is a practical way to preserve fresh foods.

Fermented food activists never subject their foods to the insult of heat in the form of a boiling water bath. Such pasteurization would kill the health benefits. "There have been no cases of

Sandor Ellix Katz

food poisoning from fermented foods," Katz counsels. "It is the safest food there is."

Katz is the guru of the fermented food movement. His book, YouTube videos, and workshops have done much to take the fear out of making fermented pickles. His earnest voice, still tinged with the New York accent of his youth, is calm as he concisely covers the ins and outs of fermentation.

Like many, he came to pickling as a gardener. His garden in Tennessee, where he lives now, produced an abundance of cabbage one year. "'Well,' I said to myself, 'it looks like now would be a good time to learn how to make sauerkraut.'" And one thing led to another.

When we spoke on the phone one December, his living room, he told me, was filled with hundreds of pounds of daikon radish. There had been a killing frost and a neighbor invited him to harvest all the daikon radishes he could, before the frost settled in. The radishes were air-drying. Next he planned to ferment the radishes by an ancient Japanese pickling method known as *takuan* (or *takuwan*).

Growing up in New York City, Katz began his love affair with pickles early. As a middle school student hungry for an after-school snack, Katz would make a stop each afternoon at Merit Farms (a chain of delis) and buy a big fat kosher dill for a quarter.

As a gardener in Tennessee, he began what has turned out to be a quest to explore different fermented food traditions. In addition to making traditional European-style cucumber pickles, he has explored making all sorts of Chinese, Japanese, Korean, and Russian pickles. "I love the diversity of traditions. You take the broad idea of fermenting food, and it has been interpreted in so many varied, quirky ways. . . . Look at kimchi. It turns out in some areas of Korea, people add fruit to their kimchi. In other parts of the country, fish is always included. In the mountainous areas, you might find kimchi made with beef broth. . . .

"I pickle whatever there is a lot of. Green beans. Okra. This past summer a Russian woman told me I could pickle cherry tomatoes. So I tried that, and they were good — just not good for long-term storage. . . . Generally cold-weather crops, like root vegetables, are best for long-term ferments. You can pickle hot-weather crops, but they don't last long."

Katz encourages people to experiment with small batches until they get the hang of what they are doing. "Fermenting is all about the dynamics of salt, time, and temperature. High salt, slow ferment. Low salt, quick ferment."

As for equipment, Katz goes low-tech. He has a nice collection of crocks, including one 55-gallon oak barrel. But for the most part, he pickles in jars or smaller crocks. He has used the highly touted Harsch crock as well as some Chinese crocks, which employ the same design to lock out air, but generally he doesn't advocate for their use. "I like to smell and taste frequently, which introduces the possibility of surface mold and defeats the purpose of the airlock. If surface mold forms, I just skim it off." He does use grape leaves or horseradish roots or leaves to add flavor and aid crisping, but he cautions that all fermented foods will soften eventually.

"We live in an era when the microbes that live in our bodies are under constant attack from antibiotics in our food and chlorinated water. Ingesting live lactic acid bacteria can aid in the digestion and assimilation of foods. You can get probiotics by eating fermented foods, and it's a lot more pleasurable than swallowing capsules."

You can learn more about "wild fermentation" by visiting Katz's website at www.wildfermentation.com.

and nifty glass weights to keep the vegetables submerged. These jars work well and come in a variety of sizes. Glass is easier to clean than ceramic crocks, and I suspect cracks in the crocks may harbor spoilage bacteria, yet another reason for using glass rather than ceramic crocks.

If you are making cucumber pickles or another whole vegetable pickle, the recipe will direct you to make enough brine to cover the vegetables. If you are working with a grated or chopped mixture (kimchi, sauerkraut, etc.), the vegetables are supposed to create their own brine from the salt you add. In that case it is okay to get rough with your vegetables — in fact, it is desirable. Use muscle to

pack the vegetables tightly in the jar. I use a 1-inch wooden dowel for tamping down the mixtures as I pack. You can improvise with a wooden spoon or your fist. Whatever you use, keep packing and pressing as you go. The vegetables should exude enough liquid to be almost covered by brine, though it may take 12 hours to get there. If after sitting overnight the vegetables are not well covered in brine, you need to make additional brine (labeled "Optional Brine") in the recipes.

When making kimchi, sauerkraut, and other pickles that create their own brine, I use 3 tablespoons salt to 5 pounds vegetable. These pickles are plenty salty; you can use less salt, but spoilage is more likely.

Temperature Is Key

Temperature is a key factor in making successful fermented pickles. Fermentation proceeds at an ideal pace between 65° and 75°F. In cooler temperatures, fermentation is slow, giving spoilage bacteria a chance to take hold. Overly fast fermentation is equally undesirable and may produce soft, slimy pickles. If you can't produce the ideal temperature, be aware that your ferment may be ready sooner or later than the recipes suggest.

In the winter, I generally ferment on my kitchen counter. In the summer, I put my ferments in the cooler basement.

Check Daily and Taste Frequently

Most of the recipes in this chapter are quick, low-salt ferments. You get to decide how long to keep them fermenting. Refrigeration slows down fermentation but doesn't halt it entirely, so your pickles will continue to age and become more sour. Since fermentation is a natural process, it

IT'S NOT JUST FOR THE CRUNCH

Of course, salt-brined pickles have better texture than pickles that have been processed in a boiling water bath. Another reason to try salt-brining is for the brine, which is perfect to use in mixed drinks. Try the Pickle Shot (page 240) and the Sheesham and Lotus (page 241).

FREESTONE FERMENTATION FESTIVAL

"Joining Culture with Agriculture" is the motto of the Freestone Fermentation Festival, which began in 2009. The festival celebrates all things fermented, from pickles to wine. It's a two-day event in Sonoma County, California, for some 1,000 fermentation fans who gather to sample the wares of some 35 fermenters, listen to live music, and learn more about making cultured food with the aid of bacteria and yeasts. Pickles and wine are notoriously hard to match, but at a fermentation festival, pickles, wine, kombucha, bread, yogurt, kefir, beer, and soda are all items of interest. For more information, go to www.freestonefermentationfestival.com.

progresses naturally — faster in warmer temperatures and faster with vegetables that contain more sugar.

Salt is the preservative for fermented pickles. Naturally occurring bacteria generate lactic acid from sugars stored in the vegetables. In the process of digesting sugars in the vegetables, carbon dioxide is given off, and you can monitor the process by watching for the gas bubbles. The lactic acid that is produced gives the fermented pickles a distinct sharp flavor, mellower than the acetic acid in the vinegar that flavors other types of pickles. The lactic acid is also a preservative.

Yeasts and Molds

It is a rare batch of fermented pickles that exists without a little yeast action. Mold is less common, but still happens on occasion. Yeast is indicated by a whitish foam that forms on the surface of the brine. It should be skimmed off daily — that's why you check — to prevent the pickles softening or developing off flavors. Mold is fuzzy looking and should be removed promptly. It is most likely to appear on the walls of the crock and can be removed with a paper towel. If your equipment is cleaned properly before use, and you take care to keep the vegetables submerged in the brine and to keep air excluded from the crock or jar, yeasts and molds shouldn't present much of a problem.

If growth does happen, don't freak out. Once you've removed any colonies of yeast or mold by skimming off, taste your pickle. As long as the pickle tastes good and isn't slimy in texture, it is safe to eat. You will know when a ferment has gone bad. Trust yourself.

Storage

Fermentation will be complete in 3 days to 4 weeks. After 4 weeks, all fermented pickles should be stored in the refrigerator. The USDA recommends canning fully fermented pickles for long-term storage, but this destroys the crisp texture of the pickle.

If fermentation went well, you can refrigerate the pickles in the original brine. Alternatively, make up fresh brine, add fresh herbs and spices, and put the pickles in the fresh brine before refrigerating.

Step-by-Step Fermented Pickles

Here's a step-by step guide to making fermented pickles.

Prepare the Vegetables and the Crock

• Wash the vegetables carefully. Scrub gently with a vegetable brush under running water or in several changes of water. Lift the vegetables out of the water; don't let the dirty water run out of the sink and redeposit dirt on the produce. Be sure to slice off the blossom end of the cucumbers, which contains enzymes that can soften the pickles.

• Drain the produce in a colander.

• To prepare the crock, scrub it well with hot soapy water and rinse with hot water. Then scald with boiling water. If you can use a dishwasher's sterilizing cycle, do so. Alternatively, you can use a

42

wine-making sanitizing solution, which is sold wherever winemaking supplies are sold.

- Weigh the produce. The weight will determine how much salt to use or how much brine to prepare.
- Slice or grate the produce as needed. Mix with the salt, if that is what the recipe requires. Work the salt into the grated or sliced produce, mixing and pounding with a potato masher or your hands to break down the cell walls. Alternatively, prepare the brine and let cool.

Pack the Jar or Crock

- Layer the vegetables and spices in the jar or crock according to the recipe. If you are using a crock, leave at least 4 inches of space at the top. If you are using a canning jar, pack up to the shoulder of the jar.

- Pour the cooled brine over the vegetables, if needed. Alternatively, tamp down the grated vegetables until they release enough liquid to cover the vegetables by an inch or two.

Cover

- If you are using a jar, fill with brine to the top and cover with the lid, then loosely place the screw band. Set the jar on a saucer to catch the

---

GROWING CUCUMBERS

As vegetables go, cucumbers are fairly easy to grow, as long as you provide the heat and moisture they crave and either room to spread or vertical trellises.

Planting. Provide a rich, loamy soil, with plenty of compost or manure worked into it. If your growing season is long enough, plant seeds ½ to 1 inch deep when the soil temperature is at least 70°F. Thin the seedlings to one plant every 12 inches in the row or three plants every 36 inches in the hill system. If you plant seedlings started indoors, plant them in warm soil 12 inches apart in the row.

Care. Provide plenty of water at all stages of growth; the plants have shallow roots and don't hunker down in dry conditions. When fruit begins setting and maturing, adequate moisture becomes especially critical. Mulch is important to help retain soil moisture. In some areas, floating row covers are necessary for protection from cucumber beetles.

Harvesting. For pickles, the smaller the better, starting when the cucumbers are 2 inches long. A cucumber is of highest quality when it is uniformly green, firm, and crisp. Do not allow cucumbers to turn yellow. Remove from the vine any missed fruits nearing ripeness so that the young fruits continue to develop. Cucumbers grow fast! They should be harvested at least every other day.

brine that will overflow once fermenting starts. Set aside any extra brine; you may need it to top off the jar.

• If you are using a crock, cover the vegetables with a plate. Weight the plate to hold the vegetables under the brine. A clean rock or a clean glass jar filled with water works well. Then cover the crock with food wrap. Alternatively, fill a food-grade plastic bag with brine and set it on the ferment to weight the vegeta-bles so they remain submerged *and* to exclude air from the vegetables.

Allow the Pickles to Cure

• Store the jar or crock where the temperatures will remain between 65° and 75°F, if you can. Fermentation should begin within a day or two, depending on the temperature. If you gently tap on the jar or crock, you should see gas bubbles rising. Check daily and remove any mold or white foam that collects on the top. Begin tasting after 3 days. Once the pickle is cured to your satisfaction, refrigerate to halt fermentation.

• Fermentation is com-plete when gas bubbles stop rising to the top of the crock. This will happen sometime between the second and fourth weeks. It is perfectly fine to refrigerate and halt the fer-mentation before the pickle is fully soured.

WHAT ABOUT WHEY?

In the current pickling revival, Sally Fallon's book *Nourishing Traditions* has had a strong impact, and you can trace to it the number of pickling recipes that incorporate whey. Whey is the watery by-product of cheese making, what is left when the milk proteins contract into curds. It turns out that whey can inoculate a brine with lactobacillius bacteria to speed up fermentation and lower the pH.

I haven't found a need to include whey in my pickles. When I began pickling, it wasn't something I ever came across, and now I feel no need to add an ingredient that will make the pickles not kosher for enjoying with meat and not vegan.

Fermented Dill Pickles

Larry Abell makes pickles at Toll a Bell Farm in East Calais, Vermont. When I first approached making fermented pickles, he was my mentor. I wrote up the following essay from his notes and my notes from our conversations.

I start with fresh cucumbers. I like to grow my own or buy fresh local produce. I prefer the black-spined cucumbers. They tend to be tougher skinned and better shaped. I think a good pickle shape is a blocky one.

The first thing I do is wash the cucumbers and reject any one that doesn't have a good shape. What's a bad shape? Well, toward the end of the season you get some that have either a pinched or swollen end. Those cucumbers have ripened unevenly. I have found I get more gas in the fermentation crock with these cucumbers, so I just reject them now.

I pack the cucumbers into a large crock. I like to put the smaller ones on the bottom. The bigger ones will hold the smaller ones down. I don't fill the crock more than two-thirds full.

Then I cover the cucumbers with a heavy weighted plate. You can use other things to weight the cucumbers down.

I cover the cucumbers with a 2.5 percent brine. I used to use a 5 percent brine. What's the difference? The difference is in the taste! The 5 percent brine is twice as salty. But the fermented cucumbers will keep better with a 5 percent brine. You'll note that I store the finished pickles in the refrigerator. It's necessary to do that; otherwise the pickles will spoil. But I've found that if I can't refrigerate the pickles — maybe I don't have the space — the pickles will keep better at the 50° to 60°F range if they are made with a 5 percent brine (¾ cup pickling salt to each gallon of water).

Anyway, I make the 2.5 percent brine (that's 6 tablespoons pickling salt for each gallon of water). I bring the salt and water to a boil and then cool it. It's easier to dissolve the salt that way. And, of course, by boiling you eliminate some of the undesirable yeast. But you have to be sure to cool your brine before pouring it over the cucumbers; otherwise you'll cook the cucumbers and kill off desirable bacteria.

I pour the cooled brine over the cucumbers, pouring just enough to cover the cucumbers

45

under the weight. Then I wait overnight. The next morning, I should find that the crock has almost overflowed with liquid that has leached from the cucumbers. If that hasn't happened, I add enough brine to make sure the plate is covered by 3 to 4 inches.

I like to keep the brine level high. It facilitates skimming off the daily scum, and it guarantees anaerobic conditions for the fermentation yeast.

I stretch a piece of plastic over the rim of the crock, just to keep dust and dirt from falling into the pickles. You can also use the lid that comes with most crocks.

The crock is left in a cool place — the stillroom is what it used to be called. Fermentation will be completed in 2 to 3 weeks, but it could happen in as little as 1 week. You have to visit the stillroom daily. This is what to look for on your daily visits:

- When you lift the cover of the crock, do the contents smell good and yeasty?
- Are there bubbles trapped under the surface skin of bacteria and fungi?
- Push on the weight. Do the contents bubble vigorously?

If your answer to the above questions are all yes, then fermentation is proceeding well, and you can remove what you can of the scum by skimming. Don't try too hard. Simply remove colonies of fungus and thicker sections of the bacterial mat. You will end up removing 1 to 2 tablespoons of brine with each skimming.

At some point, you will notice that fermentation has tapered off to almost nothing, which normally occurs after 1 to 3 weeks. Then it is time to proceed to the taste test.

Fish out a fermented cucumber. There are some qualities that all healthy pickles will display: Does the brine feel sort of ropey? Look kind of cloudy? Does it smell good? Does the cucumber have only a minimal amount of slime and sediment on it? Is its color even overall? Does it feel both firm and squeezable? Wash the cucumber off and cut it open. Does it appear evenly translucent? Is it crisp but definitely not raw? Does it smell sour?

It is dangerous to taste a pickle from a batch that has not proceeded normally. If the pickle smells bad or if it is a soft gooey mass held together by skin, throw the whole batch out; it has gone bad. But if none of this describes your pickles, and the answers to the questions in the preceding paragraph were all yes, then it is time for you to decant the fermented cukes.

You have a choice with the next step. You can make up fresh brine, or you can use the fermentation brine. If you can't refrigerate the finished pickles, it's best to make up fresh brine. Or if fermentation hasn't been ideal (especially if it went too slowly), or if the fermented cucumbers are slimy and there's a lot of sediment, then it's best to make up fresh brine. But if fermentation has gone well, I prefer to use the fermentation brine. It has a much less harsh flavor. Strain the old brine and discard the spices and garlic.

If you are making up a fresh brine, here are the proportions to use. This amount of liquid should be sufficient for 2 gallons of pickles:

6 cups water

2 cups distilled white vinegar

6 tablespoons pickling or fine sea salt

Whether you are using fresh or old brine, you'll need the following spices (these amounts are sufficient for 2 gallons of pickles):

40 garlic cloves (5 per quart)

8 tablespoons dill seeds (1 tablespoon per quart)

8 teaspoons mustard seeds (1 teaspoon per quart)

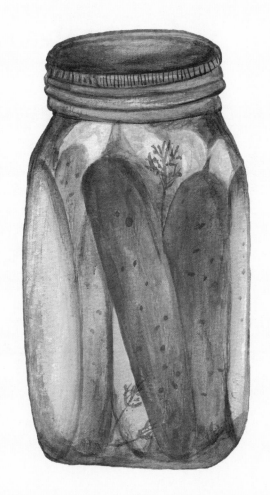

Lay the fermented cukes in gallon jars and pack them firmly, dividing the spices and garlic among the jars and layering them among the cukes.

Fill the jars to 1 inch from their tops with brine. Be sure that no fermented cucumbers float even slightly above the surface. Remove cucumbers if necessary. Fashion a floating lid by cutting a piece of plastic film, then pressing it against the surface of the liquid to exclude all air. Don't forget to release trapped bubbles of air from among the fermented cucumbers first. Protect the jar lid with another piece of plastic and seal the jar. Store in the refrigerator.

I like to decant about a week's worth of pickles into a small jar at a time, so air is not continually reintroduced into the big jar. The pickles last longer that way.

How do you know if the pickles have gone bad? You'll know easily. They get all white and slimy. But it shouldn't happen in the refrigerator.

The best flavor doesn't develop until after 2 to 3 months, and the pickles should last about a year — until it's time to start again. The first pickles you eat will taste of vinegar and salt. A few months later, the garlic flavor begins to come through, then the dill.

No-Fail Half-Sour Dill Pickles

Makes about 2 quarts

Vinegar gives a kick start to the pickling process in these quick and easy pickles, guaranteeing success. If you've never tried fermented pickles, this is definitely the recipe to start with. You can multiply this recipe as many times as you like, but these pickles are best enjoyed at 1 to 2 weeks, so it makes sense to make small batches as the cucumber season progresses.

Ingredients

- 4 cups water
- 2 tablespoons pickling or fine sea salt
- ½ cup distilled white vinegar
- 8 cups whole pickling cucumbers
- 1 dill head or 6 sprigs fresh dill
- 4 garlic cloves, peeled

1. Heat the water and salt in a saucepan, stirring until the salt is fully dissolved. Add the white vinegar and let cool to room temperature.

2. Slice ¹⁄₁₆ inch off the blossom end of each cucumber.

3. Pack a clean 2-quart canning jar or crock with the dill, garlic, and cucumbers, in that order. Pour in the brine. Weight the cucumbers so they are completely submerged in the brine.

4. Cover the container to exclude the air. Set the jar where the temperature will remain constant; 65° to 75°F is ideal.

5. Check the jar daily and remove any scum that forms on the surface.

6. The pickles will be ready in 2 to 3 days, although full flavor will not be reached for a week. If your kitchen is reasonably cool, you can leave these pickles out for up to 2 weeks. If the brine starts to become cloudy, refrigerate immediately to prevent spoiling. The flavor of the dill and garlic will continue to develop. The pickles will keep for at least 3 months in the refrigerator.

Kitchen Note

If your cucumbers are large, you may want to cut them into spears rather than leave them whole. Spears will pickle faster and more evenly than whole cucumbers.

THE KOSHER DILL PICKLE
CAPITAL OF AMERICA

Surely New York City, specifically the Lower East Side, ranks as the dill pickle capital of the United States. Pickle making here dates back at least to the Dutch settlers of the 1600s.

The golden era of pickle making dates back to the Jewish immigrants who flooded New York at the turn of the twentieth century. The most famous of these pickle makers was Izzy Guss, who began selling pickles from a pushcart and only later operated a store known as Guss' (the odd use of the apostrophe is traditional). At the heyday of pickle making, there were as many as 30 pickle shops within a few blocks.

But neighborhoods change, immigrant groups assimilate, and the Lower East Side was no longer a center of Jewish culture by the 1960s. Guss' is now owned by Andrew Leibowitz and has moved to Cedarhurst, New York. Meanwhile, Patricia Fairhurst has opened a pickle store at the original location of Guss' on Orchard Street in the Lower East Side and calls it Guss's. Alan Kaufman, a former employee of Guss', opened the Pickle Guys on nearby Essex Street. All three kept the Jewish kosher dill pickle a living tradition, selling pickles they claim are faithful to Izzy Guss' original recipe.

Meanwhile, upstart pickle makers like McClure's Pickles and Horman's New York Deli Pickles, Picklelicious (actually in New Jersey), and multitudes of home cooks are keeping the pickling tradition alive.

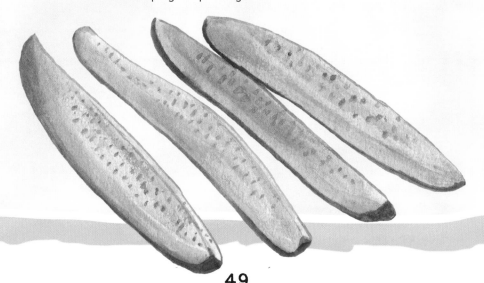

Real Deal Half-Sours

Makes 2 quarts

Lacto-fermentation makes the real deal. Because these pickles have a low-salt brine (3.6 percent solution), they are vulnerable to rapid spoilage, especially as a result of inattention to sanitation. And because these are by necessity quick pickles, you must use a generous hand with the dill and garlic to develop the flavors. I also recommend cutting the cukes into spears rather than leaving them whole, so the flavor will penetrate better.

Ingredients

- 4 cups water
- 2 tablespoons pickling or fine sea salt
- 8 cups whole pickling cucumbers
- 6 garlic cloves, peeled
- 2 dill heads or at least 12 young dill shoots

1 Heat the water and salt in a saucepan, stirring until the salt is fully dissolved. Add the garlic and dill and let cool to room temperature.

2 Slice 1/16 inch off the blossom end of each cucumber. Cut lengthwise into quarters or eighths, depending on the thickness of the cucumber.

3 Pack the garlic and dill into a clean 2-quart canning jar or crock. Pack in as many of the cucumbers as you can fit. Carefully pour in the completely cooled brine. You may not need it all; set aside any extra in a covered jar. Fill the jar to the very top with brine or weight the cucumbers so they are completely submerged in the brine.

4 Cover the container to exclude the air. Set the jar or crock where the temperature will remain constant; 65° to 75°F is ideal.

5 Check daily, and remove any scum that forms on the surface.

6 The pickles will be ready in 2 to 3 days. Refrigerate immediately. The pickles will last about 2 weeks in the refrigerator. The flavor of the dill and garlic will continue to develop.

Kitchen Note

You can double the recipe, but keep in mind that the flavor will continue to develop and the pickles will become fully sour over time.

Full-Sour Kosher Dills

Makes 1 gallon

The secret to full-sour pickles is to have a salty enough brine (5 percent is fairly standard) to enable a long, slow fermentation. Cleanliness is critical here, as are daily checks to remove any scum that might form. Pickles *must* be submerged in the brine. These pickles will be salty, but not too salty to enjoy. If you decrease the salt, the pickles will be fine, but they will not keep as long.

Ingredients

- 12 **cups water**
- 9 **tablespoons pickling or fine sea salt**
- 1 **gallon whole pickling cucumbers**
- 1 **whole head garlic, cloves separated and peeled**
- 3 **tablespoons dill seeds**
- 4 **dill heads or 24 sprigs fresh dill**
- 2 **tablespoons mixed pickling spices, store-bought or homemade (see page 18)**

1 Heat the water and salt in a saucepan, stirring until the salt is fully dissolved. Let cool to room temperature.

2 Slice off the blossom end of the cucumbers.

3 Put the garlic, dill seeds, dill heads, and mixed pickling spices in a 1-gallon jar or crock, then pack in as many cucumbers as can fit. Pour the cooled brine over the cucumbers; you will not need all of it. Fill the jar to the very top with brine or weight the cucumbers so they are submerged under the brine. Add more brine if needed to cover the pickles. Cover the crock to exclude air. Set aside any extra brine in a covered jar.

4 Set the crock in a cool place for 24 hours. It should be set in a place where it can overflow without damage to the floor. (I set my jar in a plastic crate.) Check on the pickles. The level of the brine may have risen, which is fine. If you press on the weight, bubbles should rise. Skim off any foam that forms.

5 Check daily, skimming off any foam. When fermentation tapers off, after 1 to 2 weeks, taste a pickle. When it is pleasantly sour, the pickle is ready for storage. At this point, you can make up fresh brine with fresh dill, garlic, and mixed pickling spices, or you can use the liquid in the crock.

Kitchen Note

You probably won't use all the brine, but it is handy to have extra on hand if needed. How much brine and how many cucumbers you can fit in your container depends on the shape of the jar or crock, the size and shape of the cucumbers, and how tightly you pack the container.

The King of Brine

In the southwest corner of Portland, Oregon, sits Picklopolis. The Kindom of the Brine. It is ruled by the benevolent King of Brine: Chef David Barber.

Like New York City, Portland has a history of immigrants bringing their pickling traditions from central Europe and Russia in the early part of the twentieth century. The colorful old neighborhood of South Portland was home to mom-and-pop grocery stores that featured wooden barrels of kosher dills. One mom, Mrs. Neusihin, eventually became a commercial success.

Fast-forward to today, to a vibrant restaurant scene in Portland, where pickles are as common on menus as burgers from locally sourced beef cattle.

"The locavore thing is really big here. Preserving something that has a limited supply makes sense, whether people are growing it themselves or buying it from the guy at the farmers' market", comments Barber.

"Portland is blessed — or cursed, depending on your perspective — with a really strong D.I.Y. scene. . . . People are realizing how easy pickling is. More people are cooking at home and becoming more comfortable in the kitchen. . . . Pickling is becoming demystified. Everyone experiments."

Still, a fermentation festival in 2009, organized by a committee that included Barber, drew more attention than anyone expected. More than 500 people turned out to sample everything from kimchi, natto (fermented soybeans), and kefir to potato cheese, hard cider, and kombucha. Both professionals and amateurs turned out to give demos, exchange recipes, and share tastes of their favorite ferments. Pickles, including sauerkraut and curtido, played a prominent role.

Since the goal of the festival was to educate people about making pickles, the organizers wanted to keep attendance at the festival manageable. In 2010, they charged an admission fee. In the future, they will consider mini festivals, breaking the fermented foods into categories: pickles, fermented beverages, cheeses. Barber is sure to be at the forefront of the pickle festival.

Chef and owner of the restaurant Three Square Grill, which opened in 1995, and the Picklopolis brand of pickles, Barber has loved pickles, "one of my favorite things," since he was a kid on the East Coast and in L.A., where deli foods were a frequent treat.

"I've been cooking for a really long time. Being a chef, I like to tweak things, make them better. Early on I started making pickles."

Barber's style of pickling is traditional. "Pickling is such an old thing, really. All anyone does is variations on the classics. People are playing with new flavorings. I'm not that huge on it. I'm more of a traditionalist."

His pickles include both naturally fermented garlic dill cucumber pickles, green tomatoes, and sauerkraut, and a number of vinegar-brined pickles, including garlic green beans, orange fennel pickles, spiced beets, Texas okra pickles, hot pepper pickles, and chow-chow. Pickles are offered at Three Square Grill on a sampler plate that is served as an appetizer and as an accompaniment to other dishes, such as pâtés. Under the Picklopolis label, the pickles are sold in the Portland region and online.

Anyone interested in sampling Picklopolis pickles and what is widely considered the "best cranberry sauce ever" should go to the Picklopolis website and check out the pickles and preserves available there. And link to the Three Square Grill website and see what it means to be part of a do-it-yourself culture. Besides the links to the web pages of staff and frequent customers, besides the kid's menu decorated with art made by young customers, besides a menu that features pickles and locally sourced ingredients, there is a page devoted to ingredients "Made Here."

Says the website: "We make all this stuff right here at Three Square Grill. We love great food; eating it, making it, and serving it. Many of our recipes involve labor intensive and traditional methods, which have fallen by the wayside in modern kitchens.

"We believe that these techniques, coupled with high quality local ingredients, result in a superior product hitherto unavailable to the palates of many. This is but a partial list of the items we produce in-house." In addition to burger buns and an assortment of desserts, the restaurant prepares its own black pepper–garlic sausage, turkey pastrami, hot smoked salmon, traditional-style lox, smoked duck breast, Carolina-style barbeque, molasses cured ham, honey-pepper bacon, and dry-aged prosciutto. Barber also makes strawberry, raspberry, and boysenberry preserves, Bad Monkey–brand jalapeño sauce, and garlic malt vinegar.

The Kingdom of the Brine, it turns out, is a DIY paradise, and the King of Brine, David Barber, is the talented visionary at its helm. For more information about him and the kingdom of Picklopolis, visit www.picklopolis.com.

Salt-Cured Dilly Beans

Makes 1 quart

Fast and furious is the only way to describe the green bean harvest. If you don't have the inclination to fire up the stove, you can make salt-cured beans. After fermenting, they require refrigeration. Dilly beans make a great snack, but they can also be chopped and added to salads instead of fresh cooked beans or cucumber pickles.

Ingredients

2¾ cups water

1 tablespoon pickling or fine sea salt

2 tablespoons distilled white vinegar

1 dill head or 6 sprigs fresh dill

3 garlic cloves

about 4 cups trimmed green beans

1. Heat the water and salt in a saucepan, stirring until the salt is fully dissolved. Stir in the white vinegar and let cool to room temperature.

2. Pack the dill and garlic into a clean 1-quart canning jar, then tightly pack in the green beans. Pour the cooled brine over the green beans. The brine should completely cover the beans and fill the jar to the very brim; you will probably have more brine than you need, but it is important to have the beans completely covered. Cover the jar to exclude air. Set aside any extra brine in a covered jar.

3. Place the jar on a saucer to catch the overflow that will start when fermentation begins. Set the jar where the temperature will remain constant; 65° to 75°F is ideal. Let the beans ferment for about 1 week. Check frequently and remove any scum that forms, topping off with more brine as needed. When the beans taste pleasantly pickled, store in the refrigerator. The pickles will keep at least 3 months in the refrigerator.

Kitchen Notes

- Green beans should be cut into 4-inch lengths to fit in a jar. You can cut some beans in half to fill in space at the top of the jar.
- If you have a choice, select beans that are straight, not bent, to make packing the jars easier.

Beet Kvass

Makes about 4 cups

First a disclaimer: There are those who eat to live and those who live to eat, and mostly I fall into the live-to-eat category. How something tastes is supremely important to me. And based on my usual criteria, beet kvass is not a winner. It is pleasantly sour, salty, and beet-flavored, but not something I'd drink for pleasure. But I don't think people in the United States drink it for pleasure. It is a health food, drunk by those who claim that a 4-ounce glass of kvass twice a day can promote regularity, aid digestion, cleanse the liver, and treat kidney stones.

Ingredients

- 3 pounds beets, peeled and sliced (do not grate)
- 1½ tablespoons pickling or fine sea salt
- 2 teaspoons whole allspice berries
- 3 cups water
- 1 tablespoon pickling or fine sea salt

1 Combine the beets and 1½ tablespoons salt in a large bowl and toss gently to mix. Let sit for 1 hour. Mix in the allspice berries.

2 Make the brine by heating the water and 1 tablespoon salt in a saucepan, stirring to dissolve the salt. Let cool to room temperature.

3 Pack the beets and their liquid into a clean 2-quart canning jar. Add enough brine to fill the jar to the very top. Cover the jar to exclude air.

4 Place the jar on a saucer to catch the overflow that will start when fermentation begins. Set the jar where the temperature will remain constant; 65° to 75°F is ideal.

5 Allow to ferment for 2 to 3 days and then begin tasting the brine. When it tastes pleasantly fermented, strain out the solids and refrigerate the liquid. If you like, make a second batch of kvass with the same beets (but no more than that).

Kitchen Notes

- The increased surface area of grated beets will create an overly rapid fermentation, which is why you should slice rather than grate.
- Kvass is a traditional beverage from Russia, often made with rye bread. It is worth seeking out variations if this recipe pleases you.

Sauerkraut

Makes 2 quarts

Small-batch sauerkraut is so much easier to make than you may think. I keep a batch or two going all through the winter; that way I can enjoy my sauerkraut without the hassle of making it in large batches.

Ingredients

5 **pounds trimmed fresh green or red cabbage**

3 **tablespoons pickling or fine sea salt**

OPTIONAL BRINE

4 **cups water**

1½ **tablespoons pickling or fine sea salt**

1   Quarter the cabbage and remove the central core. Thinly shred, using a food processor (use a slicing blade, not a grating blade), kraut cutting board, mandoline, or knife.

2   In a large bowl, thoroughly mix the cabbage and 3 tablespoons salt. Let stand for at least 2 hours, until the cabbage has softened and begun to release liquid. With a potato masher or meat pounder, pound the cabbage until it releases enough liquid to cover itself when pressed.

3   Pack the sauerkraut into a clean 2-quart canning jar, tamping down the cabbage very firmly as you pack. Cover to exclude air.

4   Place the jar on a saucer to catch the overflow that will start when fermentation begins. Set where the temperature remains constant; 65° to 75°F is ideal.

5   Check the sauerkraut after 24 hours. The cabbage should be completely covered in brine. If necessary, make up the optional brine by heating the salt and water in a saucepan, stirring until the salt dissolves completely. Let cool to room temperature before adding to the sauerkraut. Pour in enough brine to cover the cabbage and fill to the very top of the jar. Cover the jar to exclude air.

6   Check the sauerkraut every few days and remove any scum that appears on the surface. You should see little bubbles rising to the surface, indicating that fermentation is taking place. Start tasting the sauerkraut in about 2 weeks. It will be fully fermented in 2 to 6 weeks,

depending on the temperature. The flavor should change from salty to pickled.

7   Store fermented sauerkraut in the refrigerator for several months. For long-term storage at room temperature, process sauerkraut in 1-pint canning jars for 20 minutes or 1-quart canning jars for 25 minutes in a boiling-water bath (according to the directions on page 31). Unprocessed sauerkraut has a pleasing crunch that is lost when heat is applied.

Kitchen Notes

- If you find sauerkraut too salty to enjoy, rinse it before serving.
- Make sure you bruise your cabbage enough to create enough brine to keep the cabbage covered.
- Using a mix of red and green cabbage makes a beautiful pink sauerkraut.
- You can add 1 to 3 teaspoons (no more!) of chopped garlic, dill seeds, caraway seeds, or juniper berries to the cabbage to vary the flavor. Adding too much of the aromatics can overwhelm the flavor of the sauerkraut.
- Sauerkraut is a natural accompaniment to rich meats, especially duck (page 274) and pork (page 279).

SAUERKRAUT MATH

- Figure that 8 pounds of cabbage will fill a 1-gallon jar.

- Figure that 40 pounds of cabbage will fill a 5-gallon crock and about 1 pound of salt will be required.

Kimchi

Makes 2 quarts

The quintessential Korean pickle, kimchi is so important to the Korean diet that employers give workers time off during the fall cabbage harvest so people can put by crocks of it. Freshly made kimchi is enjoyed straight out of the crock. Aged kimchi is traditionally used in cooked dishes, such as the ones found in chapter 7. Recipes for kimchi vary widely. This one requires fish sauce — a rather tame choice compared to those versions that require raw oysters or squid. Kimchi can be addictive, irresistible, and impossible to stop eating.

Ingredients

- 1 large Chinese or napa cabbage (about 3 pounds), cut into 2-inch slices
- ½ cup pickling or fine sea salt
- 2 tablespoons rice flour
- ¾ cup water
- ½ cup Vietnamese or Thai fish sauce
- 6 garlic cloves, minced
- 1 (3-inch) piece fresh ginger, peeled and minced
- 2 tablespoons white sugar
- 2 tablespoons Korean chili powder or chili paste or 1 tablespoon sambal oelek (Indonesian chili paste) or Chinese chili paste with garlic, or more to taste
- 1 apple or Asian pear, peeled
- 1 (6-inch) piece daikon radish, peeled
- 6 scallions, white and green parts, sliced on an angle into 2-inch slices

1　Mix together the cabbage and salt in a large bowl. Use your hands to massage the salt into the cabbage. Add ice water to cover and set aside for at least 2 hours, and up to 6 hours.

2　Meanwhile, begin making the chili paste. Combine the rice flour and water in a small saucepan over low heat. Bring to a boil and stir until the mixture is a thick paste, 1 to 2 minutes. Let cool to room temperature.

3　Drain the cabbage and press on it to squeeze out as much excess water as possible. Set aside to continue draining.

4　To finish the chili paste, stir in the fish sauce, garlic, ginger, sugar, and chili powder. Grate the apple and daikon and stir into the sauce along with the scallions.

5　Combine the chili paste mixture and cabbage, mixing with your hands to blend. Pack into a clean 2-quart canning jar, cover to exclude air, and place in a cool, dark place.

6　Begin tasting the kimchi after 24 hours. If it is pleasingly sour and spicy, it is done and can be stored in the refrigerator, where it will last for at least 3 months. If you like your kimchi more strongly flavored, let it ferment a few days longer (I like a 3-day ferment) before storing it in the refrigerator, where it will continue to ferment but will remain pleasing for several months.

Kitchen Notes

- Rice flour can be found in natural food stores. The rice flour paste helps distribute the spicing evenly. It can be omitted if a chili paste is used rather than the chili powder.

- Korean chili powder is found where Korean foods are sold. If you don't live in a large city with large Korean population, you will have to order it online or use a substitute.

- Both Korean chili paste and sambal oelek have brighter color than the Chinese chili paste, so they are preferred. Use your judgment about how much to add since tastes vary, as do brands of chili paste. A jar that has been opened for a while loses some of its heat. In a pinch, cayenne can substitute for the chili powder (use ½ to 1 teaspoon), but the color of the kimchi will be off.

Napa Cabbage and Carrot Kimchi

Makes 2 quarts

Korean chili paste makes this recipe. On its own, it replaces the rice-flour paste and chili powder of the previous recipe. Because it is combined with rice flour and other ingredients, Korean chili paste is milder than other chili pastes.

Ingredients

- 1 large head Chinese or napa cabbage (2–3 pounds), discolored or loose outer leaves discarded
- ½ cup pickling or fine sea salt
- 1 head garlic, cloves separated and peeled
- 1 (2-inch) piece fresh ginger, peeled
- ¼ cup sugar
- 2 tablespoons Vietnamese or Thai fish sauce
- 2 tablespoons Korean chili paste or 1 tablespoon sambal oelek (Indonesian chili paste) or Chinese chili paste with garlic, or to taste
- 6 scallions, trimmed and julienned
- 2 carrots, julienned

1 Cut the bottom inch off the head of cabbage. Stack the leaves into a couple of piles. Cut each pile of cabbage leaves lengthwise in half, then cut the halves crosswise in half. Transfer to a large bowl.

2 Toss the cabbage with the salt. Add ice water to cover. Let stand for at least 2 hours, and up to 6 hours.

3 Meanwhile, combine the garlic and ginger on a cutting board or in a food processor and chop until finely minced. Transfer to a large bowl and mix in the sugar, fish sauce, and chili paste.

4 Lift the cabbage out of the brine. Reserve the brine and add the cabbage to the bowl with the seasoning mixture. Add the scallions and carrots and mix well, using your hands to distribute the seasoning evenly.

5 Pack the mixture into a clean 2-quart canning jar. Add enough reserved brine to fill the jar to the very top. Cover to exclude air.

6 Place the jar on a saucer to catch any overflow that happens when fermentation begins. Set in a cool, dark place.

7 Begin tasting after 1 day, and refrigerate after 3 to 5 days. The kimchi will continue to age and develop flavor. It will keep for several months.

Kitchen Note

I began making kimchi with the easily found Chinese chili paste with garlic. It works, but the color of the resulting kimchi is dull. Sambal oelek has brighter color, so it is a better substitute. Korean chili paste, found online or in Asian markets in large cities, is best.

Mild Kimchi

Makes 2 quarts

If you like your kimchi hot, increase the amount of chili paste. The Korean chili paste I use is much milder than my other chili pastes, but that might not always be the case, so proceed with caution and add to taste.

Ingredients

- 1 large head Chinese or napa cabbage (about 3 pounds), cut into 2-inch pieces
- 1 (4-inch) piece daikon radish, peeled and thinly sliced
- 1 carrot, thinly sliced
- ½ cup pickling salt
- 4 garlic cloves, minced
- 2 tablespoons Korean chili paste or 2 teaspoons Chinese chili paste with garlic
- 1 teaspoon peeled minced fresh ginger
- 1 teaspoon sugar

1 Combine the cabbage, daikon, carrot, and pickling salt in a large bowl. Mix to distribute the salt evenly. Add ice water to cover. Let stand for at least 2 hours, and up to 6 hours.

2 Drain, reserving the brine. Add the garlic, chili paste, ginger, and sugar to the cabbage mixture and mix well. Use your hands to distribute the seasoning mixture evenly.

3 Pack the mixture into a clean 2-quart canning jar. Add enough of the reserved brine to cover the mixture and fill to the top of the jar. Cover to exclude air.

4 Set the jar on a saucer to catch any overflow that happens when fermentation begins. Place in a cool, dark place.

5 Begin tasting after 1 day, and refrigerate after 3 to 5 days. The kimchi will continue to age and develop flavor. It will keep for several months.

KIMCHI FAVORITES

Kimchi is very "moreish" — the more you eat, the more you want. It will keep in the refrigerator for several months, if only it lasted. Try these kimchi-licious recipes to feed your habit:

- Kimchi Rice Salad with Tofu (page 252)
- Kimchi Fried Rice (page 260)
- Kimchi Noodle Bowl (page 262)
- Kimchi Fish Stew (page 268)
- Kimchi Chicken Stir-Fry (page 272)
- Korean Bulgogi Tacos with Kimchi (page 284)

Curtido

Makes 2 quarts

Sometimes called the Salvadoran version of sauerkraut, curtido is lightly fermented cabbage, flavored with onion and oregano. The result is tasty and even surprising if you are expecting plain old sauerkraut. Curtido is the traditional Salvadoran accompaniment to pupusas, which are stuffed pancakes made from masa harina.

Ingredients

- 2 **pounds green cabbage (1 small to medium head), cored and very thinly sliced**
- 2 **carrots, grated**
- 1 **onion, thinly sliced**
- 2 **fresh red or green jalapeños, seeded and finely chopped**
- 2 **teaspoons pickling or fine sea salt**
- 2 **teaspoons dried oregano (preferably Mexican)**

OPTIONAL BRINE

- 1 **cup water**
- 1 **teaspoon pickling or fine sea salt**

1   Combine the cabbage, carrots, onion, and jalapeños in a large bowl. Add the salt and mix well. Let stand for 30 minutes.

2   Using a potato masher or your fists, pound and press the vegetables until they release their liquid and are quite wet. Add the oregano and toss to distribute.

3   Pack the mixture tightly into a clean 2-quart canning jar, tamping down the vegetables with a wooden dowel or your fingertips with as much force as you can until the level of liquid rises above the vegetables.

4   If the vegetables do not make enough liquid to cover themselves, make up the optional brine. Heat the salt and water in a saucepan, stirring until the salt dissolves completely. Let cool to room temperature before adding to the jar; you should not need more than a couple of tablespoons. Cover the jar to exclude air.

5   Set the jar on a saucer to catch any overflow that happens when fermentation starts. Place where the temperature remains constant; 65° to 75°F is ideal. Let ferment for 2 to 3 days. Taste; when pleasingly sour, refrigerate.

Curtido with Cilantro

Makes 1 quart

The flavor of curtido is here enhanced with the fresh flavor of cilantro. Use curtido as a winter salad or as a topping for Fish Tacos (page 269) or Korean Bulgogi Tacos (page 284).

Ingredients

1½ **pounds green cabbage (1 small head), cored and grated or thinly sliced**

2 **carrots, grated**

2 **fresh red or green jalapeños, seeded and finely chopped**

2 **scallions, white and tender green parts, chopped**

2 **teaspoons pickling or fine sea salt**

½ **cup chopped fresh cilantro**

1 **teaspoon dried oregano (preferably Mexican)**

OPTIONAL BRINE

1 **cup water**

1 **teaspoon pickling or fine sea salt**

1 Combine the cabbage, carrots, jalapeños, and scallions in a large bowl. Add the salt and mix well. Let stand for 30 minutes.

2 Using a potato masher or your fists, pound and press the vegetables until they release their liquid and are quite wet. Add the cilantro and oregano and toss to mix.

3 Pack the mixture tightly into a clean 1-quart canning jar, tamping down the vegetables with a wooden dowel or your fingertips with as much force as you can until the level of liquid rises above the vegetables.

4 If the vegetables do not make enough liquid to cover themselves, make up the optional brine. Heat the salt and water in a saucepan, stirring until the salt dissolves completely. Let cool to room temperature before adding to the jar; you should not need more than a couple of tablespoons. Fill the jar to the very top with the brine. Cover to exclude air.

5 Set the jar where the temperature remains constant; 65° to 75°F is ideal. Let ferment for 2 to 3 days. Taste; when pleasingly sour, refrigerate.

Fermented Asian-Style Turnips and Carrots

Makes 1 quart

Purple-topped turnips and daikon radishes are reasonably interchangeable, especially when the turnips are freshly harvested. So use whichever makes sense in your kitchen. This pickle ages nicely and mellows over time. I like it best at about 1 month.

Ingredients

- 2 turnips or 1½ pounds daikon radish, peeled and grated
- 2 carrots, grated
- 2 teaspoons pickling or fine sea salt
- 1 fresh red or green chile
- 2 large garlic cloves, minced
- 1 (½-inch) piece fresh ginger, peeled and minced

OPTIONAL BRINE

- 1 cup water
- 1 teaspoon pickling or fine sea salt

1   Combine the turnips, carrots, and salt in a large bowl. Toss to mix and set aside for at least 30 minutes, and up to 4 hours.

2   Using a potato masher or your fists, pound and press the vegetables until they release their liquid and are quite wet. Add the chile, garlic, and ginger and toss to distribute.

3   Pack the mixture tightly into a clean 1-quart canning jar, tamping down the vegetables with a wooden dowel or your fingertips with as much force as you can until the level of liquid rises above the vegetables.

4   If the vegetables do not make enough liquid to cover themselves, make up the optional brine by heating the salt and water in a saucepan, stirring until the salt dissolves completely. Let cool to room temperature before adding to the jar; you should not need more than a couple of tablespoons. Reserve the extra in a covered jar. Fill the jar with the brine to the very top. Cover the jar to exclude air.

5   Place the jar on a saucer to catch any overflow that happens when fermentation begins. Set the jar where the temperature remains constant; 60° to 70°F is ideal. Let ferment for 2 to 3 days, topping off with additional brine if needed. Taste; when pleasingly sour, refrigerate.

Kitchen Note

If you use a food processor to grate the vegetables (recommended!), then you may as well mince the garlic and ginger in there as well. There is no need to wash the bowl of the food processor in between.

Spiced Carrot Sticks

Makes 1 quart

Bring back the old relish tray with these carrots, celery sticks, and olives — and, of course, some vinegar-brined pickles from chapters 3 and 4. Because these carrots are never exposed to heat, they retain a delightful crunch.

Ingredients

- 2 garlic cloves
- 2 bay leaves
- 2 teaspoons mixed pickling spices, store-bought or homemade (page 18)
- 2 teaspoons fennel seeds
- 1 tablespoon pickling or fine sea salt
- 4 cups carrot sticks (about 1 pound)
- 1 cup distilled white vinegar
- water

1 Pack the garlic, bay leaves, mixed pickling spices, fennel seeds, and salt into a clean 1-quart canning jar. Pack in the carrots. Add the vinegar, then pour in water to cover.

2 Cover the jar firmly and shake to distribute the spices evenly. Release the lid so it is no longer tight. Set the jar in a room where the temperature remains constant; 65° to 75°F is ideal.

3 Let the carrots ferment for 10 to 14 days. Fermentation is complete when the carrots all sink to the bottom of the jar. If you tap the jar, no bubbles should rise to the top.

4 Store in the refrigerator.

THAT LAST LONELY PICKLE

When you get to the end of a jar, that last pickle seems to linger, getting more and more sour. Chop it up and slip it into:

- Dilly Mustard Coleslaw (page 250)
- Creamy Dilled Smoked Fish Pasta Salad (page 254)
- Dilled Potato and Egg Salad (page 255)
- Pickled German Potato Salad (page 256)

Korean-Style Pickled Garlic

Makes 1 pint

Extraordinary patience is required for these pickled garlic cloves. The garlic remains delightfully crunchy and the flavor mellows over time. Give these a good 6 months before tasting. Wait a year to get a better idea of their potential. Needless to say, the garlic-infused soy sauce makes a sublime dipping sauce.

Ingredients

FIRST PICKLING

- 5 heads garlic
- 1 tablespoon pickling or fine sea salt
- 1 cup water

SECOND PICKLING

- ⅓ cup soy sauce
- ⅓ cup water
- ⅓ cup rice vinegar
- 2 tablespoons firmly packed brown sugar

1 Peel the garlic by putting the heads in a bowl and covering them with boiling water. Let stand for 3 minutes. Drain, break the heads into cloves, and peel them, cutting off the hard root end of each clove. Pack the garlic into a clean 1-pint canning jar or crock.

2 For the first pickling, combine the salt and water in a small saucepan and heat, stirring until the salt is dissolved. Let cool to room temperature.

3 Pour the brine over the garlic to the top of the jar. Cover the jar to exclude air and let stand for 4 days. The garlic should taste very mildly fermented. Drain off the brine and discard.

4 For the second pickling, stir together the soy sauce, water, rice vinegar, and brown sugar. Pour over the garlic. Cover the jar to exclude air and let stand for at least 6 months.

5 Store in the refrigerator or at room temperature (which is what I do).

Dilled Kohlrabi

Makes 1 quart

A fresh kohlrabi is said to taste like a cross between an apple and a cabbage, although the comparison to an apple is more about texture than flavor. When pickled, kohlrabi's mustardy flavor, evidence of its cabbage family origins, strengthens.

Ingredients

- 6 kohlrabi, peeled and thinly sliced
- 1 tablespoon pickling or fine sea salt
- 6 sprigs fresh dill or 1 dill head
- 1 tablespoon dill seeds
- 2 garlic cloves
- water

1 Combine the kohlrabi and salt in a large bowl. Toss to mix. Let stand for at least 2 hours, and up to 6 hours.

2 Pack the fresh dill, dill seeds, and garlic in a clean 1-quart canning jar. Fill with the kohlrabi. Add water to completely fill the jar. Cover to exclude air.

3 Set the jar on a saucer to catch the overflow that happens when fermentation begins. Place where the temperature remains constant; 65° to 75°F is ideal. Let the kohlrabi ferment for about 1 week. When the kohlrabi tastes pleasantly pickled, store in the refrigerator. The pickles will keep for at least 3 months in the refrigerator.

Kitchen Note

Substitute traditional sauerkraut seasonings (1 tablespoon caraway seeds or juniper berries) for the dill if you prefer.

Pickled Mustard Greens

Makes 1 quart

Many classic Szechuan dishes are made with pickled mustard greens. While American mustard greens have a stronger flavor than the mellower Chinese mustard, they make a more than adequate substitute. These greens are essential for Szechuan Green Beans (page 276). They are also very good in Shrimp Congee (page 267).

Ingredients

2 pounds fresh mustard greens

1 tablespoon pickling or fine sea salt

1 teaspoon sugar

OPTIONAL BRINE

1 cup water

1 teaspoon pickling or fine salt

1 Trim off the brown stem ends of the greens. Thinly slice the leaves and stems.

2 In a very large bowl or crock, mix the greens, salt, and sugar thoroughly. Let stand for at least 2 hours, and up to 6 hours, until the greens have softened, begun to release liquid, and lost a considerable amount of volume. With your hands or a potato masher, work the greens until they release enough liquid to cover themselves when pressed.

3 Pack the greens into a clean 1-quart canning jar, tamping them down very firmly. Cover to exclude air. Set the jar where the temperatures remain fairly constant; 65° to 75°F is ideal.

4 Check the greens after 24 hours. The greens should be completely covered in brine. If necessary, make up the optional brine by heating the salt and water in a saucepan, stirring until the salt dissolves completely. Let the brine cool, then pour enough brine into the jar to fill the jar completely.

5 Check the greens every few days and remove any scum that appears on the surface. You should see little bubbles rising to the surface, indicating that fermentation is taking place. Start tasting the greens in 3 to 4 days, and refrigerate when they taste pleasantly sour to you. They'll keep in the refrigerator for several months.

Kitchen Notes

- If you find the greens too salty to enjoy, rinse before serving.

- A bowl of reheated leftover rice, a couple of forkfuls of these greens, a drizzle of sesame oil, and a splash of soy sauce makes a great breakfast. A poached egg on top is heavenly.

Classic Hot Pepper Sauce

Makes ½ pint

You get to choose how hot to make your hot sauce by choosing the chiles. Jalapeños make a *relatively* mild sauce; and I do emphasize the relativity of that statement. Obviously, habaneros make a hotter sauce. A mix of chiles is fine, but my palate finds that the hottest chile dominates.

Ingredients

- ¾ **pound (scant) fresh red chiles, stemmed, halved, and seeded**

- 2 **teaspoons pickling or fine sea salt**

1 Purée the chiles with the salt in a food processor until liquid. Open the food processor carefully (do not breathe in the chile fumes).

2 Pour into a clean half-pint canning jar. Seal the jar to exclude air.

3 Set aside to ferment for 30 days in a dark spot where the temperature remains constant; 65° to 75°F is ideal.

4 Keep in the refrigerator for long-term storage.

Kitchen Notes

- After pureeing, you may have a tablespoon extra that won't fit in the jar. You can use it within a day or so to spice up a dish.
- Light will cause the color of the sauce to fade, which is why it is a good idea (but not absolutely critical) to ferment in a dark spot.

Sauer-Roots

Makes about 2 quarts

If you ferment just turnips or rutabagas, you'll end up with sauereuben. But why stop there? This pickle can be made with whatever root veggies you have on hand — beets, carrots, parsnips, turnips, rutabagas. When fermentation is complete, the vegetables taste of themselves, only better. Warning: Do not use more than one small beet; otherwise fermentation will be too rapid.

Ingredients

5 **pounds root vegetables**

3 **tablespoons pickling or fine sea salt**

OPTIONAL BRINE

4 **cups water**

1½ **tablespoons pickling or fine sea salt**

1 Peel all the vegetables and grate on the coarse side of a box grater or in a food processor.

2 Transfer the vegetables to a big bowl. Sprinkle with salt and mix well with your hands, squeezing and pressing on the vegetables as you go. You should be able to see the vegetables begin to release liquid.

3 When the mixture is moist, pack into a clean 2-quart canning jar, tamping down the vegetables firmly. Continue to press down on the vegetables until they are submerged in the brine. If the vegetables have dried out in the field or in a root cellar and don't release enough liquid, make up the optional brine by heating the salt and water in a saucepan, stirring until the salt dissolves completely. Let the brine cool, then pour enough brine into the jar to cover the vegetables and fill the jar. Cover to exclude air.

4 Set the jar on a saucer to catch any overflow that happens when fermentation begins. Place the jar where the temperature remains constant; 65° to 75°F is ideal.

5 Let the vegetables ferment for 1 to 3 weeks. Check every few days and remove any scum that forms. When the vegetables taste pleasantly pickled, store in the refrigerator. The pickles will keep for at least 3 months in the refrigerator.

Salt-Brined Green Tomatoes

Makes 1 quart

Old-style Jewish delis used to stock barrels of pickled green tomatoes right next to the barrels of pickled cucumbers. Everyone knew that green tomatoes meant unripe tomatoes. But the popularity of heirloom tomatoes has made sweet, ripe green tomatoes commonplace. Let me be perfectly clear: This recipe is what you make when the frost has brought an abrupt end to the growing season and you have unripe green tomatoes on your hands.

Ingredients

2¾ cups water

1 tablespoon pickling or fine sea salt

2 tablespoons distilled white vinegar

1 dill head or 6 sprigs fresh dill

1 tablespoon dill seeds

3 garlic cloves

about 4 cups green unripe cherry or small plum tomatoes

1 Combine the water and salt in a saucepan and heat, stirring until the salt dissolves. Stir in the white vinegar and let cool to room temperature.

2 Pack the dill, dill seeds, and garlic in a clean 1-quart canning jar. Tightly pack with the tomatoes. Pour the cooled brine over the tomatoes to completely fill the jar. Cover to exclude air.

3 Place the jar on a saucer to catch any overflow that happens when fermentation begins. Set the jar where the temperature will remain constant; 65° to 75°F is ideal.

4 Let the tomatoes ferment for about 1 week. Check every few days and remove any scum that forms. When the tomatoes taste pleasantly pickled, store in the refrigerator. The pickles will keep for at least 3 months in the refrigerator.

Kitchen Note

If you are short on refrigerator space, the pickles will hold up on the counter or in a cool basement for a couple of weeks but will continue to ferment. The flavor will become more sour and the texture of the pickle will soften.

Chapter 3

Single Jar Pickles

Kosher Dill Spears • Baby Kosher Dills • Dill Chips • Classic Bread and Butters • Curried Cucumber Pickles • Vermont Maple Sweet Pickles • Lemon Cukes • Dilled Asparagus • Lemon Pickled Asparagus • Dilly Beans • Chile Dilly Beans • Bread and Butter Beans • Basil Beans • Tarragon Beans • Italian-Style Pickled Green Beans • Caraway Pickled Beets • Orange Pickled Beets • Spiced Pickled Carrots • Rosy Middle-Eastern Caraway Cauliflower • Golden Spiced Pickled Cauliflower • Sweet Spiced Cauliflower Pickles • Pickled Cauliflower with Pomegranate Molasses • Spiced Pickled Fennel • Dilled Fiddleheads • Pickled Garlic Scapes • Dilled Jerusalem Artichokes • Spicy Dilled Okra • Sweet Pickled Okra • Zesty Sweet Pickled Okra • Pickled Pears • Roasted Pickled Peppers • Mixed Pickled Peppers • Spiced Prune Plums • Ramp Pickles • Pickled Tomatillos • Sweet Green Tomato Wheels • Zucchini Dill Chips • Zucchini Bread and Butters • Curried Zucchini Pickles • Herbed Jardinière • Sweet Mixed Pickles

When I started making pickles, I was often frustrated by recipes that required making pickles in big batches, usually seven jars at a time, a canner load. If it was my first time working with a recipe, how would I know whether I'd like the end product enough to eat my way through seven jars? Working in large batches took effort, especially in the heat of summer. And if I only had enough produce for, say, five jars, the math was excruciating.

Then I had an idea: Why not figure out how to make pickles a single jar at a time? Initially, my goal was to introduce more variety to my pickle shelf and make the math simpler, but as I undertook the project, more and more advantages came to light.

By working in small quantities, I could take advantage of the limited amount of surplus my garden produced, while the vegetables were still at their peak. No waiting around until the refrigerator filled with cucumbers or beans. I could make pickles whenever I had an extra quart of fresh vegetables kicking around. When I had a little of this and a little of that, I could make a jar of mixed pickles, turning odds and ends into very delicious and showy pickles.

Experimenting with new recipes and new ideas became very easy with small batches. If it turned out I didn't really like a particular recipe, there were no extra jars of an unpopular pickle. And when I chose to work with a large quantity, I just multiplied the recipe — the math was easy! Thus, my second book, *Summer in a Jar,* was born.

That book is now out of print. But small-batch pickle making remains popular with many. I was a little ahead of the curve when I wrote *Summer in a Jar;* since then small-batch canning has become the rule rather than the exception. It's just one more trend in pickle making that has made our preserving efforts different from the way our ancestors used to approach the task.

The recipes in this chapter have been designed to fill one jar at a time, but they are easily multiplied to fill jar after jar. In fact, I expect that you will be multiplying your efforts most of the time. Eventually, I hope, you will find a few that you love to make year after year, whether your harvests are big or small.

Please note that all of the recipes in this chapter are suitable for making with Pickle Crisp Granules (see Crisping Agents, page 22). I did not mandate it in each recipe because the recipe will be successful without it, *but it is highly recommended,* especially for cucumbers and zucchini.

Recipes for cucumbers and zucchini generally call for a quick soak in salted ice water. The salt draws excess moisture from the vegetable, resulting in a crisper pickle. If you multiply a recipe for cucumbers or zucchini, don't use more than 6 tablespoons salt in the soak. Taste the vegetable after draining. If it is pleasantly salty, all is well. If it tastes too salty, give it a quick rinse in fresh water, until it tastes pleasantly salty to you. An undersalted pickle tastes flat.

The recipes in this chapter are arranged more or less alphabetically by main ingredient. They do start, however, with cucumber pickles, and they end with pickles that use a mixture of vegetables. If you are new to canning, take a minute to review the canning instructions on pages 29 to 32. The recipes in this chapter are designed to be processed in a boiling water bath for long-term storage, but you can skip the canning step and refrigerate the jars instead. If you choose this option, omit the Pickle Crisp Granules.

Canning pickles isn't necessary. With single-jar recipes, it may make more sense to store the pickles in the refrigerator rather than deal with a full-size canner for one jar.

THE BLOSSOM END

The blossom end of the cucumber contains enzymes that will soften a pickle, so it should be sliced off. The blossom end is opposite the stem end and often has a dimple that is lightly colored. Can't tell which is which? Slice both ends off.

Kosher Dill Spears

By the quart

When cucumbers are coming on fast and furious, this is an excellent pickle to make, multiplying the recipe as needed for the amount of cucumbers you have. This is as close as you can get to a deli pickle with vinegar and water bath canning.

Ingredients

- **4 cups pickling cucumber spears, blossom ends removed (about five 4-inch cucumbers)**
- **1 tablespoon plus 2 teaspoons pickling or fine sea salt, or more if necessary**
- **4 garlic cloves**
- **2 tablespoons dill seeds**
- **6 sprigs fresh dill or 1 dill head**
- **1 teaspoon celery seeds**
- **1 teaspoon mustard seeds**
- **½ teaspoon black peppercorns**
- **1 cup distilled white vinegar**
- **1 cup water**
- **Pickle Crisp Granules (optional)**

1 Combine the cucumbers and 1 tablespoon salt in a bowl. Cover with ice water and let stand for at least 2 hours, and up to 6 hours. Drain. Taste a spear of cucumber. If it isn't decidedly salty, toss the cucumbers with an additional 1 to 2 teaspoons pickling salt. If it is too salty (which it never is for me), rinse in water.

2 Pack the garlic, dill seeds, fresh dill, celery seeds, mustard seeds, and peppercorns into a clean hot 1-quart canning jar. Pack in the cucumbers, leaving ½ inch headspace.

3 Combine the white vinegar, water, and remaining 2 teaspoons salt in a saucepan and bring to a boil, stirring to dissolve the salt. Pour the hot vinegar mixture into the jar, leaving ½ inch headspace. Add a rounded ¼ teaspoon of Pickle Crisp to the jar, if using. Remove any air bubbles and seal.

4 Process in a boiling-water bath for 10 minutes, according to the directions on page 31. Let cool undisturbed for 12 hours. Store in a cool, dry place. Do not open for at least 6 weeks to allow the flavors to develop.

Kitchen Notes

- If you have the refrigerator space, don't process these pickles in a boiling water bath — or don't process all of them. Pickles that have not been subjected to heat will be crisper than those that are.
- It often happens that cucumbers are ready for harvest after the dill has already gone by. Use dill in any form: fresh foliage, mature seed head, or dried.
- I pack as many whole spears as possible into the jar vertically, then cut remaining spears into halves and pack those horizontally in the jar.

Baby Kosher Dills

By the quart

There's no debate: boiling water bath canning results in a softer-texture pickle compared to salt-curing. Which is why I prefer to use tiny cucumbers for this recipe. The small size means more crisp skin compared to soft flesh and results in a crisper pickle. With a recipe that can be made 1 quart at a time, there's no excuse for not picking your cucumbers when they are about 2 inches long, and certainly no bigger than 3 inches.

Ingredients

- water
- 1 dill head or 6 sprigs fresh dill
- 4 garlic cloves
- 1 (1-inch) piece horseradish (optional)
- 1 tablespoon dill seeds
- 1 teaspoon black peppercorns
- 1½ teaspoons pickling or fine sea salt
- 4 cups tiny pickling cucumbers, blossom ends removed
- 1½ cups distilled white vinegar
- Pickle Crisp Granules (optional)

1   Bring a kettle of water to a boil. Pack the dill head, garlic, horseradish (if using), dill seeds, peppercorns, and salt into a clean hot 1-quart canning jar. Pack in the cucumbers and pour in the white vinegar. Fill with boiling water, leaving ½ inch headspace. Add a rounded ¼ teaspoon of Pickle Crisp to the jar, if using. Remove any air bubbles and seal.

2   Process in a boiling-water bath for 15 minutes, according to the directions on page 31. Let cool undisturbed for 12 hours. Store in a cool, dry place. Do not open for at least 6 weeks to allow the flavors to develop.

Kitchen Note

European pickling cucumbers are the varieties of choice for pickling small, but any pickling cucumber can be used.

Dill Chips

By the pint

Sandwich-ready dill chips are handy to have in the pantry. I can't even imagine a tuna fish sandwich without them.

Ingredients

2¼–2½ cups thinly sliced pickling cucumbers, blossom ends removed

½ small onion, thinly sliced

1 tablespoon pickling or fine sea salt, or more if necessary

6 tablespoons distilled white vinegar

6 tablespoons water

1 teaspoon sugar

1 tablespoon dill seeds

1 tablespoon chopped fresh dill or 1 teaspoon dried

3 garlic cloves

½ teaspoon mustard seeds

½ teaspoon black peppercorns

Pickle Crisp Granules (optional)

1 Combine the cucumbers, onion, and salt in a large bowl. Mix well. Cover the vegetables with ice water and let stand for at least 2 hours, and up to 6 hours. Drain. Taste a slice of cucumber. If it isn't decidedly salty, toss the vegetables with an additional 1 to 2 teaspoons pickling salt. If it is too salty (which it never is for me), rinse the vegetables in water.

2 Combine the white vinegar, water, and sugar in a saucepan and bring to a boil, stirring to dissolve the sugar.

3 Pack the dill seeds, fresh dill, garlic, mustard seeds, and peppercorns into a clean hot 1-pint canning jar. Pack in the cucumbers. Pour in the hot vinegar mixture, leaving ½ inch headspace. Add a rounded ⅛ teaspoon of Pickle Crisp, if using. Remove any air bubbles and seal.

4 Process in a boiling-water bath for 10 minutes, according to the directions on page 31. Let cool undisturbed for 12 hours. Store in a cool, dry place. Do not open for at least 6 weeks to allow the flavors to develop.

Kitchen Note

The thinner you slice the cukes, the more you will be able to pack into the jars. If you are cutting by hand, you will probably fit only about 2 cups of chips in each pint jar.

The Psychology of Pickles

A young man grows up in the small town of Barnard, Vermont (population 938, as of 2000). Like many rural New England families, his has a vegetable garden, and pickle making is a summer ritual.

"My pickle training was with my family. We made two kinds of very traditional, very old-school, New England–style pickles: sliced dill pickles and pickled green beans, what we called 'dilly beans.' But full disclosure," admits Rick Field, the CEO and pickler-in-chief at Rick's Picks in New York City, "I was more of a consumer than manufacturer in those days."

Rick Field

and still live, near the Grand Army Plaza Farmers' Market [in Brooklyn]. I was finding all this great produce and making interesting relationships with farmers. I built out a repertoire of twenty recipes and then whittled it to nine.

"My watershed moment, my sign from the heavens, was when I won a pickle contest in 2001." It was at the Rosendale Pickle Festival, and he won again in 2002.

Then the bright lights of the city exerted their magic allure, and Field found himself pursuing a career in TV at VH1 and Comedy Central, in the "info-tainment" field, which he found stimulating and fun, but never as though he'd found his place.

And so, at "a crossover time" in his life, Field found himself "pursuing a classic story. What started as a hobby became an obsession and then went beyond obsession." Rick's Picks was created. "I did it for fun in the mid-'90s. I started replicating family recipes. At the time I was living,

A distinguishing feature of Rick's Picks products is that they are all old-fashioned vinegar-brined pickles with bold new flavors and very appealing names. A sampling includes Bee 'N' Beez (bread and butters), Pepi Pep Peps (pickled peppers), Handy Corn (corn relish), Hotties (spicy Sriracha-habanero cucumber pickles), Windy City Wasabeans (wasabi and soy–flavored green beans), Kool Gherks, Slices of

Life (sliced dills), Whup Asp (pickled asparagus), Smokra (pickled okra flavored with smoked okra), and Spears of Influence (cumin-lime dill pickle spears).

Do the pickles begin with the name? Surprisingly, no. Field takes a fairly businesslike approach to developing new pickles. "I look first at the spectrum of products I already have. Then I look at a specific ingredient or a secondary spice and then I just listen to people. I do tons of demos and I listen to what people say. . . . Then I have an 'aha' moment." Which is how The People's Pickle came about. People kept asking for a garlic dill pickle. How could he refuse?

Rick's Picks employs four people full-time in his office in the Lower East Side of Manhattan, the traditional epicenter of American pickling. During the summer pickling season, anywhere from 5 to 15 people will be hand-packing pickles into jars in a manufacturing kitchen located in Poughkeepsie, New York. All of the ingredients come from a 250-mile radius around New York City, which means the production work is all seasonal. But because the pickles are shelf-stable, they can be purchased year-round, from the Rick's Picks website, a number of New York City farmers' markets, the Whole Foods supermarket chain, and many stores nationwide (a listing is available on the website).

Despite what must be the fun of the business — coming up with recipes, dreaming up the names, working with farmers — Field admits it is a stressful business. "I've become a complete insomniac. When I was in television, I slept like a baby."

Perhaps as a result of never sleeping, Rick's Picks website includes a great pickle blog, full of just the kind of helpful advice that amateur pickle makers can take advantage of, including how to choose a pickle gift for everyone in your life. Sure, it's specifically tailored for Rick's Picks pickles. But who would disagree that spicy pickled green beans would suit "straight-shooters" who are "funny, frank, and loyal" or a super-hot pickle would be the perfect gift for "the thrill-seeker who blazes off the beaten path in search of authentic, local eats before it's discovered by the masses"? I know I'll be giving gifts of bread and butter pickles to the "sweet, playful, and happy-go-lucky" in my life.

The psychology of pickles is an unexplored region, but Rick's Pick is ahead of the curve on that, as well as on spicing up the old-fashioned pickle.

For more on the psychology of pickles and other pickle pleasures, visit Rick's Picks website at www.rickspicksnyc.com.

Classic Bread and Butters

By the pint

A farmhouse classic, bread and butters are essential to the pickler's pantry: sweet, spiced, crunchy. They make an excellent addition to Sweet Pickle Macaroni Salad (page 251).

Ingredients

2¼–2½ cups thinly sliced pickling cucumbers, blossom ends removed

½ small onion, thinly sliced

1 tablespoon pickling or fine sea salt, or more if needed

½ cup cider vinegar

⅓ cup firmly packed brown sugar

¼ teaspoon ground turmeric

water

1 teaspoon mixed pickling spices, store-bought or homemade (page 18)

½ teaspoon celery seeds

Pickle Crisp Granules (optional)

1 Combine the cucumbers, onion, and salt in a large bowl. Mix well. Cover the vegetables with ice water and let stand for at least 2 hours, and up to 6 hours. Drain. Taste a slice of cucumber. If it isn't decidedly salty, toss the vegetables with an additional 1 to 2 teaspoons pickling salt. If it is too salty (which it never is for me), rinse the vegetables in water.

2 Combine the cider vinegar, brown sugar, and turmeric in a saucepan. Heat to boiling, stirring to dissolve the sugar. Bring a kettle of water to a boil.

3 Pack the mixed pickling spices and celery seeds into a clean hot 1-pint canning jar. Pack in the cucumbers and onions. Pour in the vinegar mixture. The vinegar mixture will not cover the vegetables, so top off with the boiling water, leaving ½ inch headspace. Add a rounded ⅛ teaspoon of Pickle Crisp to the jar, if using. Remove any air bubbles and seal.

4 Process in a boiling-water bath for 10 minutes, according to the directions on page 31. Let cool undisturbed for 12 hours. Store in a cool, dry place. Do not open for at least 6 weeks to allow the flavors to develop.

Kitchen Notes

- If you slice your cucumbers paper-thin on a mandoline or other device, you will fit 2½ cups of salted slices into a pint jar. If the slices are thicker, less will fit in.
- Extra salted cucumber slices are tasty in salads or enjoyed plain.

Curried Cucumber Pickles

By the pint

I love to watch the faces of people trying these pickles for the first time. First there is surprise, then delight because the flavors are both delicious and unexpected. Make these pickles when the usual dills and bread and butters evoke yawns.

Ingredients

2¼–2½ cups thinly sliced pickling cucumbers, blossom ends removed

½ onion, thinly sliced

1 tablespoon pickling or fine sea salt, or more if needed

½ cup cider vinegar

½ cup sugar

3 tablespoons raisins

1½ teaspoons curry powder

½ teaspoon coriander seeds

½ teaspoon mustard seeds

Pickle Crisp Granules (optional)

1 Combine the cucumbers, onion, and salt in a bowl. Add ice water to cover and let soak for at least 2 hours, and up to 6 hours. Drain. Taste a slice of cucumber. If it isn't decidedly salty, toss with 1 to 2 teaspoons pickling salt. If it is too salty (which it never is for me), rinse in water.

2 Combine the cider vinegar, sugar, raisins, curry powder, coriander seeds, and mustard seeds in a small saucepan. Heat to boiling, stirring to dissolve the sugar.

3 Pack the cucumbers into a clean hot 1-pint canning jar. Pour in the hot vinegar mixture, leaving ½ inch headspace. Add a rounded ⅛ teaspoon of Pickle Crisp to the jar, if using. Remove any air bubbles and seal.

4 Process in a boiling-water bath for 10 minutes, according to the directions on page 31. Let cool undisturbed for 12 hours. Store in a cool, dry place. Do not open for at least 6 weeks to allow the flavors to develop.

CUCUMBER MATH

Three average pickling cucumbers equal 2¼ to 2½ cups thinly sliced, which after brining will fit into a 1-pint jar.

Vermont Maple Sweet Pickles

By the pint

Vermonters take their maple syrup seriously.
Very seriously. So, if you are going to use maple syrup in a recipe, it better be pure maple syrup, not pancake syrup made of corn syrup and maple flavoring. And the darker the grade of syrup, the better. Vermont Fancy (US Grade A Light Amber) syrup, made from the first collected sap, is lightest in color and flavor. As the season progresses, the sap darkens and the syrup maker makes Vermont Grade A Medium Amber maple syrup, then Vermont Grade A Dark Amber maple syrup, and finally Vermont Grade B maple syrup: the strongest and darkest table-grade syrup. That's the grade I prefer for these pickles, but any grade can be used. The flavor of these pickles has a subtle maple sweetness.

Ingredients

- **2 cups cucumbers cut into ¾-inch chunks, blossom ends removed**
- **½ small onion, sliced**
- **2 teaspoons pickling or fine sea salt, or more if needed**
- **½ cup cider vinegar**
- **¼ cup pure maple syrup**
- **water**
- **1 teaspoon mixed pickling spices, store-bought or homemade (page 18)**
- **1 teaspoon coriander seeds**
- **Pickle Crisp Granules (optional)**

1 Combine the cucumbers, onion, and salt in a large bowl. Mix well. Cover the vegetables with ice water and let stand for at least 2 hours, and up to 6 hours. Drain. Taste a piece of cucumber. If it isn't decidedly salty, toss with 1 to 2 teaspoons pickling salt. If it is too salty (which it never is for me), rinse in water.

2 Combine the cider vinegar and maple syrup in a saucepan and bring to a boil, stirring to dissolve the maple syrup. Bring a kettle of water to a boil.

3 Pack the mixed pickling spices and coriander seeds into a clean hot 1-pint canning jar. Pack in the cucumbers and onions. Pour in the hot vinegar mixture. It will not cover the vegetables, so top off with the boiling water, leaving ½ inch headspace. Add a rounded ⅛ teaspoon of Pickle Crisp to the jar, if using. Remove any air bubbles and seal.

4 Process in a boiling-water bath for 10 minutes, according to the directions on page 31. Let cool undisturbed for 12 hours. Store in a cool, dry place. Do not open for at least 6 weeks to allow the flavors to develop.

Kitchen Notes

- Any type of cucumber can be used for a sweet pickle, even salad cucumbers with their slightly tougher skins. I find that salad cucumbers do better in pickle recipes that call for cutting them into chunks, rather than pickling them whole or in thin slices.
- If your cucumbers are fully mature, scrape away the seeds before cutting into chunks.

KOOL-AID PICKLES

File this one under "Now I've Heard Everything. . . . "

Pickle recipes from the South are often sweeter than northern versions, but some might say the Mississippi-developed Kool-Aid pickle goes too far. Here's how to make it: Take a quart of dill pickles, drain off all the brine, and slice the pickles in half. Return the pickles to the jar. Make a double-strength batch of Kool-Aid; use any flavor, but cherry or tropical fruit (red) and lemon-lime (green) are popular choices. Pour it over the pickles. Refrigerate for at least a week. The pickles will take on the vibrant Kool-Aid color.

And the flavor? They say the sugar and the vinegar cancel each other out, leaving behind a fruity, sweet, tangy, highly crunchy cucumber. Kids love it.

According to the *New York Times*, which ran a story about Kool-Aid pickles in 2007, the Kool-Aid pickles are famous for selling out at fairs and school fund-raisers. For the going price of fifty cents to a dollar, wouldn't you try a bright red pickle?

Lemon Cukes

By the pint

The lemon in these pickles gives them an unusual fruity tart-ness, quite different from the traditional vinegar pickles — and quite delicious.

Ingredients

2¼–2½ cups thinly sliced pickling cucumbers, blossom ends removed

½ cup sliced red or green bell pepper

1 tablespoon pickling or fine sea salt, or more if necessary

3 tablespoons bottled lemon juice

3 tablespoons distilled white vinegar

3 tablespoons water, plus extra for topping off jar

2 tablespoons sugar

1 lemon slice

¼ teaspoon allspice berries

Pickle Crisp Granules (optional)

1 Combine the cucumbers, bell pepper, and salt in a large bowl. Mix well. Cover the vegetables with ice water and let stand for at least 2 hours, and up to 6 hours. Drain. Taste a slice of cucumber. If it isn't decidedly salty, toss with 1 to 2 teaspoons pickling salt. If it is too salty (which it never is for me), rinse in water.

2 Combine the lemon juice, white vinegar, 3 tablespoons water, and sugar in a saucepan and bring to a boil, stirring to dissolve the sugar. Bring a kettle of water to a boil.

3 Pack the lemon slice and allspice berries into a clean hot 1-pint canning jar. Pack in the cucumbers and bell peppers. Pour in the vinegar mixture; it will not cover the vegetables, so top off with the boiling water, leaving ½ inch headspace. Add a rounded ⅛ teaspoon of Pickle Crisp to the jar, if using. Remove any air bubbles and seal.

4 Process in a boiling-water bath for 10 minutes, according to the directions on page 31. Let cool undisturbed for 12 hours. Store in a cool, dry place. Do not open for at least 6 weeks to allow the flavors to develop.

Kitchen Note

Use bottled, not fresh, lemon juice in pickles. The acidity is consistent and, therefore, safer. Also, the nuanced flavor of fresh lemon juice is lost in the pickling and canning process.

Dilled Asparagus

By the pint

The "dilly bean" treatment is delicious with all manner of green vegetables, especially asparagus. Dilled asparagus has a nutty, green flavor that distinguishes it from dilly beans.

Ingredients

- ½ **pound asparagus (about 10 spears)**
- ¾ **cup distilled white vinegar**
- ¾ **cup water**
- 1½ **teaspoons sugar**
- 2 **garlic cloves**
- 1 **shallot or pearl onion**
- 2 **teaspoons dill seeds**
- 1 **teaspoon pickling or fine sea salt**

1 Trim the woody ends from the asparagus. Cut the asparagus into 2-inch lengths.

2 Combine the white vinegar, water, and sugar in a saucepan and heat to boiling, stirring to dissolve the sugar.

3 Pack the garlic, shallot, dill seeds, and salt into a clean hot 1-pint canning jar. Pack in the asparagus. Pour in the hot vinegar mixture, leaving ½ inch headspace. Remove any air bubbles and seal.

4 Process in a boiling-water bath for 10 minutes, according to the directions on page 31. Let cool undisturbed for 12 hours. Store in a cool, dry place. Do not open for at least 6 weeks to allow the flavors to develop.

Kitchen Note

Pickled asparagus makes a lovely addition to a crudités platter. Or serve on a bed of greens with crumbled hard-cooked egg sprinkled on top for a lovely looking, delicious salad.

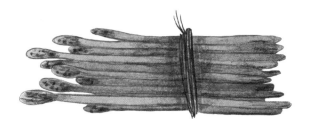

Lemon Pickled Asparagus

By the pint

Pickled asparagus will never be as pretty as the fresh vegetable because the spears turn olive green. But the flavor — and the treat of having local asparagus in the gloom of winter — makes it worthwhile.

Ingredients

- ½ pound asparagus (about 10 spears)
- ¾ cup distilled white vinegar
- ¾ cup water
- 1½ teaspoons sugar
- 1 (3-inch) strip lemon zest
- 2 garlic cloves
- 1 teaspoon coriander seeds
- 1 teaspoon pickling or fine sea salt

1 Trim the woody ends from the asparagus. Cut the asparagus into 2-inch lengths.

2 Combine the white vinegar, water, and sugar in a saucepan and heat to boiling, stirring to dissolve the sugar.

3 Pack the lemon zest, garlic, coriander seeds, and salt into a clean hot 1-pint canning jar. Pack in the asparagus. Pour in the hot vinegar mixture, leaving ½ inch headspace. Remove any air bubbles and seal.

4 Process in a boiling-water bath for 10 minutes, according to the directions on page 31. Let cool undisturbed for 12 hours. Store in a cool, dry place. Do not open for at least 6 weeks to allow the flavors to develop.

Dilly Beans

By the pint

Harvest snap beans daily to prevent them from getting overripe (when you can see the shape of the beans within the pod). An overripe bean can be pickled, but it will not be as tender as less mature beans. This recipe makes the classic dilly bean.

Ingredients

- ¾ **cup distilled white vinegar**
- 6 **tablespoons water**
- 1 **tablespoon sugar**
- 1 **teaspoon pickling or fine sea salt**
- 2 **garlic cloves**
- 6 **sprigs fresh dill, 1 dill head, or 1 tablespoon dill seeds**
- 2 **cups trimmed green beans (about 6 ounces)**

1   Combine the white vinegar, water, sugar, and salt in a saucepan and bring to a boil, stirring to dissolve the sugar and salt.

2   Pack the garlic, dill, and beans into a sterilized hot 1-pint canning jar. Pour in the hot vinegar mixture, leaving ½ inch headspace. Remove any air bubbles and seal.

3   Process in a boiling-water bath for 5 minutes, according to the directions on page 31. Let cool undisturbed for 12 hours. Store in a cool, dry place. Do not open for at least 6 weeks to allow the flavors to develop.

Chile Dilly Beans

By the pint

A hot red pepper adds zing to a classic recipe. My son, who has been a pickle aficionado since his highchair days, thinks this might be the best dilly bean recipe ever created.

Ingredients

- ¾ **cup distilled white vinegar**
- 6 **tablespoons water**
- 1 **tablespoon sugar**
- 1 **teaspoon pickling or fine sea salt**
- 2 **garlic cloves**
- 6 **sprigs fresh dill, 1 dill head, or 1 tablespoon dill seeds**
- 1 **dried red chile or ½ teaspoon crushed red pepper flakes**
- 2 **cups trimmed green beans (about 6 ounces)**

1 Combine the white vinegar, water, sugar, and salt in a saucepan and bring to a boil, stirring to dissolve the sugar.

2 Pack the garlic, dill, chile, and beans into a sterilized hot 1-pint canning jar. Pour in the hot vinegar mixture, leaving ½ inch headspace. Remove any air bubbles and seal.

3 Process in a boiling-water bath for 5 minutes, according to the directions on page 31. Let cool undisturbed for 12 hours. Store in a cool, dry place. Do not open for at least 6 weeks to allow the flavors to develop.

Bread and Butter Beans

By the pint

We get stuck in our thinking. Dilly beans are so terrific, we don't think of experimenting with other seasonings for our pickles. I am here to tell you that your favorite sweet pickle can be made with green beans.

Ingredients

- 2 cups trimmed green beans (about 6 ounces)
- ½ small onion, thinly sliced
- ⅔ cup cider vinegar
- ⅓ cup water
- ½ cup firmly packed brown sugar
- 1 teaspoon pickling or fine sea salt
- 1 teaspoon mustard seeds
- ½ teaspoon mixed pickling spices, store-bought or homemade (page 18)
- ¼ teaspoon ground turmeric

1 Mix the beans with the onion.

2 Combine the cider vinegar, water, brown sugar, salt, mustard seeds, mixed pickling spices, and turmeric in a saucepan and bring to a boil, stirring to dissolve the sugar.

3 Pack the beans and onion into a sterilized hot 1-pint canning jar. Pour in the hot vinegar mixture, leaving ½ inch headspace. Remove any air bubbles and seal.

4 Process in a boiling-water bath for 5 minutes, according to the directions on page 31. Let cool undisturbed for 12 hours. Store in a cool, dry place. Do not open for at least 6 weeks to allow the flavors to develop.

Basil Beans

By the pint

The classic flavoring is dill, of course. But other herbs can make a wonderful marriage with beans. Aromatic basil makes a haunting contribution to these pickles.

Ingredients

- ¾ **cup distilled white vinegar**
- 6 **tablespoons water**
- 1 **tablespoon sugar**
- 1 **teaspoon pickling or fine sea salt**
- 2 **garlic cloves**
- 1 **large sprig fresh basil**
- 2 **cups trimmed green beans (about 6 ounces)**

1   Combine the white vinegar, water, sugar, and salt in a saucepan and bring to a boil, stirring to dissolve the sugar.

2   While the brine heats, pack the garlic, basil, and beans into a sterilized hot 1-pint canning jar. Pour in the hot vinegar mixture, leaving ½ inch headspace. Remove any air bubbles and seal.

3   Process in a boiling-water bath for 5 minutes, according to the directions on page 31. Let cool undisturbed for 12 hours. Store in a cool, dry place. Do not open for at least 6 weeks to allow the flavors to develop.

Tarragon Beans

By the pint

Grow the aromatic and delicately flavored French tarragon (*Artemisia dracunculus*), rather than Russian tarragon (*Artemesia dracunculoides*), which has coarser, paler leaves and a bitter flavor. You'll appreciate its aniselike flavor. Tarragon is frequently used to flavor vinegar, so why not pickled beans? Try it! I think you'll like it. Finely chopped Tarragon Beans makes an intriguing contribution to homemade tartar sauce.

Ingredients

- ¾ cup distilled white vinegar
- 6 tablespoons water
- 1 tablespoon sugar
- 1 teaspoon pickling or fine sea salt
- 2 garlic cloves
- 2 sprigs fresh tarragon
- 2 cups trimmed green beans (about 6 ounces)

1 Combine the white vinegar, water, sugar, and salt in a saucepan and bring to a boil, stirring to dissolve the sugar.

2 While the brine heats, pack the garlic, tarragon, and beans into a sterilized hot 1-pint canning jar. Pour in the hot vinegar mixture, leaving ½ inch headspace. Remove any air bubbles and seal.

3 Process in a boiling-water bath for 5 minutes, according to the directions on page 31. Let cool undisturbed for 12 hours. Store in a cool, dry place. Do not open for at least 6 weeks to allow the flavors to develop.

Italian-Style Pickled Green Beans

By the quart

These taste wonderful! The olive oil and fresh herbs make this an unusually flavorful pickle. The oil will float to the top of the jar, so just before removing the beans, give the jar a good shake to mix the oil into the brine. Then remove the beans and serve in your grandmother's glass pickle dish.

Ingredients

- 1½ cups white wine vinegar
- ¾ cup water
- 2 teaspoons pickling or fine sea salt
- 4 cups trimmed 4-inch-long green beans (about 12 ounces)
- 2 garlic cloves
- 1 large sprig fresh basil, oregano, rosemary, or thyme
- extra-virgin olive oil

1 Combine the white wine vinegar, water, and salt in a saucepan and bring to a boil, stirring to dissolve the salt.

2 Pack the beans, garlic, and basil into a clean hot 1-quart canning jar, shaking the jar as you pack to settle the beans and create space for more. Leave about ½ inch headspace. Pour in the hot vinegar mixture. Top off with olive oil, completely covering the beans and leaving ½ inch headspace. Remove any air bubbles and seal.

3 Process in a boiling-water bath for 10 minutes, according to the directions on page 31. Let cool undisturbed for 12 hours. Store in a cool, dry place. Do not open for at least 6 weeks to allow the flavors to develop.

Kitchen Note

Pack the beans in tightly. You can chop some beans in half to fill in space at the top of the jar. It helps to hold the jar at an angle and add the beans vertically, shaking the jar to help them settle in.

Caraway Pickled Beets

By the quart

Caraway seeds add a buttery flavor to the pickled beets. Enjoy as a side dish with a dollop of sour cream on top.

Ingredients

- 1 cup distilled white vinegar
- ½ cup water
- ½ cup sugar
- 1 teaspoon pickling or fine sea salt
- 4 cups sliced cooked beets (see box)
- 1 small onion, thinly sliced
- 1 tablespoon caraway seeds

1 Combine the white vinegar, water, sugar, and salt in a small saucepan and heat to boiling, stirring to dissolve the sugar.

2 Pack the beets, onion, and caraway seeds into a clean hot 1-quart canning jar. Pour in the hot vinegar mixture, leaving ½ inch headspace. Remove any air bubbles and seal.

3 Process in a boiling-water bath for 30 minutes, according to the directions on page 31. Let cool undisturbed for 12 hours. Store in a cool, dry place. Do not open for at least 6 weeks to allow the flavors to develop.

Kitchen Notes

- Beets are one of the few vegetables that can be pickled at your convenience. They keep well in the refrigerator for 2 to 3 weeks. Gently brush off the beets before storing, but do not wash.
- Dill seeds can replace the caraway seeds for a similar flavor.

COOKING BEETS

To cook beets, scrub them well. Remove the greens, leaving about 2 inches of stem. Leave about 2 inches of taproot. Cook the beets in boiling water to cover for 20 to 40 minutes, depending on the size. The beets are done when a fork can easily pierce them. Let cool, then peel.

Orange Pickled Beets

By the pint

The sweet flavor of beets lends itself to playing with sweet spices — in this case, allspice. Allspice berries were discovered in the Caribbean by Christopher Columbus, who thought he had found yet another "pepper." The name was later changed to "allspice" because the berries have the flavor and aroma of a mix of cloves, cinnamon, and nutmeg with a hint of peppery heat.

Ingredients

- ¼ cup distilled white vinegar
- ¼ cup water
- 1 teaspoon pickling or fine sea salt
- 1 teaspoon sugar
- Zest from ½ orange, cut into thin strips
- 2 allspice berries
- 2 cups cubed cooked beets (see page 93)

1 Combine the white vinegar, water, salt, and sugar in a small saucepan and bring to a boil, stirring to dissolve the sugar.

2 Pack the orange zest and allspice into a clean hot 1-pint canning jar, followed by the beets. Pour in the hot vinegar mixture, leaving ½ inch headspace. Remove any air bubbles and seal.

3 Process in a boiling-water bath for 30 minutes, according to the directions on page 31. Let cool undisturbed for 12 hours. Store in a cool, dry place. Do not open for at least 6 weeks to allow the flavors to develop.

Kitchen Note

Beets vary tremendously in size. Figure that 4 to 5 medium-size beets make a pound and that each pound will yield 2 to 3 cups of cubed beets.

Spiced Pickled Carrots

By the quart

The sweet, snappy goodness of a freshly harvested carrot is without comparison. But toward the spring, carrots can show signs of age. Perhaps they are trying to break dormancy by growing little root hairs, or perhaps your local farm market is selling 5-pound bags at a big discount. When that happens, it is time to make carrot pickles.

Ingredients

- 1 cup distilled white vinegar
- 1 cup water, plus more as needed
- 3 tablespoons sugar
- 1½ teaspoons pickling or fine sea salt
- 1 small dried chile or ⅛ teaspoon crushed red pepper
- 1 cinnamon stick
- 2 garlic cloves
- 4 whole cloves
- 1 teaspoon mixed pickling spices, store-bought or homemade (page 18)
- ¼ teaspoon fennel seeds
- ¼ teaspoon seeds fenugreek
- 1 pound carrots, cut into thin sticks

1 Combine the white vinegar, water, sugar, and salt in a small saucepan. Bring to a boil, stirring to dissolve the sugar.

2 While the vinegar mixture heats, pack a clean 1-quart canning jar with the chile, cinnamon, garlic, cloves, mixed pickling spices, fennel seeds, and fenugreek seeds. Pack the carrots into the jar. Pour in the hot vinegar mixture, leaving ½ inch headspace (top off with additional water if necessary). Remove any air bubbles and seal.

3 Process in a boiling-water bath for 20 minutes, according to the directions on page 31. Let cool undisturbed for 12 hours. Store in a cool, dry place. Do not open for at least 6 weeks to allow the flavors to develop.

Kitchen Notes

- How many carrots can be packed into a jar varies considerably, depending on the size of the carrots and how tightly you can pack the jar. I usually fit in about 1 pound, which means 4 to 6 carrots, depending on their size.
- Fenugreek is a wonderful, underutilized spice that adds an almost buttery flavor. It is traditionally used in curries and pickles. It is also used in the making of imitation maple syrup, though I find the connection difficult to fathom.

Rosy Middle-Eastern Caraway Cauliflower

By the quart

Beets give this pickle its unusual color; caraway provides its unusual flavor.

Ingredients

- 1 small to medium beet, peeled and chopped (¼–½ cup)
- 1⅓ cups distilled white vinegar
- 1⅓ cups water
- 1 tablespoon sugar
- 2 teaspoons pickling or fine sea salt
- 1 teaspoon caraway seeds
- ½ teaspoon celery seeds
- 3½ cups cauliflower florets

1 Combine the beet, white vinegar, water, sugar, and salt in a small saucepan. Bring almost to a boil, then simmer for 5 minutes, stirring to dissolve the sugar.

2 While the vinegar mixture heats, pack a clean 1-quart canning jar with the caraway seeds, celery seeds, and cauliflower.

3 Strain the vinegar mixture, reserving the liquid and discarding the beet. Pour the hot liquid over the cauliflower, leaving ½ inch headspace. Remove any air bubbles and seal.

4 Process in a boiling-water bath for 15 minutes, according to the directions on page 31. Let cool undisturbed for 12 hours. Store in a cool, dry place. Do not open for at least 6 weeks to allow the flavors to develop.

CAULIFLOWER

- Cauliflower is perfect for pickling because it retains a pleasing texture in the jar and absorbs flavors well. It's a good thing it makes such a fine pickle because cauliflower does not store well. It has a refrigerator shelf life of about 1 week, so it should be pickled as soon as possible after harvest.

- Cauliflower heads vary widely in size and weight. Homegrown cauliflower is often smaller than commercially grown cauliflower. Figure that a 6-inch-diameter head, with the leaves and stem removed, weighs about a pound and yields 4 cups of florets.

- A small homegrown head will make about 1 quart of pickles; an average-size (8-inch-diameter) commercial cauliflower will yield about 2 quarts.

Golden Spiced Pickled Cauliflower

By the quart

Turmeric dyes the cauliflower yellow, a promise of the spice that flavors these delicious pickles. Feel free to add to the mix of vegetables. Green beans, wax beans, and more pearl onions are all good choices.

Ingredients

- 1⅓ **cups distilled white vinegar**
- 1⅓ **cups water**
- 1 **tablespoon sugar**
- 1 **teaspoon pickling or fine sea salt**
- ¼ **teaspoon ground turmeric**
- 1 **small dried chile or ⅛ teaspoon crushed red pepper**
- 1 **pearl onion or shallot**
- 1 **garlic clove**
- 1 **cardamom pod**
- ½ **teaspoon mixed pickling spices, store-bought or homemade (page 18)**
- ¼ **teaspoon coriander seeds**
- ¼ **teaspoon cumin seeds**
- 3–3½ **cups cauliflower florets**
- 1 **carrot, thinly sliced**

1 Combine the white vinegar, water, sugar, salt, and turmeric in a small saucepan. Bring almost to a boil, then simmer for 5 minutes, stirring occasionally.

2 While the vinegar mixture heats, pack a clean 1-quart canning jar with the chile, onion, garlic, cardamom, mixed pickling spices, coriander, and cumin.

3 Mix together the cauliflower and carrot and pack into the jar. Pour in the hot vinegar mixture, leaving ½ inch headspace. Remove any air bubbles and seal.

4 Process in a boiling-water bath for 15 minutes, according to the directions on page 31. Let cool undisturbed for 12 hours. Store in a cool, dry place. Do not open for at least 6 weeks to allow the flavors to develop.

Kitchen Note

The turmeric tends to settle on the bottom of the jar. For even coloring of the cauliflower, give the jar a shake every couple of days after processing.

Sweet Spiced Cauliflower Pickles

By the quart

The recipe title says it all: a sweet pickle, delicately spiced. If a blast of chile heat isn't to your taste, this pickle is for you.

Ingredients

- 1¼ **cups cider vinegar**
- 1¼ **cups water**
- ½ **cup sugar**
- 2 **teaspoons pickling or fine sea salt**
- ½ **teaspoon ground turmeric**
- 2 **teaspoons mixed pickling spices, store-bought or homemade (page 18)**
- 1 **teaspoon black peppercorns**
- 3–3½ **cups cauliflower florets**
- ½ **small onion, thinly sliced**

1 Combine the cider vinegar, water, sugar, salt, and turmeric in a small saucepan and bring to a boil, stirring to dissolve the sugar.

2 While the brine heats, pack a clean 1-quart canning jar with the mixed pickling spices and black peppercorns. Mix the cauliflower and onion and pack into the jar. Pour in the hot vinegar mixture, leaving ½ inch headspace. Remove any air bubbles and seal.

3 Process in a boiling-water bath for 15 minutes, according to the directions on page 31. Let cool undisturbed for 12 hours. Store in a cool, dry place. Do not open for at least 6 weeks to allow the flavors to develop.

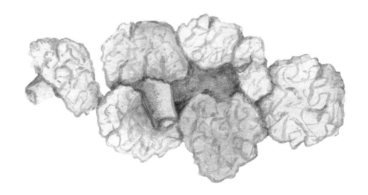

Pickled Cauliflower with Pomegranate Molasses

By the quart

Pomegranate molasses, a concentrate of pomegranate juice, gives these pickles an elusive tart and fruity flavor reminiscent of tamarind.

Ingredients

- 1¼ **cups distilled white vinegar**
- 1¼ **cups water**
- 2 **tablespoons pomegranate molasses**
- ½ **cup sugar**
- 2 **teaspoons pickling or fine sea salt**
- 1 **cardamom pod**
- 2 **teaspoons coriander seeds**
- 3–3½ **cups cauliflower florets**
- ½ **onion, thinly sliced**

1 Combine the white vinegar, water, pomegranate molasses, sugar, and salt in a saucepan. Bring to a boil, stirring until the sugar dissolves.

2 While the vinegar mixture heats, pack a clean 1-quart canning jar with the cardamom and coriander. Mix the cauliflower and onion and pack into the jar. Pour in the hot vinegar mixture, leaving ½ inch headspace. Remove any air bubbles and seal.

3 Process in a boiling-water bath for 15 minutes, according to the directions on page 31. Let cool undisturbed for 12 hours. Store in a cool, dry place. Do not open for at least 6 weeks to allow the flavors to develop.

POMEGRANATE MOLASSES

Pomegranate molasses is available wherever Middle Eastern foods are sold. You can also find it at natural food stores. Pomegranates are a powerhouse of nutrition, but if you can't find any, a mixture of 2 tablespoons sugar to 1 tablespoon lemon juice makes an adequate substitute.

Spiced Pickled Fennel

By the pint

Crunchy, sweet, and mysteriously spiced, these pickles make a fine accompaniment to chicken and pork. The red wine vinegar gives the brine a rosy hue. The five-spice powder, found wherever Chinese foods are sold, is a mixture of cinnamon, cloves, fennel seeds, star anise, and Szechuan peppercorns.

Ingredients

- 2 fennel bulbs
- 2¾ teaspoons pickling or fine sea salt, or more if necessary
- ¾ cups red wine vinegar
- ½ cup water
- 2 tablespoons honey
- ½ teaspoon Chinese five-spice powder

1 Remove the fronds and stems from the fennel and set aside. Slice the bulbs in half vertically; remove and discard the cores. Thinly slice the bulbs vertically. You should have about 2 cups sliced fennel.

2 Combine the fennel and salt in a bowl and toss to combine. Cover with ice water and let sit for at least 2 hours, and up to 6 hours. Taste a slice of fennel. If it isn't decidedly salty, toss with 1 to 2 teaspoons pickling salt. If it is too salty (which it never is for me), rinse in water.

3 Combine the red wine vinegar, water, honey, and five-spice powder in a small saucepan and bring to a boil, stirring to dissolve the honey.

4 While the vinegar mixture heats, drain the fennel. Pack a clean hot 1-pint canning jar with a few fennel fronds. Then pack the fennel into the jar. Pour in the hot vinegar mixture, leaving ½ inch headspace. Remove any air bubbles and seal.

5 Process in a boiling-water bath for 10 minutes, according to the directions on page 31. Let cool undisturbed for 12 hours. Store in a cool, dry place. Do not open for at least 6 weeks to allow the flavors to develop.

Kitchen Note

Fennel is sometimes labeled "Florence fennel" in the supermarket and seed catalogs to distinguish it from fennel that is grown for its seeds.

Dilled Fiddleheads

By the pint

Wild food enthusiasts know that fiddleheads emerge shortly after wild leeks (ramps) in the spring. The sprout of the ostrich fern looks a lot like the tuning end of a fiddle, hence the name. These ferns have a distinctive brown papery covering, which is how you can distinguish them from other less tasty ferns. Fiddleheads are best cooked (sauté in butter) or pickled; they have a green flavor that some describe as a cross between asparagus and spinach.

Ingredients

- 2 cups fiddleheads
- ½ cup distilled white vinegar
- ½ cup water
- 1 teaspoon sugar
- 2 garlic cloves
- 1½ teaspoons dill seeds
- 1 teaspoon pickling or fine sea salt

1. Wash the fiddleheads in several changes of water until no papery brown skin remains. Trim off the woody or discolored ends from the stems.

2. Combine the white vinegar, water, and sugar in a saucepan and heat to boiling, stirring to dissolve the sugar.

3. While the vinegar mixture heats, pack the garlic, dill, and salt into a clean hot 1-pint canning jar. Pack in the fiddleheads. Pour in the hot vinegar mixture, leaving ½ inch headspace. Remove any air bubbles and seal.

4. Process in a boiling-water bath for 10 minutes, according to the directions on page 31. Let cool undisturbed for 12 hours. Store in a cool, dry place. Do not open for at least 6 weeks to allow the flavors to develop.

Kitchen Notes

- Look for fiddleheads on the banks of streams and rivers. Harvest while the fronds are tightly curled, taking care not to damage the crown of the plant (at the base). Or find them in produce sections of upscale markets in mid-spring.
- Look for fiddleheads with a tight coil and only an inch or two of stem. Take care to remove all of the brown papery covering, which is a carcinogen. Start the cleaning process outdoors by lightly shaking them in an open wire basket. Then wash in several changes of water, rubbing off any paper chaff that remains.

Pickled Garlic Scapes

By the pint

The first time I grew garlic, I was shocked because I was expecting scapes and none emerged. It turns out I had planted a soft-neck variety. Only the stiff-neck garlic plant sends up a scape from its central woody stem a few weeks before harvest. The scape is a thin, green, curled extension of the stalk with a small bulbil, or swelling, several inches from its end. The swelling looks like a flower bud, but inside the bulbil are more than 100 tiny cloves that are genetically identical to the parent bulb beneath. If left on the plant, the scape will eventually die and fall over, and the tiny cloves will spill onto the ground, seeding new garlic plants. However, cutting off the scapes keeps the plant's energy from forming the bulbil and therefore encourages larger bulbs. Until recently the scapes were simply composted, but lately cooks have been experimenting with them. It turns out they make a delightful pickle, quite similar to dilly beans. The smaller the scape, the more tender the pickle.

Ingredients

- 1 cup distilled white vinegar
- ½ cup water
- 2 teaspoons sugar
- 1 teaspoon pickling or fine sea salt
- 6 sprigs fresh dill
- 2 cups trimmed 4-inch garlic scapes

1 Combine the white vinegar, water, sugar, and salt in a small saucepan and heat to boiling, stirring to dissolve the sugar.

2 While the vinegar mixture heats, pack the dill into a clean hot 1-pint canning jar. Pack in the scapes. Pour in the hot vinegar mixture, leaving ½ inch headspace. Remove any air bubbles and seal.

3 Process in a boiling-water bath for 10 minutes, according to the directions on page 31. Let cool undisturbed for 12 hours. Store in a cool, dry place. Do not open for at least 6 weeks to allow the flavors to develop.

Kitchen Notes

- Use the scapes as you would any pickle. They make a lovely and unexpected garnish for a Bloody Mary.
- I usually have enough scapes to fill some jars with the straight ends of the scapes and some with the curly tops.

ARTICHOKE PICKLE PASSION: A SONNET

Beverly Fields Burnette enjoys the challenge of taking intimidating poetry and bringing it into the realm of "everyday life." She uses poetry and storytelling as vehicles for teaching history, exposing positive feelings, healing wounds, and bridging gaps. Her career included writing for a children's television program, editing a weekly advice column titled "Ask Miz Bee," social work, and teaching. Published in several poetry anthologies, Burnette is a founding member of both the Carolina African American Writers' Collective and the North Carolina Association of Black Storytellers.

This particular poem came out of a childhood experience she had under the watchful eye of Flossie, one of her mother's sisters. Flossie was the matriarch of the family and directed the harvesting, pickling, and canning operation.

In southern springs we dug for artichokes
In Miz Olivia's tall and weedy yard.
She dipped her snuff, but never, ever smoked;
At eighty-five, she wasn't avant-garde.
Her 'bacco spittings grew the vegetable;
Well nourished were the tubers, strong, the stalks.
And even though their worth was questionable,
With hoe in hand, we dug, postponing talk.
Once washed, soaked, sliced, they met some torrid brine.
Aromas flew on steamy clouds of heat.
When canned, the waiting was the longest time.
How many weeks or months before we eat?
In southern springs, we dug the precious root,
And still, this day, it is my passion fruit.

From *Catch the Fire!!! A Cross-Generational Anthology of Contemporary African-American Poetry*, edited by Derrick I. M. Gilbert. (Reprinted by permission of the author.)

GROWING SUNCHOKES

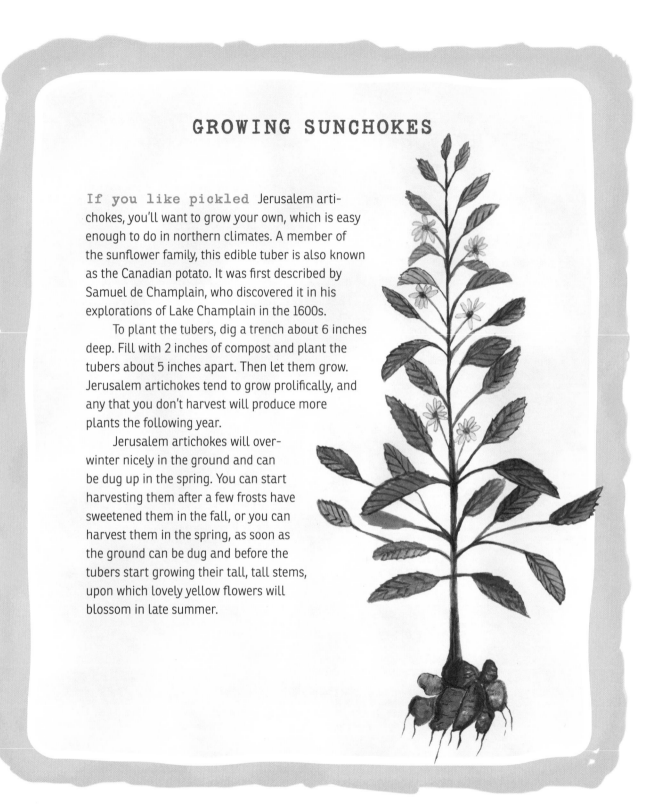

If you like pickled Jerusalem arti-
chokes, you'll want to grow your own, which is easy
enough to do in northern climates. A member of
the sunflower family, this edible tuber is also known
as the Canadian potato. It was first described by
Samuel de Champlain, who discovered it in his
explorations of Lake Champlain in the 1600s.

To plant the tubers, dig a trench about 6 inches
deep. Fill with 2 inches of compost and plant the
tubers about 5 inches apart. Then let them grow.
Jerusalem artichokes tend to grow prolifically, and
any that you don't harvest will produce more
plants the following year.

Jerusalem artichokes will over-
winter nicely in the ground and can
be dug up in the spring. You can start
harvesting them after a few frosts have
sweetened them in the fall, or you can
harvest them in the spring, as soon as
the ground can be dug and before the
tubers start growing their tall, tall stems,
upon which lovely yellow flowers will
blossom in late summer.

Dilled Jerusalem Artichokes

By the pint

The pickling season winds down once the first frosts hit, but Jerusalem artichokes are good for harvesting as long as you can still get a shovel into the ground. The natural sweet flavor and crisp texture of the Jerusalem artichoke make it a good candidate for pickling. Indeed, pickling or roasting is the best thing you can do to this odd little tuber.

Ingredients

- 2 cups Jerusalem artichokes
- 2 tablespoons pickling or fine sea salt
- 1 cup distilled white vinegar plus 2 tablespoons for the soak
- ½ cup water
- 1 tablespoon sugar
- 2 tablespoons dill seeds
- 1 garlic clove
- 1 teaspoon mixed pickling spices, store-bought or homemade (page 18)

1 Scrub or peel the Jerusalem artichokes and cut into ¼-inch slices. Combine them with the salt and cover with ice water. Add 2 tablespoons white vinegar to prevent the Jerusalem artichokes from darkening. Let stand overnight, then drain.

2 Combine the remaining 1 cup white vinegar, water, and sugar in a small saucepan and heat to boiling, stirring to dissolve the sugar.

3 While the vinegar mixture heats, pack a clean hot 1-pint canning jar with the dill seeds, garlic, and mixed pickling spices. Pack in the Jerusalem artichokes. Pour in the hot vinegar mixture, leaving ½ inch headspace. Remove any air bubbles and seal.

4 Process in a boiling-water bath for 10 minutes, according the directions on page 31. Let cool undisturbed for 12 hours. Store in a cool, dry place. Do not open for at least 6 weeks to allow the flavors to develop.

Kitchen Note

Jerusalem artichoke can be harvested in the spring, before the plant begins to grow, or in the fall, after a couple of light frosts.

Spicy Dilled Okra

By the pint

Okra pickles: Either you love them or you hate them, depending on how you feel about okra in the first place. To me, okra pickles taste wonderfully green and, well, rather like okra.

Ingredients

2 **cups okra pods**

water

½ **cup distilled white vinegar**

1 **tablespoon sugar**

1 **teaspoon pickling or fine sea salt**

1 **small dried red pepper**

1 **dill head or 6 sprigs fresh dill**

1 **teaspoon dill seeds**

½ **teaspoon celery seeds**

1 Wash the okra. Trim off the stems, but do not cut into the okra pods. Bring a kettle of water to a boil.

2 Combine the white vinegar, sugar, and salt in a small saucepan and bring to a boil, stirring to dissolve the sugar.

3 While the vinegar mixture heats, pack a clean hot 1-pint canning jar with the red pepper, fresh dill, dill seeds, celery seeds, and okra. Pour in the hot vinegar mixture, leaving ½ inch headspace. Top off with boiling water, if needed. Remove any air bubbles and seal.

4 Process in a boiling-water bath for 10 minutes, according to the directions on page 31. Let cool undisturbed for 12 hours. Store in a cool, dry place. Do not open for at least 6 weeks to allow the flavors to develop.

Kitchen Notes

- Try to select similar-size pods.
- Whether you will need to top off the jars with boiling water depends on the size of the okra pods and how tightly you pack them in.
- As with all pickles, the fresher the vegetable, the better the pickle. You can judge the age of an okra pod by its tip. A soft, dark tip indicates an older pod.

Sweet Pickled Okra

By the pint

Like other green vegetables, okra can be regarded as a blank canvas on which to paint the pickling flavors, with okra contributing the "green" flavor.

Ingredients

2 cups okra pods

water

½ cup cider vinegar

2 tablespoons firmly packed brown sugar

1 teaspoon pickling or fine sea salt

½ teaspoon mixed pickling spices, store-bought or homemade (page 18)

1 Wash the okra. Trim off the stems, but do not cut into the okra pods. Bring a kettle of water to a boil.

2 Combine the cider vinegar, brown sugar, and salt in a small saucepan and bring to a boil, stirring to dissolve the sugar.

3 While the vinegar mixture heats, put the mixed pickling spices into a clean hot 1-pint canning jar. Pack in the okra pods. Pour in the hot vinegar mixture, leaving ½ inch headspace. Top off with boiling water, if needed. Remove any air bubbles and seal.

4 Process in a boiling-water bath for 10 minutes, according to the directions on page 31. Let cool undisturbed for 12 hours. Store in a cool, dry place. Do not open for at least 6 weeks to allow the flavors to develop.

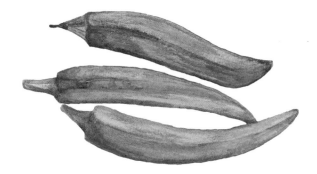

Zesty Sweet Pickled Okra

By the pint

Bring on the sweet! These pickles are sweet and spicy, channeling my inner Southern nature.

Ingredients

2 cups okra pods

water

½ cup cider vinegar

½ cup sugar

1 teaspoon pickling or fine sea salt

1 teaspoon crushed red pepper flakes

1 teaspoon mustard seeds

¼ teaspoon peppercorns

1 bay leaf

1 Wash the okra. Trim off the stems, but do not cut into the okra pods. Bring a kettle of water to a boil.

2 Combine the cider vinegar, sugar, and salt in a small saucepan and bring to a boil, stirring to dissolve the sugar.

3 While the vinegar mixture heats, pack a clean hot 1-pint canning jar with the red pepper flakes, mustard seeds, peppercorns, and bay leaf. Pack in the okra pods. Pour in the hot vinegar mixture, leaving ½ inch headspace. Top off with boiling water, if needed. Remove any air bubbles and seal.

4 Process in a boiling-water bath for 10 minutes, according to the directions on page 31. Let cool undisturbed for 12 hours. Store in a cool, dry place. Do not open for at least 6 weeks to allow the flavors to develop.

Pickled Pears

By the quart

Pears have perfect ripeness for about one minute, but you don't have to worry about that with this recipe because it works best with slightly underripe, firm pears. Small Seckel pears are the perfect choice. Named for the eighteenth-century Pennsylvania farmer who introduced the diminutive pear, the small, russet-colored fruit has a firm texture and sweet, spicy flavor. The pear's crisp texture makes it perfect for canning, so it is worth seeking it out at farmers' markets.

Ingredients

- 4 cups peeled, quartered, and cored pears
- 2 tablespoons lemon juice
- 1 cup cider vinegar
- ½ cup water
- ½ cup honey
- 1 tablespoon whole cloves
- 1 cinnamon stick

1   Put the pears in a large bowl and add water to cover. Add the lemon juice to prevent browning.

2   Combine the cider vinegar, water, and honey in a small saucepan and bring to a boil, stirring to dissolve the honey.

3   Meanwhile, stick 1 whole clove into each pear quarter, and pack the pears into a clean 1-quart canning jar, along with the cinnamon stick. Pour in the hot vinegar mixture, leaving ½ inch headspace. Remove any air bubbles and seal.

4   Process in a boiling-water bath for 20 minutes, according to the directions on page 31. Let cool undisturbed for 12 hours. Store in a cool, dry place. Do not open for at least 6 weeks to allow the flavors to develop.

Kitchen Notes

- When coring the pears, be sure to remove the blossom end (the end opposite the stem), which contains enzymes that can soften the fruit.
- Pickled pears make an interesting addition to roasted poultry, particularly duck. Drain off the syrup before serving.

Roasted Pickled Peppers

By the pint

My mountaintop garden probably *could* yield red peppers with a lot of intervention on my part, but I prefer to let the farmers in the valley handle this crop. And when their pepper plants yield an abundance of beautiful red bell peppers, I snatch them up at bargain prices for putting by. The time it takes to roast the peppers is more than offset by the fact that the result is a delicious, recipe-ready roasted pepper.

Ingredients

- 3 red bell peppers
- 1 teaspoon pickling or fine sea salt
- 2 garlic cloves
- 1 large sprig fresh basil, oregano, rosemary, or thyme (optional)
- ¼ cup white wine vinegar, plus more if needed

1 Put the peppers on a sheet pan and broil as close to the flame as possible, until charred all over, about 10 minutes per side, or 40 minutes total. Timing will vary depending how close they are to the flame. Put the charred peppers in a paper bag or covered bowl to steam for about 10 minutes.

2 Pack the salt, garlic, and herbs (if using) into a clean hot 1-pint canning jar. Remove the skins and seeds from the peppers and cut into quarters. Fold the peppers and pack into the jar, pressing as you pack to create space for more.

3 Heat the white wine vinegar in a saucepan or microwave until almost boiling. Pour the hot vinegar into the jar, leaving ½ inch headspace. Remove any air bubbles, add additional vinegar as needed, and seal.

4 Process in a boiling-water bath for 15 minutes, according to the directions on page 31. Let cool undisturbed for 12 hours. Store in a cool, dry place. Do not open for at least 6 weeks to allow the flavors to develop.

Kitchen Note

Try the peppers in Pickled Pepper Pasta with Goat Cheese (page 264) or Pickled Pepper Spinach Salad (page 249). The peppers make a fine addition to any salad, particularly pasta salads, potato salads, grain salads, and bean salads. Or cut them into bite-size pieces for an antipasto plate.

Mixed Pickled Peppers

By the quart

It is the mixture of colors and the slight variations in flavor that make these mixed peppers so appealing. Including hot peppers in the mix adds heat. How much depends on the type of chile and whether it is left whole (for mild spice) or halved (for more heat).

Ingredients

1¼ **cups cider vinegar**

1¼ **cups water, plus more water as needed**

1 **tablespoon sugar**

1 **teaspoon pickling or fine sea salt**

4 **cups seeded and quartered or halved mixed sweet peppers (red, yellow, orange, green, or chocolate bell peppers or other sweet peppers)**

1–2 **hot chiles, left whole or halved and seeded (optional)**

1 Combine the cider vinegar, water, sugar, and salt in a saucepan. Bring to a boil, stirring to dissolve the sugar. Bring a kettle of water to a boil.

2 While the vinegar mixture heats, pack a clean hot 1-quart canning jar with the peppers so their outer skins face out in the jar (it looks pretty that way). Pour in the hot vinegar mixture, leaving ½ inch headspace. Top off with boiling water, if needed. Remove any air bubbles and seal.

3 Process in a boiling water bath for 10 minutes, according to the directions on page 31. Let cool undisturbed for 12 hours. Store in a cool, dry place. Do not open for at least 6 weeks to allow the flavors to develop.

Kitchen Note

Pickled peppers are terrific on top of crackers and cheese or added to cheese sandwiches. They can be julienned and added to salads of all types. They are also pretty tasty straight out of the jar.

Spiced Prune Plums

By the quart

Plums can be divided into two basic families: European and Japanese. The European plums, also know as Italian plums, prune plums, or Stanley plums, are small and ovoid, with purple skins and green flesh. These are excellent plums to use in cooking and baking. Japanese plums come in various colors and are rounder, juicier, and often sweeter.

Ingredients

- 5 **cups prune plums (about 1¾ pounds)**
- ½ **cup red or white wine vinegar**
- ¼ **cup water**
- ½ **cup sugar**
- ¼ **teaspoon pickling or fine sea salt**
- 4 **thin slices peeled fresh ginger or Pickled Ginger (page 229)**
- 1 **cinnamon stick**
- 1 **teaspoon allspice berries**
- ¼ **teaspoon whole cloves**

1 With a small paring knife, cut the fruit through to the pit, following the natural indent of the plum. Twist each half in the opposite direction to separate the halves. Remove and discard the pits.

2 Combine the wine vinegar, water, sugar, and salt in a saucepan and bring to a gentle boil, stirring to dissolve the sugar. Add the plums and return to a boil.

3 Pack the ginger, cinnamon, allspice, and cloves into a clean hot 1-quart canning jar. With a slotted spoon, add the hot plums, pressing down to pack them all into the jar. Add the hot vinegar mixture, leaving ½ inch headspace. Remove any air bubbles and seal.

4 Process in a boiling-water bath for 10 minutes, according to the directions on page 31. Let cool undisturbed for 12 hours. Store in a cool, dry place. Do not open for at least 6 weeks to allow the flavors to develop.

Kitchen Notes

- Pack the jar tightly to avoid floating fruit, though some floating is inevitable.
- Serve with rich meats, such as roasted duck or pork.

Ramp Pickles

By the quart

Ramps, or wild leeks, as they are called in New England, are one of the first wild foods to emerge from the forest when the snow melts in the spring. The leaves look quite a bit like wild lilies of the valley, but their strong onion scent is unmistakable. Despite the strong aroma, the flavor is quite delicate, more like scallions or garden leeks than yellow onions. If you are walking in the woods in early spring and get a strong whiff of onion, stop and look around; undoubtedly you have come across a patch of ramps.

Ingredients

- about ½ pound ramps
- 2 cups cider vinegar
- 1 cup water
- 3 tablespoons sugar
- 1 teaspoon pickling or fine sea salt
- 2 tablespoons mixed pickling spices, store-bought or homemade (page 18)
- 1 teaspoon coriander seeds
- 1 teaspoon allspice berries

1 Prepare the ramps by trimming off the root ends and washing in several changes of cold water (it is not a bad idea to do the first washing in a forest stream if you are collecting in the wild). Make sure to swish the ramps in the water to dislodge any soil trapped in the leaves. Peel off any discolored, bruised, or slippery skin on the stems. Trim off the root ends and the stems, to about 6½ inches in length.

2 Combine the cider vinegar, water, sugar, and salt in a small saucepan and bring to a boil, stirring to dissolve the sugar.

3 Pack the mixed pickling spices, coriander, and allspice into a clean hot 1-quart canning jar. Pack in the ramps. Pour in the hot vinegar mixture, leaving ½ headspace. Remove any air bubbles and seal.

4 Process in a boiling-water bath for 10 minutes according to the directions on page 31. Let cool undisturbed for 12 hours. Store in a cool, dry place. Do not open for at least 6 weeks to allow the flavors to develop.

Kitchen Note

The leaves you trim off the ramps make good eating — raw or cooked. Treat them like scallion greens and add to salads and stir-fries.

Pickled Tomatillos

By the quart

Like Mexican flavors in general, tomatillos were late to arrive in New England, and they are still sometimes met with confusion. The fruit of the tomatillo, inside its papery husk, is green and about the size of a large cherry tomato. The husks should be discarded and the tomatillos washed to remove the sticky substance that coats the fruit. Tomatillos are fully ripe when green, but the flavor is quite acidic. I like them best when they are yellow and somewhat sweeter.

Ingredients

- 1⅛ **cups cider vinegar**
- ½ **cup water**
- 2½ **tablespoons sugar**
- 1¼ **teaspoons pickling or fine sea salt**
- ⅛ **teaspoon ground turmeric**
- 1 **tablespoon mixed pickling spices, store-bought or homemade (page 18)**
- ½ **teaspoon coriander seeds**
- ½ **teaspoon mustard seeds**
- **about 4 cups tomatillos, husked and washed**

1 Combine the cider vinegar, water, sugar, salt, and turmeric in a saucepan and bring to a boil, stirring to dissolve the sugar.

2 Pack the mixed pickling spices, coriander seeds, and mustard seeds into a clean hot 1-quart canning jar. Pack in the tomatillos, pressing firmly to pack in as much as possible. Pour in the hot vinegar mixture, leaving ½ inch headspace. Remove any air bubbles and seal.

3 Process in a boiling-water bath for 15 minutes, according to the directions on page 31. Let cool undisturbed for 12 hours. Store in a cool, dry place. Do not open for at least 6 weeks to allow the flavors to develop.

Kitchen Notes

- Sometimes I open jars before the 6 weeks are up, but not with this recipe. The pickles need the full 6 weeks — or more — to achieve a harmonious balance of flavors.
- You may have leftover brine, which should just be discarded. The amount of brine that will fit into the jar depends on the size of the tomatillos and how tightly the jar is packed. In the unlikely event you don't have enough brine, top off with boiling water.

Sweet Green Tomato Wheels

By the quart

A little sweet, a little sharp, the flavor varies depending on the tomato because some will be a little more ripe than others. These look like wheels when you work with green plum tomatoes or other small tomatoes that can be neatly sliced.

Ingredients

1⅛ **cups cider vinegar**

½ **cup water**

2½ **tablespoons sugar**

2 **teaspoons pickling or fine sea salt**

⅛ **teaspoon ground turmeric**

1 **tablespoon mixed pickling spices, store-bought or homemade (page 18)**

½ **teaspoon coriander seeds**

½ **teaspoon mustard seeds**

about 4 cups sliced small green tomatoes (½-inch slices)

1 **onion, sliced**

1   Combine the cider vinegar, water, sugar, salt, and turmeric in a saucepan and bring to a boil, stirring to dissolve the sugar.

2   Pack the mixed pickling spices, coriander seeds, and mustard seeds into a clean hot 1-quart canning jar. Mix the tomatoes with the onion and pack into the jar. Press firmly on the tomatoes to pack in as much as possible. Pour in the hot vinegar mixture, leaving ½ inch headspace. Remove any air bubbles and seal.

3   Process in a boiling-water bath for 10 minutes, according to the directions on page 31. Let cool undisturbed for 12 hours. Store in a cool, dry place. Do not open for at least 6 weeks to allow the flavors to develop.

Kitchen Note

Measuring cups don't always include eighths. An eighth of a cup equals 2 tablespoons.

115

Zucchini Dill Chips

By the pint

I plant only two zucchini plants each year and still I get more than I need. Small-batch pickles are particularly good for keeping up with the harvest.

Ingredients

2–2¼ cups thinly sliced zucchini

1½ teaspoons pickling or fine sea salt, plus more to taste

water

½ cup distilled white vinegar

½ teaspoon sugar

6 sprigs fresh dill or 1 dill head

2 teaspoons dill seeds

1 garlic clove

Pickle Crisp Granules (optional)

1 Combine the zucchini and salt in a bowl. Toss to mix well. Add ice water to cover. Let stand for at least 2 hours, and up to 6 hours. Taste a slice of zucchini. If it isn't decidedly salty, toss with 1 to 2 teaspoons pickling salt. If it is too salty (which it never is for me), rinse in water.

2 Drain well. Spread out the zucchini on a large clean towel. Top with a second towel and roll together. Squeeze to press out as much water as possible.

3 Bring a kettle of water to a boil. Combine the white vinegar and sugar in a saucepan and bring to a boil, stirring to dissolve the sugar.

4 Pack the fresh dill, dill seeds, and garlic into a clean hot 1-pint canning jar. Pack the zucchini into the jar. Add the hot vinegar mixture, then top off the jar with the boiling water if necessary, leaving ½ inch headspace. Add a rounded ⅛ teaspoon of Pickle Crisp, if using. Remove any air bubbles and seal.

5 Process in a boiling-water bath for 10 minutes, according to the directions on page 31. Let cool undisturbed for 12 hours. Store in a cool, dry place. Do not open for at least 6 weeks to allow flavors to develop.

Kitchen Note

The recipe can be used for zucchini or cucumber pickles. You can use it for other summer squash varieties, but only zucchini yields slices of regular diameter, which look best in the jar.

ZUCCHINI:
A PROBLEM OF OVERABUNDANCE

It is always best to harvest zucchini and summer squash when small, when the flesh is firm and the seeds are small. Also, harvesting squash when small encourages the plant to produce more. If you end up working with larger zucchini, remove the seeds.

Yes, you can use zucchini — or any variety of summer squash — in any cucumber pickle recipe, but remember that zucchini pickles will always be less crunchy than their cucumber counterparts. For the best texture, use zucchinis that are small to medium in size and be sure to add Pickle Crisp Granules.

Figure that a 6-inch zucchini will yield 2 to 2½ cups of slices.

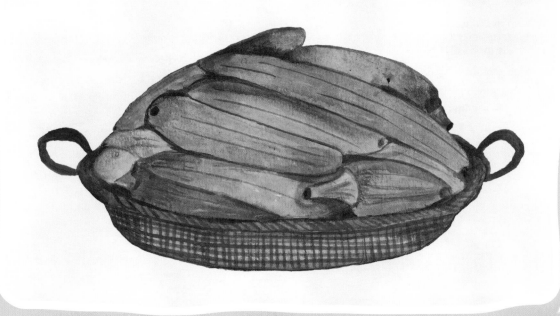

Zucchini Bread and Butters

By the pint

Anything you can do to a cucumber, you can do to a zucchini. The zucchini is perfect for small-batch pickling: a 6- to 8-inch zucchini should fit in a pint jar.

Ingredients

- 2¼ cups thinly sliced zucchini
- ½ small onion, thinly sliced
- 2 teaspoons pickling or fine sea salt
- ½ cup cider vinegar
- ½ cup firmly packed brown sugar
- ½ teaspoon mustard seeds
- ½ teaspoon mixed pickling spices, store-bought or homemade (page 18)
- ¼ teaspoon ground turmeric
- Pickle Crisp Granules (optional)

1 Combine the zucchini, onion, and salt in a medium bowl. Mix thoroughly, cover with ice water, and set aside for at least 2 hours, and up to 6 hours.

2 Drain well. Spread out the zucchini and onion on a large clean towel. Top with a second towel and roll together. Squeeze to press out as much water as possible.

3 Combine the cider vinegar, brown sugar, mustard seeds, mixed pickling spices, and turmeric in a saucepan and bring to a boil, stirring to dissolve the sugar.

4 Pack the zucchini and onion into a clean hot 1-pint canning jar. Pour in the hot vinegar mixture, leaving ½ inch headspace. Add a rounded ⅛ teaspoon of Pickle Crisp to the jar, if using. Remove any air bubbles and seal.

5 Process in a boiling-water bath for 10 minutes, according to the directions on page 31. Let cool undisturbed for 12 hours. Store in a cool, dry place. Do not open for at least 6 weeks to allow the flavors to develop.

Curried Zucchini Pickles

By the pint

Pomegranate molasses is a concentration of pomegranate juice. It gives an interesting tart-sweet edge to these pickles.

Ingredients

2¼ cups thinly sliced zucchini

½ small onion, thinly sliced

2 teaspoons pickling or fine sea salt

½ cup cider vinegar

2 tablespoons pomegranate molasses (see page 99)

¼ cup sugar

1½ teaspoons curry powder

½ teaspoon Chinese five-spice powder

½ teaspoon coriander seeds

Pickle Crisp Granules (optional)

1 Combine the zucchini, onion, and salt in a bowl. Mix thoroughly, cover with ice water, and set aside for at least 2 hours, and up to 6 hours.

2 Drain well. Spread out the zucchini and onion on a large clean towel. Top with a second towel and roll together. Squeeze to press out as much water as possible.

3 Combine the cider vinegar, pomegranate molasses, sugar, curry powder, and five-spice powder in a small saucepan. Heat to boiling, stirring to dissolve the sugar.

4 Pack the coriander seeds into a clean hot 1-pint canning jar. Pack in the zucchini and onions. Pour in the hot vinegar mixture, leaving ½ inch headspace. Add a rounded ⅛ teaspoon of Pickle Crisp to the jar, if using. Remove any air bubbles and seal.

5 Process in a boiling-water bath for 10 minutes, according to the directions on page 31. Let cool undisturbed for 12 hours. Store in a cool, dry place. Do not open for at least 6 weeks to allow the flavors to develop.

Herbed Jardinière

By the quart

Jardinière (French) or giardinara (Italian):
Whatever you call them, these layered pickles look beautiful in jars, and they taste just as wonderful. Choose your vegetables with an eye to color and take the time to pack the jar in layers. Use at least four different types of vegetables.

Ingredients

- 1¼ **cups distilled white vinegar**
- ¾ **cup water**
- 3 **tablespoons sugar**
- 1½ **teaspoons pickling or fine sea salt**
- 1 **large sprig basil or tarragon**
- 1 **garlic clove**
- 4 **cups assorted firm vegetables (cauliflower florets, chopped green beans, green cherry tomatoes, any color bell pepper cut into squares or strips, pearl onions, diagonally sliced carrots, okra, cooked sliced golden beets, sliced fennel)**

1 Combine the white vinegar, water, sugar, and salt in a saucepan and bring to a boil, stirring to dissolve the sugar.

2 Pack the basil and garlic into a clean hot 1-quart canning jar. Carefully pack the vegetables in layers. A chopstick will help you arrange and hold the vegetables in their position as you pack. Press firmly on the vegetables to pack in as much as possible. Pour in the hot vinegar mixture, leaving ½ inch headspace. Remove any air bubbles and seal.

3 Process in a boiling-water bath for 15 minutes, according to the directions on page 31. Let cool undisturbed for 12 hours. Store in a cool, dry place. Do not open for at least 6 weeks to allow the flavors to develop.

Kitchen Notes

- It is important to pack in as many vegetables as possible. Press firmly on each layer to create as much space as possible and fill to ½ inch of the top. This helps prevent "floating" vegetables in the jar.
- Cooked golden beets can be added to the mix of vegetables. If you add red beets, they will dye all the vegetables and the brine a purple color, taking away from the beauty of the jar.
- You don't have to layer the vegetables. They can be all jumbled together if you prefer.
- To give this recipe an exotic twist, make Sweet Spiced Jardinière: Add ½ teaspoon ground turmeric to the vinegar solution in step 1. In step 2, omit the basil or tarragon and pack in 1 tablespoon mixed pickling spices (page 18) instead.

Sweet Mixed Pickles

By the quart

Use up small amounts of vegetables with this lovely, balanced pickle. The choice of vegetables is quite broad.

Ingredients

1½ cups cider vinegar

¾ cup water

½ cup sugar

2 teaspoons pickling or fine sea salt

¼ teaspoon ground turmeric

¼ teaspoon mixed pickling spices, store-bought or homemade (page 18)

4 allspice berries

4 whole cloves

¼ teaspoon crushed red pepper flakes (optional)

4 cups assorted firm vegetables (chopped green beans, diagonally sliced carrots, cauliflower florets, any color bell peppers cut in strips or squares, pearl onions, green cherry tomatoes, sliced fennel, sliced cooked golden beets)

1 Combine the cider vinegar, water, sugar, salt, and turmeric in a saucepan and heat to boiling, stirring to dissolve the sugar.

2 Pack the mixed pickling spices, allspice berries, cloves, and red pepper flakes, if using, into a clean hot 1-quart canning jar. Add the vegetables, pressing firmly to pack in as many as possible. Pour in the hot vinegar mixture, leaving ½ inch headspace. Remove any air bubbles and seal.

3 Process in a boiling-water bath for 15 minutes, according to the directions on page 31. Let cool undisturbed for 12 hours. Store in a cool, dry place. Do not open for at least 6 weeks to allow the flavors to develop.

Chapter 4

Big-Harvest Fresh-Pack Pickles

The recipes in this chapter are mostly traditional, old-fashioned vinegar-cured pickles, developed by (mostly) women who were responsible for feeding large households year-round with food they raised in their gardens. Some of the recipes are my own variations on classics, while others were collected from other Storey Publishing authors.

I love to read food histories, and I always turn to the index first to find mentions of pickling. I love to read about farm women who took incredible pride in their stores of food, often kept in the cellar. When survival depended on putting by enough food to get a family through the winter, rows and rows of pantry shelves filled with pickles was a beautiful sight to behold. And while pickles weren't as crucial to survival as sacks of grain and dried beans, or hams hanging in the smokehouse, they sure did make a fairly monotonous diet more interesting.

We have access to modern conveniences that our ancestors never dreamed of, such as food processors and refrigerators. Even the stove has been improved, with power burners that bring the water bath canner to a boil faster than ever.

Old-fashioned recipes using lime and alum to make pickles crisp involved several days of soaking and rinsing. Those steps have been replaced by Pickle Crisp (see Crisping Agents, page 22), which I highly recommend using in all the cucumber and zucchini recipes in this chapter.

Don't forget that some of your big harvest can be made into relishes, salsas, and chutneys. There are plenty of large-scale recipes in chapter 5. And chapter 3, Single Jar Pickles, contains recipes that can be multiplied to handle big harvests just as easily as small ones.

Big Harvest Dill Pickles

Makes 6 quarts

Year after year, for many this is the only pickle worth making. It works with a large quantity, gets the job done easily, and is a favorite for snacking.

Ingredients

7½–8 **pounds (3- to 5-inch) pickling cucumbers, quartered lengthwise, blossom ends removed**

1 **cup pickling or fine sea salt**

5 **cups distilled white vinegar**

4 **cups water**

¼ **cup sugar**

12 **garlic cloves, sliced**

18 **sprigs fresh dill or 12 dill heads**

6 **tablespoons dill seeds**

2 **tablespoons mixed pickling spices, store-bought or homemade (see page 18)**

Pickle Crisp Granules (optional)

1 In a large bowl, toss the cucumbers with ½ cup of the salt. Cover with ice water and let sit for at least 8 hours, and up to 12 hours. Drain the cucumbers.

2 Combine the white vinegar, water, sugar, and remaining ½ cup salt in a saucepan and bring to a boil, stirring to dissolve the sugar and salt.

4 While the vinegar mixture heats, divide the garlic, fresh dill, dill seeds, and mixed pickling spices among six clean hot 1-quart canning jars. Pack in the cucumbers. Pour in the vinegar mixture, leaving ½ inch headspace. Add a rounded ¼ teaspoon of Pickle Crisp to each jar, if using. Remove any air bubbles and seal.

5 Process in a boiling-water bath for 15 minutes, according to the directions on page 31. Let cool undisturbed for 12 hours. Store in a cool, dry place. Do not open for at least 6 weeks to allow the flavors to develop.

Kitchen Notes

- I pack as many whole spears vertically as possible into the jars, then cut the remaining spears in half and pack those horizontally in the jars.
- With sweet pickles, you can get by with letting the pickles stand for less than the recommended 6 weeks before opening. But dill is slow to infuse, and it requires the full 6 weeks.

CUCUMBER MATH

One average Kirby cucumber is 4 to 5 inches in length.

One average Kirby cucumber yields about ¾ cup chopped cucumber.

Keeping the Harvest
Bread and Butter Pickles

Makes 7 pints

This is a classic recipe, originally published in *Keeping the Harvest* by Nancy Chioffi and Gretchen Mead, and slightly adapted. It is the standard by which I judge all other bread and butters.

Ingredients

16 **cups sliced pickling cucumbers (about 6 pounds), blossom ends removed**

1½ **cups sliced onions (about 1 pound)**

2 **large garlic cloves**

½ **cup pickling or fine sea salt**

3 **cups cider vinegar**

4½ **cups sugar**

2 **tablespoons mustard seeds**

1½ **teaspoons celery seeds**

1½ **teaspoons ground turmeric**

Pickle Crisp Granules (optional)

1 Combine the cucumbers, onions, and garlic in a large bowl. Mix in the salt. Cover with ice water and let stand for at least 2 hours, and up to 6 hours. Rinse and drain the vegetables. Remove the garlic.

2 Combine the cider vinegar, sugar, mustard seeds, celery seeds, and turmeric in a large saucepan over high heat, stirring to dissolve the sugar. When the mixture is almost boiling, stir in the cucumbers and onions and heat for 5 minutes.

3 Pack the hot pickles and vinegar mixture into clean hot 1-pint canning jars, leaving ½ inch headspace. Add a rounded ¼ teaspoon of Pickle Crisp to each jar, if using. Remove any air bubbles and seal.

4 Process in a boiling-water bath for 10 minutes, according to the directions on page 31. Let cool undisturbed for 12 hours. Store in a cool, dry place. Do not open for at least 6 weeks to allow the flavors to develop.

Kitchen Notes

If you like, add 2 green or red bell peppers, sliced. The yield will increase to 8 pints, a canner load for a large canner.

Priscilla Heindel's Bread and Butter Pickles

Makes 8 pints

There are thousands of recipes for bread and butter pickles, with slight variations of spices and proportions, each making a slightly different variation on a theme. This recipe came to me from my friend Judy Chaves, who got it from her mother-in-law. With white vinegar instead of cider vinegar, and no turmeric, the brine is clear and the flavor a little sharper and crisper than in the previous recipe.

Ingredients

- 6 **quarts thinly sliced pickling cucumbers (about 7½ pounds), blossom ends removed**
- 6 **medium onions, sliced**
- ¾ **cup pickling or fine sea salt**
- 4 **cups distilled white vinegar**
- 2 **cups water**
- 4 **cups sugar**
- 2 **tablespoons celery seeds**
- 2 **tablespoons mustard seeds**
-   **Pickle Crisp Granules (optional)**

1   Arrange the cucumber and onion slices in layers in a large bowl or crock, sprinkling each layer with salt. Cover and let sit for at least 2 hours, and up to 6 hours. Drain the liquid that accumulates.

2   Combine the white vinegar, water, sugar, celery seeds, and mustard seeds in a large saucepan and bring to a boil, stirring to dissolve the sugar. Add the cucumbers and onions and mix well.

3   Pack the mixture into clean hot 1-pint canning jars, leaving ½ inch headspace. Add a rounded ⅛ teaspoon of Pickle Crisp to each jar, if using. Remove any air bubbles and seal.

4   Process in a boiling-water bath for 10 minutes, according to the directions on page 31. Let cool undisturbed for 12 hours. Store in a cool, dry place. Do not open for at least 6 weeks to allow the flavors to develop.

Kitchen Note

Wondering what you will do with all the sweet pickles? When fresh lettuce and tomatoes are a distant summer memory, sweet (or dill) pickles make a perfect addition to a cheese sandwich made with mustard and raw onion.

Spicy Sweet Slices

Makes 10 pints

Nutmeg adds a distinctive flavor to these sweet pickles. Freshly grated nutmeg is more flavorful than the ground nutmeg sold in jars.

Ingredients

- **5 quarts thinly sliced pickling cucumbers (about 6½ pounds), blossom ends removed**
- **5 bell peppers of any color, seeded and cut into thin strips**
- **½ cup pickling or fine sea salt**
- **6 cups cider vinegar**
- **3 cups honey**
- **1 tablespoon coriander seeds**
- **½ teaspoon ground cardamom**
- **½ teaspoon freshly grated nutmeg**
- **Pickle Crisp Granules (optional)**

1 Combine the cucumbers, bell peppers, and salt in a large bowl. Mix well and cover with ice water. Let stand for at least 2 hours, and up to 6 hours. Drain well.

2 Combine the cider vinegar, honey, coriander seeds, cardamom, and nutmeg in a large saucepan and bring to a boil, stirring to dissolve the honey. Add the vegetables and mix well.

3 Pack the vegetables and vinegar mixture into clean hot 1-pint canning jars, leaving ½ inch headspace. Add a rounded ⅛ teaspoon of Pickle Crisp to each jar, if using. Remove any air bubbles and seal.

4 Process in a boiling-water bath for 10 minutes, according to the directions on page 31. Let cool undisturbed for 12 hours. Store in a cool, dry place. Do not open for at least 6 weeks to allow the flavors to develop.

TOO MUCH BRINE?

Before you assume a recipe generated too much of the vinegar mixture, check to make sure there are no air bubbles packed in the jars with your vegetables. Often, once you release all the bubbles, there is room for most of the remaining vinegar mixture.

Oh, Do You Know the Pickle Man?

If you were walking down a city street and a man in a pickle costume offered to sell you the best pickle in the world, you'd try it, wouldn't you?

Of course you would. You love pickles. That's why you are looking at this book. You love pickles so much, you'd try it even if the pickle man wasn't wearing a green suit.

But to build a business, a pickle suit might be necessary. That's what Travis Grillo found when he donned his pickle suit and began selling pickles made with his great-grandfather's Italian dill pickle recipe. He built a cart and parked it in front of a T stop in Boston.

"I'd be shouting myself hoarse: 'Taste the best pickle in the world.' Okay, I went out on a limb. But it got people's attention."

But if the pickle suit and showmanship attracted the first purchase, it was the flavor of the pickles that created repeat customers and helped Grillo place his pickles in Whole Foods stores from Maine to New Jersey.

"I was eating my father's pickles one summer and I said to myself, 'This is the best pickle in the world.'" Two years later, Grillo was making about 4,000 quarts of pickles each month and looking to expand.

Grillo calls these pickles Italian because the recipe originated in Bari, Italy. Unlike the classic kosher dill, these are not fermented, salt-cured

Travis Grillo

cucumbers. Grillo takes fresh Kirby cukes, slices them into spears ("Whole cucumbers," he explains, "get soft"), and puts them in a brine of distilled white vinegar, spring water, garlic, salt, and fresh dill. A final touch: To each plastic container of pickles, he adds a wine grape leaf.

"The grape leaves keep them crunchy. It gives them a distinct, earthy flavor."

What is truly distinctive about these pickles is that they are sold fresh and have a refrigerated shelf life of 1½ to 2 months. As the pickles age, flavor develops.

"You can interact with a natural pickle. A chemical pickle is consistent. My pickles are consistent but they change. They are good after three days. I like the pickles the best at the one-month mark. After two months, the color goes. You won't lose the crunch, though. But at the end, it's like a whole other thing. Some customers I have, they hold them for three to four months. By then the pickles are tan in color. Of course, it doesn't harm them; it's what they like."

The business has expanded to employ Grillo's dad, his cousin, and his sister. "My friends and my family helped me through the whole process. The business wouldn't have happened without them. It was just a dream and a drive and a lotta, lotta time spent at the pickle cart as days turned into months and months turned into years."

"Making pickles can be a hobby or it can be a business," reflects Grillo. "If making pickles is your hobby, then trial and error is everything. You gotta make sure everything is clean, so wash everything with vinegar. Bacteria is what makes a pickle funky. You make the brine in a big vat or in the jar, as long as it is all clean. You can add anything you like — carrots, cauliflower, peppers — it is all good. A red pepper is really, really good."

Although Grillo's recipe is based on tradition, his marketing efforts are strictly modern. He still dons the pickle suit, but the cart appears only on fair-weather days, and its appearance and location are announced on Twitter and Facebook. So, too, are the pickle parties Grillo stages in the Boston area. Who can resist a party of pickle aficionados, eating their fill of pickles and French fries, or pickles and Pabst? Friend Grillo on Facebook, and you can find out just how much fun pickles can be.

You can learn more about Grillo's Pickles at www.grillospickles.com.

IN A PICKLE

Shakespeare knew a pickle when he saw one. He was among the first to use the phrase "in a pickle," in *The Tempest* (Act V, Scene 1) in 1610:

ALONSO:
And Trinculo is reeling ripe: where should they
Find this grand liquor that hath gilded 'em?
How camest thou in this pickle?

TRINCULO:
I have been in such a pickle since I saw you last that, I fear me, will never out of
my bones: I shall not fear fly-blowing.

Jane's Hillside Pickles

Makes 9 pints

Seventh-generation Vermonter Jane Dwinell believes in self-sufficiency and self-reliance. Naturally, preserving garden foods is part of her ethos. In her favorite pickle recipe, the combination of cider vinegar, brown sugar, and cinnamon gives these pickles warm, home-style flavor.

Ingredients

- **18 cups thinly sliced pickling cucumbers, blossom ends removed**
- **¼ cup pickling or fine sea salt**
- **6 cups cider vinegar**
- **6 cups firmly packed brown sugar**
- **3 tablespoons mixed pickling spices, store-bought or homemade (page 18)**
- **1 teaspoon ground cinnamon**
- **1 teaspoon ground cloves**
- **Pickle Crisp Granules (optional)**

1 Mix the cucumbers and salt in a large bowl or crock. Cover with ice water and let stand for at least 2 hours, and up to 6 hours. Drain well.

2 Combine the cider vinegar, brown sugar, mixed pickling spices, cinnamon, and cloves in a large saucepan and bring to a boil, stirring to dissolve the sugar. Add the cucumbers and mix well.

3 Pack the cucumbers and vinegar mixture into clean hot 1-pint canning jars, leaving ½ inch headspace. Add a rounded ⅛ teaspoon of Pickle Crisp to each jar, if using. Remove any air bubbles and seal.

4 Process in a boiling-water bath for 10 minutes, according to the directions on page 31. Let cool undisturbed for 12 hours. Store in a cool, dry place. Do not open for at least 6 weeks to allow the flavors to develop.

A FOUNDING FATHER ON PICKLES

According to the Food Museum of New York City, pickles inspired Thomas Jefferson to write, "On a hot day in Virginia, I know nothing more comforting than a fine spiced pickle, brought up trout-like from the sparkling depths of the aromatic jar below the stairs of Aunt Sally's cellar."

Two-Day Tongue Pickles

Makes 2 pints

It is nearly impossible to avoid having some of your cucumber crop become overripe because cucumbers seem to hide under the leaves of the vine. Miss one during your daily harvest and before you know it, the cucumber has become huge, rounded, hard-skinned, and yellow. But that is no reason for despair. Our fore-mothers, who let nothing go to waste, came up with a family of pickle recipes to put such monsters to good use. Some called them tongue pickles — the crescent-shaped cucumber pieces retain a certain crisp texture but look somewhat floppy, like a tongue. Some called them sunshine pickles. By any name, the pickles are usually sweet.

Ingredients

- 7½–8 pounds overripe cucumbers (7 or 8 cucumbers)
- 2 cups distilled white vinegar
- 3 cups firmly packed brown sugar
- 1 tablespoon pickling or fine sea salt
- 1 tablespoon whole cloves
- 2 cinnamon sticks
- 1 (1-inch) piece fresh ginger, peeled and sliced, or 1-inch stack Pickled Ginger (page 229)
- 1 teaspoon black peppercorns

1 Peel the cucumbers and halve lengthwise. Scoop out and discard the seeds, and slice into ½-inch chunks.

2 Combine the cucumbers, white vinegar, brown sugar, salt, cloves, cinnamon sticks, ginger, and peppercorns in a large saucepan. Bring to a boil, stirring to dissolve the sugar. Decrease the heat and simmer until most of the cucumbers appear translucent, 1 to 1¼ hours.

3 Cover and let stand overnight.

4 The next day, reheat the pickles until the vinegar mixture comes to a boil. Pack the cucumbers with a slotted spoon into clean hot 1-pint canning jars. Strain the pickling liquid to remove the whole spices and pour in over the cucumbers, leaving ½ inch headspace. Remove any air bubbles and seal.

5 Process in a boiling-water bath for 10 minutes, according to the directions on page 31. Let cool undisturbed for 12 hours. Store in a cool, dry place. Do not open for at least 6 weeks to allow the flavors to develop.

Kitchen Notes

- Overripe pickling cucumbers weigh about 1 pound each.
- The yield is low considering that you start with so many cucumbers. But much is lost when you discard the peels and seeds.

Overnight Sunshine Pickles

Makes 8 pints

The reason to make these pickles is that they just might turn out to be your grandmother's pickles, and such recipes should not be lost to history. Sunshine pickles and tongue pickles are two names for the class of recipes made from overripe cucumbers, which turn yellow on the vine (hence the sunshine in the title).

The cucumbers should be weighed after you have peeled and seeded them, which means you need to start with about 18 pounds overripe cucumbers, or about 18 overripe cucumbers.

Ingredients

- 10 pounds peeled and seeded overripe cucumbers
- 3 cups distilled white vinegar
- 4 cups brown sugar, firmly packed
- 3 cups white sugar
- 2 teaspoons pickling or fine sea salt
- 1 teaspoon ground cinnamon
- 1 teaspoon ground cloves
- 1 teaspoon ground ginger
- 1 teaspoon freshly ground black pepper

1 Slice the cucumbers into 2-inch pieces and put in a large saucepan. Add the white vinegar, brown and white sugars, salt, cinnamon, cloves, ginger, and pepper. Set over medium heat and cook, stirring to dissolve the sugar. Continue to simmer until the most of cucumbers appear translucent, 1½ to 2 hours.

2 Cover and let stand overnight.

3 The next day, reheat the pickles just to the boiling point. Pack into clean hot 1-pint canning jars, leaving about ½ inch headspace. Remove any air bubbles and seal.

4 Process in a boiling-water bath for 10 minutes, according to the directions on page 31. Let cool undisturbed for 12 hours. Store in a cool, dry place. Do not open for at least 6 weeks to allow the flavors to develop.

Keeping the Harvest Dilly Beans

Makes 4 pints

Here's another classic recipe from Nancy Chioffi and Gretchen Mead, the authors of Garden Way's *Keeping the Harvest*, adapted slightly. Older recipes are often quite salty. In this one, I reduced the salt. In vinegar pickles, such as this one, it is safe to play around with the salt amounts.

Ingredients

- 2½ cups distilled white vinegar
- 2½ cups water
- 2 tablespoons pickling or fine sea salt
- 1 teaspoon cayenne pepper
- 4 garlic cloves
- 4 dill heads
- 2 pounds green beans, trimmed (about 8 cups)

1 Combine the white vinegar, water, salt, and cayenne in a saucepan and bring to a boil.

2 Pack the garlic and dill heads into sterilized hot 1-pint canning jars. Pack in the beans. Pour the hot vinegar mixture over the beans, leaving ½ inch headspace. Remove any air bubbles and seal.

3 Process in a boiling-water bath for 5 minutes, according to the directions on page 31. Let cool undisturbed for 12 hours. Store in a cool, dry place. Do not open for at least 6 weeks to allow the flavors to develop.

Kitchen Note

If your dill is not mature when the beans are ready, pack each jar with 6 large sprigs of fresh dill instead of 1 mature dill head.

TRIMMING GREEN BEANS

When we want to trim green beans, some cooks say to "top and tail" the beans. The phrase is British in origin and so much more descriptive than simply asking for trimming the beans, but that is what is meant. Simply cut off the pointy ends and stem ends of all the beans. If the beans are straight, grab a handful and place on a cutting board. Tap with the flat side of a chef's knife to align and then cut off the ends. Tap to align the second side and trim the other ends. If you are planning to can them, cut them into 4-inch lengths.

Spiced Apples

Makes 12 pints

This is an old family recipe collected from Lewis Hill of Greensboro, Vermont. Lewis was a descendant of one of Greensboro's 1781 original settlers, Peleg Hill, Sr. A noted orchardist, Lewis was a pioneer in Vermont's nursery business and was among the first to grow plants in containers for summer sales. He developed and introduced to the trade nine new daylilies, two new black currants, and two new elderberries. With his wife, Nancy, Lewis wrote numerous magazine and newspaper articles, as well as 14 books. *Secrets of Plant Propagation* was chosen by the American Horticultural Society as one of the best garden books of the past 75 years. Lewis told me that this recipe was originally made in 5-gallon stone crocks, and he recommended using Duchess Beacon apples, an heirloom variety.

Ingredients

- 9 pounds tart apples
- about 1 cup whole cloves
- 4 cups cider vinegar
- 4 cups water
- 1 cup maple syrup
- 4 cups firmly packed brown sugar
- 1 cup white sugar
- 2 teaspoons pickling or fine sea salt
- 8 cinnamon sticks

1 Halve and core the apples, but do not peel. Stick two whole cloves in each piece.

2 Combine the cider vinegar, water, maple syrup, brown and white sugars, salt, and cinnamon in a large saucepan and bring to a boil, stirring to dissolve the sugars. Add the apples and simmer for 5 minutes.

3 Using a slotted spoon, pack the apples tightly into clean hot 1-pint canning jars. Remove the cinnamon sticks from the syrup with a slotted spoon and discard. Cover the apples with the hot syrup, leaving ½ inch headspace. Remove any air bubbles and seal.

4 Process in a boiling-water bath for 10 minutes, according to the
   directions on page 31. Let cool undisturbed for 12 hours. Store in a
   cool, dry place. Do not open for at least 6 weeks to allow the flavors to
   develop.

Kitchen Note

The best apples for preserving are ones that are super-crisp. My favorites are
Northern Spy, Rome, Gravenstein, Winesap, and Golden Delicious.

Big Harvest Pickled Beets

Makes 7 pints

Beets are baked rather than boiled in this recipe developed by Janet Chadwick. It was originally published in *The Busy Person's Guide to Preserving Food*. I have adapted it slightly.

Ingredients

- 10–12 **pounds beets (without greens)**
- 4 **cups cider vinegar**
- 1 **cup water**
- ⅔ **cup sugar**
- 2 **tablespoons pickling or fine sea salt**

1 Preheat the oven to 400°F. Arrange a couple of wire racks in a large roasting pan.

2 Cut the beet tops and roots off flush with the beets. Scrub thoroughly. Arrange the beets in a single layer on the wire racks. Bake until tender, about 1 hour if the beets are medium-size.

3 When the beets are tender, fill the roasting pan with cold water to cool off the beets. Slip the skins off the beets and discard. You can leave the beets whole or cut them into wedges. Pack the beets into clean hot 1-pint canning jars, leaving ½ inch headspace.

4 Combine the cider vinegar, water, sugar, and salt in a saucepan and bring to a boil, stirring to dissolve the sugar. Pour the hot vinegar mixture over the beets, leaving ½ inch headspace. Remove any air bubbles and seal.

5 Process in a boiling-water bath for 30 minutes, according to the directions on page 31. Let cool undisturbed for 12 hours. Store in a cool, dry place. Do not open for at least 6 weeks to allow the flavors to develop.

Mustard Cauliflower Pickles

Makes 6 pints

Cauliflower will keep for a week or two after harvest — then it is time to pickle it! Cauliflower is just too fussy to grow to waste any, and pickled cauliflower is one of the best ways to enjoy it.

Ingredients

- 3 small heads cauliflower (4½–5 pounds), cut into florets
- 6 cups distilled white vinegar
- 3 cups water
- 1½ cups sugar
- 3 tablespoons mustard seeds
- 3 tablespoons mixed pickling spices, store-bought or homemade (page 18)
- 1 tablespoon pickling or fine sea salt

1 Bring a large pot of salted water to a boil. Add the cauliflower and blanch for 1 minute. Drain immediately and transfer into an ice-water bath to stop the cooking.

2 Combine the white vinegar, water, sugar, mustard seeds, mixed pickling spices, and salt in a saucepan and bring to a boil, stirring to dissolve the sugar. Simmer for about 3 minutes.

3 Drain the cauliflower and pack into clean hot 1-pint canning jars. Pour in the hot vinegar mixture, leaving ½ inch headspace. Remove any air bubbles and seal.

4 Process in a boiling-water bath for 10 minutes, according to the directions on page 31. Let cool undisturbed for 12 hours. Store in a cool, dry place. Do not open for at least 6 weeks to allow the flavors to develop.

Kitchen Note
The blanching in step 1 is optional. It will reduce the bite of the cauliflower but isn't necessary.

CAULIFLOWER MATH

Cauliflower heads vary widely in size and weight. Figure that 1 pound of trimmed cauliflower (leaves and stem removed) equals 4 cups of florets. This is roughly equivalent to a 6-inch-diameter head.

The Pickle Freak

There are pickle lovers, and then there are extreme pickle lovers. Take Katy, who blogs under the name Pickle Freak. She never goes anywhere without pickles. She's an extreme fan of the sour crunch.

"People mail me pickles all the time. Or someone might give me a jar of pickles at work, or maybe I want a pickle martini. I'm not embarrassed anymore about whipping out a jar of pickles and handing it to some bartender."

Asked if her obsession with pickles is a recent phenomenon, Katy says, "I like to tell people I was born this way. I remember being very young and left alone for some reason and I ate a whole jar of pickles. I can still sit down and eat a whole jar.

"Growing up in Mississippi, my mom and grandmother always made pickles, but that kind of ended after a while . . . I made a couple of jars of pickles when I was in college. Then I moved to New York City and it was more difficult — a tiny kitchen, hauling bags of produce home from the farmers' market. But it makes sense to make my own," she reflects, since she now lives in New Orleans. "With the longer growing season in Louisiana, I'll be able to grow my own cukes. I have to feed my habit."

Katy, the Pickle Freak

Katy's preference is for vinegar-brined pickles. "For me it is all about a strong flavor." Southerners, she thinks, like strong flavors; they make sweet tea and sweet pickles. She tells me about pickle candy — you strain the brine from a jar of pickle slices, reserving it, pour a bag of sugar into the jar over the pickles, and then return some of the brine. The sugar crystallizes around the slices. We both shudder.

When Katy isn't eating pickles, she is on the lookout for pickles and pickle fun. "I can spot a pickle a block away." One of the weirdest places she's found pickles is at her local hardware store.

On reflection, maybe it wasn't so weird. When she was growing up in a small town in Mississippi, a local farm family sold homemade pickles at the hardware store.

Katy is always up for a pickle adventure, which is why people are always sending her great pickle memorabilia. In her home right now she has pickle-flavored mints, pickle-shaped green Band-aids, and an electronic yodeling pickle. She travels with a camera wherever she goes, which is great for her blog, because she never knows what she might be posting next, like the "pickles in a can" (not a mason jar but a can), a picture she took on a trip to Germany — land of pickles.

Pickles, in the Pickle Freak's world, are more than just nourishment (she is a picky eater, except for the pickles). It is also about community. To give back to the "pickle community," she volunteered at the ninth annual Pickle Festival in New York City in 2010. "Along with the Pickle Girl, who no longer blogs, we were able to create a photo booth with a giant papier mâché pickle and the festival banner. People could have their picture taken with the giant pickle. Or wearing a pickle barrel we had — with holes cut out for arms and legs and heads. Or with a radish or a carrot. Then we uploaded the photos on Flickr."

And that pickle community? Katy explained that Brooklyn is the epicenter for all things pickled — with all the vendors from the Pickle Festival, including Rick's Picks, the Pickle Guys, McClure's, Horman's. "Picklers are some of the nicest people. Sometimes we have coordinated social events. It was easy for me to be right in the midst of all these people."

Unfortunately for Katy, returning to live in the South has meant giving up her pickle community in Brooklyn. But Katy has plans. "Once I really settle in, then I'd like to organize events." Since moving to New Orleans, Katy has discovered pickle juice sno-cones (why didn't I think of that?) and pickled mirlitons. (Outside of New Orleans, those one-seeded summer squash are called chayote.) Stayed tuned for the First Pickled Mirliton Festival in New Orleans? If it happens, you can read about it at the Pickle Freak's blog.

To read about Katy's ongoing pickle adventures, go to www.picklefreak.com.

Star Anise Pickled Pineapple

Makes 3 pints

Okay, this is an oddball recipe. Unless you live in Hawaii where pineapples are grown, you are unlikely to have a glut of fresh pineapple to deal with. For many of us, it is hard to find a fresh pineapple with good flavor. They may be too acidic or simply too bland. Pickling is the cure. The spicy tangy-sweet pickling syrup infuses the pineapple with wonderful flavor. The star anise adds a whiff of mystery.

Ingredients

½ **cup distilled white vinegar**

½ **cup water**

1½ **cups sugar**

8 **cups fresh pineapple chunks (about 2 small pineapples)**

3 **cinnamon sticks**

3 **whole star anise**

1 Combine the white vinegar, water, and sugar in a large saucepan. Bring to a boil, stirring to dissolve the sugar, and boil for 3 minutes. Add the pineapple, cinnamon sticks, and star anise. Simmer for 20 minutes, until the pineapple is tender. Remove the cinnamon sticks and star anise and discard.

2 Pack the pineapple into clean hot 1-pint canning jars, pressing down on the pineapple firmly. Add the hot vinegar mixture, leaving ½ inch headspace. Remove any air bubbles and seal.

3 Process in a boiling-water bath for 10 minutes, according to the directions on page 31. Let cool undisturbed for 12 hours. Store in a cool, dry place. Do not open for at least 6 weeks to allow the flavors to develop.

Kitchen Notes

• To prepare the pineapple, slice off the top of the pineapple, including the leaves. Slice off the bottom of the pineapple so the fruit will stand on a cutting board. Starting at the top, slice off the outer husk in 3- to 4-inch-wide slices, cutting just enough to remove the inedible husk but not so much that you lose too much fruit. After removing the husk, use the tip of a paring knife to remove the little "eyes" that remain. Vertically cut the pineapple into quarters. Slice the core from each quarter and discard. Slice the quarters into thirds and slice these into bite-size chunks.

• Serve with ham and other meats, especially when a teriyaki marinade is in play. It really shines as a dessert or cocktail garnish instead of a maraschino cherry.

Summer Squash Pickles

Makes 4 pints

Zucchini and all summer squash originated in the Americas and were brought to Europe as part of the Columbian exchange. But zucchini wasn't typically grown in the United States until it was brought back to America by Italian immigrants in the early 1900s. A surge in backyard gardening that accompanied the back-to-the-land hippie culture of the 1960s brought zucchini to mainstream America. This bland vegetable, Americans discovered, grew prolifically even when neglected, could be cooked every which way, and made a fine pickle. This recipe first appeared in Garden Way's best-selling *Zucchini Cookbook* by Nancy Ralston and Marynor Jordan. I had the fun of revising the cookbook for its 25th anniversary edition.

Ingredients

- 8 cups sliced summer squash or zucchini
- 2½ cups sliced onions
- 1 cup diced green bell pepper
- 1 tablespoon pickling or fine sea salt
- 2 cups distilled white vinegar
- 3 cups sugar
- 1½ teaspoons mustard seeds
- 1 teaspoon celery seeds
- Pickle Crisp Granules (optional)

1 Combine the summer squash, onions, bell pepper, and salt in a large bowl. Mix well, cover with ice water, and let stand for at least 2 hours, and up to 6 hours.

2 Combine the white vinegar, sugar, mustard seeds, and celery seeds in a saucepan and bring to a boil, stirring to dissolve the sugar.

3 Pack the vegetables into clean hot 1-pint canning jars. Pour in the hot vinegar mixture, leaving ½ inch headspace. Add a rounded ⅛ teaspoon of Pickle Crisp to each jar, if using. Remove any air bubbles and seal.

4 Process in a boiling-water bath for 10 minutes, according to the directions on page 31. Let cool undisturbed for 12 hours. Store in a cool, dry place. Do not open for at least 6 weeks to allow the flavors to develop.

Sweet Summer Squash Pickles

Makes 4 to 5 pints

Any type of summer squash — or a mixture of squash — can be used in this delightful pickle. Use different colors of bell peppers for maximum eye appeal. I collected this recipe from Jack M. Sherman of Dallas, Texas.

Ingredients

- 4 cups cubed summer squash or zucchini
- 4 cups sliced onions
- 4 cups diced bell peppers of any color
- 1 cup pickling or fine sea salt, or more if necessary
- 6 cups distilled white vinegar
- 3 cups water
- 5 cups sugar
- 1 tablespoon mixed pickling spices, store-bought or homemade (page 18)
- Pickle Crisp Granules (optional)

1 Combine the squash, onions, bell peppers, and salt in a large bowl. Mix well and cover with ice water. Let stand for at least 2 hours, and up to 6 hours. Rinse in cold water and drain. Taste a slice of squash. If it isn't decidedly salty, toss with 1 to 2 teaspoons pickling salt. If it's too salty, rinse again.

2 Combine the white vinegar, water, sugar, and mixed pickling spices in a saucepan and bring to a boil, stirring to dissolve the sugar.

3 Pack the vegetables into clean hot 1-pint canning jars. Pour in the hot vinegar mixture, leaving ½ inch headspace. Add a rounded ⅛ teaspoon of Pickle Crisp to each jar, if using. Remove any air bubbles and seal.

4 Process in a boiling-water bath for 10 minutes, according to the directions on page 31. Let cool undisturbed for 12 hours. Store in a cool, dry place. Do not open for at least 6 weeks to allow the flavors to develop.

Kitchen Note

This recipe is perfect for medium to large summer squash. Cut the squash into long strips, discard the middle strips that are full of seeds, and cube the rest.

Dilled Green Cherry Tomatoes

Makes 6 quarts

If you live in the North Country, you hope and hope that all your tomatoes ripen before the first frost. Sometimes you just aren't that lucky.

Ingredients

- 6 quarts green cherry tomatoes
- ¼ cup mixed pickling spices, store-bought or homemade (page 18)
- 8 cups water
- 2 cups distilled white vinegar
- ¾ cup pickling or fine sea salt
- 12 grape leaves
- 12 garlic cloves
- 24 peppercorns
- 6 dill heads

1 Remove the stems from the tomatoes. Put the mixed pickling spices in a spice bag (see How to Make a Spice Bag, page 20).

2 Combine the water, white vinegar, and salt in a saucepan. Add the spice bag and bring to a boil. Simmer for 15 minutes.

3 Meanwhile, put 2 grape leaves, 2 garlic cloves, 4 peppercorns, and 1 dill head in each clean hot 1-quart canning jar. Pack in the tomatoes. Pour in the hot brine, leaving ½ inch headspace. Remove any air bubbles and seal.

4 Process in a boiling-water bath for 15 minutes, according to the directions on page 31. Let cool undisturbed for 12 hours. Store in a cool, dry place. Do not open for at least 6 weeks to allow the flavors to develop.

LEAF PRESERVATION

If your opportunities to collect grape leaves and the like are limited, you can preserve your harvest in salt. Wash the leaves well and dry completely. Layer with salt in a clean, dry crock. Cover and store in a cool, dry place. When you are ready to use them, rinse the dried leaves in several changes of cold water.

Big Harvest Sweet Green Wheels

Makes about 10 pints

The good thing about green tomatoes is that they tend to be small, so they are easily sliced for the canning jar. And really, they are simply a blank canvas, ready for the flavor of the vinegar mixture. This old-fashioned recipe has several steps but results in a very full-flavored, delicious sweet pickle.

Ingredients

35–40   small green tomatoes, sliced ¼ inch thick

10   small onions, sliced

FIRST BRINE

8   cups water

½   cup pickling or fine sea salt

SECOND BRINE

3   cups water

1   cup cider vinegar

CANNING SYRUP

1   tablespoon whole cloves

2   cinnamon sticks

2   tablespoons mixed pickling spices, store-bought or homemade (page 18)

4   cups cider vinegar

3   cups honey

1. Layer the green tomatoes and onions in a large bowl. Make the first brine by combining the water and salt. Pour over the tomatoes and onions and let stand overnight.

2. In the morning, drain the tomatoes and onions. Rinse well in cold water and drain again. The tomatoes should taste pleasantly salty.

3. To make the second brine, pour the tomatoes and onions into a large saucepan; add the water and cider vinegar. Simmer the tomatoes for about 1 hour, until they look light and slightly translucent.

4. To make the canning syrup, tie the cloves, cinnamon, and mixed pickling spices in a spice bag (see How to Make a Spice Bag, page 20). Combine the cider vinegar and honey in a saucepan. Add the spice bag and bring to a boil, stirring to dissolve the honey. Boil for 10 minutes. Discard the spice bag.

5. Pack the tomatoes and onions into clean hot 1-pint canning jars, leaving ½ inch headspace. Pour in the hot syrup, leaving ½ inch headspace. Remove any air bubbles and seal.

6. Process in a boiling-water bath for 15 minutes, according to the directions on page 31. Let cool undisturbed for 12 hours. Store in a cool, dry place. Do not open for at least 6 weeks to allow the flavors to develop.

Old-Fashioned Watermelon Rind Pickles

Makes 6 pints

Among the (perhaps) unintended consequences of breeding the ever more popular seedless watermelons has been the thinning of the watermelon rind. You'll want the big old-fashioned seeded watermelon for making these. The pickling process is a two-day affair, but that should come as no surprise — it takes time to imbue flavor into something you would ordinarily compost.

Ingredients

- rind from 1 large watermelon
- ½ cup pickling or fine sea salt
- water
- 2 cinnamon sticks
- 1 teaspoon allspice berries
- 1 teaspoon whole cloves
- 2 cups distilled white vinegar
- 3 cups white or firmly packed brown sugar
- 1 lemon, thinly sliced

1 To prepare the watermelon rind, use a sharp knife to remove the dark green skin and any pink flesh from the rind. Cut the rind into 1-inch cubes or chunks. Dissolve the salt in 8 cups water in a large bowl. Add the watermelon rind and let soak overnight.

2 The next day, drain the watermelon rind. Return it to the bowl and cover with fresh water. Drain again. Transfer the rind to a large saucepan and cover with fresh water. Bring to a boil, then simmer until fork-tender, 5 to 10 minutes. Drain.

3 Tie together the cinnamon, allspice, and cloves in a spice bag (see How to Make a Spice Bag, page 20). Combine the white vinegar, sugar, and lemon in a large saucepan. Add the spice bag and bring to a boil, stirring to dissolve the sugar. Simmer for 5 minutes. Add the watermelon rind and simmer until translucent, about 1 hour. Remove the spice bag and lemon, and discard.

4 Pack the watermelon rind into clean hot 1-pint canning jars. Pour in the hot vinegar mixture, leaving ½ inch headspace. Remove any air bubbles and seal.

5 Process in a boiling-water bath for 10 minutes, according to the directions on page 31. Let cool undisturbed for 12 hours. Store in a cool, dry place. Do not open for at least 6 weeks to allow the flavors to develop.

Zucchini Bread and Butter Pickles

Makes 6 pints

Pickling mixtures that work for cucumbers will work for zucchini, though the texture of zucchini pickles is somewhat less crisp. For this, I particularly recommend adding Pickle Crisp (see Crisping Agents, page 22) to each jar.

Ingredients

- **12 cups thinly sliced small zucchini or other summer squash**
- **2 onions, thinly sliced**
- **¼ cup pickling or fine sea salt**
- **4 cups cider vinegar**
- **2 cups sugar**
- **2 teaspoons celery seeds**
- **2 teaspoons mustard seeds**
- **2 teaspoons ground turmeric**
- **Pickle Crisp Granules (optional)**

1 Combine the zucchini, onions, and salt in a large bowl. Mix thoroughly, cover with ice water, and let stand for at least 2 hours, and up to 6 hours. Drain well.

2 Combine the cider vinegar, sugar, celery seeds, mustard seeds, and turmeric in a saucepan and bring to a boil, stirring to dissolve the sugar. Let simmer while you pack the jars.

3 Pack the vegetables into clean hot 1-pint canning jars. Pour in the hot vinegar mixture, leaving ½ inch headspace. Add a rounded ⅛ teaspoon of Pickle Crisp to each jar, if using. Remove any air bubbles and seal.

4 Process in a boiling-water bath for 10 minutes, according to the directions on page 31. Let cool undisturbed for 12 hours. Store in a cool, dry place. Do not open for at least 6 weeks to allow the flavors to develop.

Kitchen Note

Aim to slice the vegetables about ⅛ inch thick. A food processor makes the job quick and easy.

Two-Day Mustard Pickles

Makes 5 to 6 quarts

This old-fashioned recipe is perfect for using up small amounts of a variety of vegetables — all of which ripen together at the end of the summer.

Ingredients

DAY 1

½ cup pickling or fine sea salt

12 cups cold water

1 head cauliflower, broken into florets (about 6 cups)

4 cups small white onions

4 cups sliced pickling cucumbers, zucchini, or other summer squash

4 cups green cherry or small plum tomatoes

2 large green bell peppers, seeded and cut into squares (about 2 cups)

2 large red bell peppers, seeded and cut into squares (about 2 cups)

DAY 2

1½ cups firmly packed brown sugar

⅔ cup ClearJel (see page 151) or all-purpose flour

2 teaspoons ground turmeric

8 cups cider vinegar

6 tablespoons yellow ballpark mustard

1   Day One: Dissolve the salt in the water. Add the vegetables and weight them to completely submerge them in the liquid. Cover and let sit for 24 hours.

2   Day Two: Drain the vegetables in a colander, capturing the brine in a large saucepan. Heat the brine to boiling and pour over the vegetables in the colander. Let the vegetables drain in a sink, discarding the salt brine.

3   Combine the brown sugar, ClearJel, and turmeric in the saucepan used in the previous step and stir until well mixed. Stir in the cider vinegar and mustard, then heat gradually, stirring constantly, until the mixture is thick and smooth. Add the drained vegetables and cook briefly until the vegetables are just fork-tender, about 10 minutes. Keep stirring to prevent scorching.

4   Pack the vegetables and vinegar mixture into clean hot 1-quart canning jars, leaving ½ inch headspace. Remove any air bubbles and seal.

5   Process in a boiling-water bath for 10 minutes, according to the directions on page 31. Let cool undisturbed for 12 hours. Store in a cool, dry place. Do not open for at least 6 weeks to allow the flavors to develop.

Kitchen Note

The hardest part of this recipe is peeling the onions. To make it easy, put the onions in a bowl and cover with boiling water. Let the onions sit in the water for about 5 minutes. Then drain. The skins should slip off easily.

Chapter 5

Salsas

Relishes

Chutneys

Mustard Pickle Relish • Dilled Dog Relish • Classic Sweet Pickle Relish • Apple Chutney • Apple Raisin Chutney • Apricot Date Chutney • Russian Beet Relish • Red Cabbage and Apple Relish • Candied Carrot Relish • Sweet Honey Corn Relish • Chili Corn Relish • Savory Cranberry-Apple Relish • Traditional Cranberry Relish • Horseradish Relish • Homemade Mustard • Rosemary Onion Confit • Peach Ginger Chutney • Ginger Pear Chutney • Classic Pepper Relish • Smoky Red Hot Sauce • Green Chile Sauce • Five-Spice Plum Chutney • Sweet-Tart Rhubarb Chutney • Helen Nearing's Rhubarb Chutney • Curried Summer Squash Relish • Tomatillo Salsa • Tomato Ketchup • Classic Homemade Tomato Ketchup • Simple Salsa • Chipotle Salsa • Barbecue Sauce • Betty Jacob's Red Tomato Chutney • Sweet Chili Sauce • Italian Tomato Relish • Green Tomato Pickle Relish • Keeping the Harvest Green Tomato Mincemeat • Janet Ballentyne's Green Tomato Mincemeat • Old-Fashioned Green Tomato Mincemeat with Suet • Busy Person's Zucchini Relish • Keeping the Harvest Piccalilli • Chow-Chow • Pennsylvania Chow-Chow • Homemade Branston-Style Pickle Relish • Old-Time Hot Dog Relish • Mixed Fruit Chutney

Relishes, salsas, and chutneys belong to the end of the gardening season. Most of the fruits and vegetables called for in the recipes assembled here — apples, beets, cabbages, carrots, cauliflower, chiles, corn, onions, green and red bell peppers — ripen at the end of the growing season, in late summer or fall.

Relishes and chutneys are forgiving. You can often use slightly overgrown or less-than-mature produce in them. Slightly woody beets, for example, are fine to use in beet relish; green tomatoes are desirable in some recipes.

When chopping vegetables and fruit for this chapter, take advantage of the labor-saving food processor. For best results, first chop the fruits and veggies coarsely by hand. Then chop finely using the pulsing action. Chop each type of fruit or veggie separately; otherwise the soft ones will become a puree before the hard ones are finely chopped. Don't bother to wash out the food processor in between batches.

You'll note that many of the recipes do not include the familiar caution to wait six weeks before opening to allow the flavor to develop. Most of these recipes include cooking, during which time most of the flavor that is going to develop does. What you taste going into the jar is pretty much what you get. So be sure to taste and adjust the sugar and salt if you like.

If it is too hot or you are too busy at the end of the summer to make relishes, consider freezing the vegetables until the timing works for you. You don't even have to blanch the vegetables first, though you will notice a slight loss of texture and color. I don't recommend cucumbers for this treatment, but other vegetables can be used.

Relish and chutney recipes tend to be big-batch projects with lots of ingredients, so consider them more "big harvest" recipes. You can find even more relishes and sauces in the salt-brined chapter, too.

If you are wondering whether you will be able to make good use of these relishes and chutneys, chapter 7 has plenty of ideas for you. I like to use pickle relishes as a winter replacement for lettuce and tomatoes on sandwiches. Pickle relishes and chutneys also liven up crackers and cheese — enough to make that simple combination company worthy.

This chapter includes several recipes for cucumbers, green tomatoes, and summer squash. I don't think any garden-focused cookbook can include too many recipes for these "problem" vegetables. The recipes here are arranged in alphabetical order by main vegetable or fruit, with cucumbers at the start and vegetable mixtures at the end of the chapter.

Mustard Pickle Relish

Makes 5 half-pints

If the perfect topping for your hot dog includes pickle relish and mustard, this is the recipe for you. The relish also makes a fine addition to potato salad, egg salad, cold-cut sandwiches, macaroni salad, and grilled (or not) cheese sandwiches.

Ingredients

- **6 cups coarsely chopped cucumbers**
- **1 bell pepper of any color, seeded**
- **1 onion**
- **1½ teaspoons pickling or fine sea salt**
- **1 cup cider vinegar**
- **½ cup sugar**
- **2 tablespoons yellow ballpark mustard**
- **1 tablespoon ClearJel or all-purpose flour**
- **¼ teaspoon ground turmeric**
- **1 tablespoon chopped fresh dill**

1 Finely chop the cucumbers in a food processor using the pulsing action. Transfer to a large colander. Then, each in turn, finely chop the bell pepper and then the onion, using the pulsing action, and transfer to the colander with the cucumbers. Add the salt and toss to mix well. Let sit for at least 30 minutes, and up to 60 minutes. Press on the mixture to remove excess liquid and transfer to a large saucepan.

2 Add the cider vinegar and bring to a boil.

3 Meanwhile, mix together the sugar, mustard, ClearJel, and turmeric to form a paste. Stir into the saucepan. Bring back to a boil, then remove from the heat and stir in the dill.

4 Pack the mixture into clean hot half-pint canning jars, leaving ½ inch headspace. Remove any air bubbles and seal. ·

5 Process in a boiling-water bath for 10 minutes, according to the directions on page 31. Let cool undisturbed for 12 hours. Store in a cool dry place.

CLEARJEL

ClearJel is a modified food starch approved for use in home canning. It is easy to use, thickens without clouding, and doesn't break down when exposed to high temperatures. It is the only product approved by the USDA for thickening canned pie fillings, which is how it crept into the pickling world. It also doesn't clump like flour; to replace flour in a recipe, use an equal amount of ClearJel. It is available online from sites that carry canning supplies.

Dilled Dog Relish

Makes 8 to 9 half-pints

Don't let the recipe title limit your impulse to slather this relish everywhere. I can never have too many jars of this versatile relish. I love it on a bun with Pulled Chicken Barbecue (page 271). I add it to Thousand Island Dressing (page 248), Dilly Mustard Coleslaw (page 250), and tuna fish salad. But keep that hot dog in mind while preparing the cucumbers and chop finely so the relish doesn't fall off the hot dog, but not so finely that the pieces of crunchy cucumber are unidentifiable.

Ingredients

- 6 cups finely chopped cucumbers (about 12 pickling cucumbers)
- 2 onions, finely chopped
- ¼ cup pickling or fine sea salt
- 3 cups distilled white vinegar
- 1 cup water
- 1 cup sugar
- 6 sprigs fresh dill, chopped (about ¼ cup)
- 1 head garlic, cloves separated, peeled, and chopped
- 1 teaspoon mustard seeds
- ½ teaspoon freshly ground black pepper

1 Combine the cucumbers and onions in a large bowl. Sprinkle with the salt and cover with ice water. Let stand for at least 2 hours, and up to 6 hours. Drain the vegetables in a colander, pressing out any liquid.

2 Combine the white vinegar, water, sugar, dill, garlic, and mustard seeds in a saucepan and bring to a boil, stirring to dissolve the sugar. Add the drained vegetables and stir until well combined. Simmer until hot, about 5 minutes.

3 Pack the mixture into clean hot half-pint canning jars, leaving ½ inch headspace. Remove any air bubbles and seal.

4 Process in a boiling-water bath for 10 minutes, according to the directions on page 31. Let cool undisturbed for 12 hours. Store in a cool, dry place. Do not open for at least 6 weeks to allow the flavors to develop.

Kitchen Note

If you aren't a big fan of garlic, reduce the number of cloves, but don't omit it entirely.

RELISHING HOT DOGS

July is National Hot Dog Month. Have you made plans to honor this American icon?

Americans eat a yearly average of 60 hot dogs per person, according to the National Hot Dog and Sausage Council, which also notes that more than seven billion hot dogs will be eaten by Americans between Memorial Day and Labor Day. During the July 4th weekend alone (the biggest hot-dog holiday of the year), 155 million hot dogs will be slid into buns, doused with relish, and enjoyed.

Adults generally go for mustard on their dogs (but it doesn't have to be that boring bright-yellow glop — see Homemade Mustard, page 169), while kids tend to prefer ketchup (see pages 182–183). I used to be a sauerkraut person (see page 56) but lately my allegiance is to Mustard Pickle Relish (page 151). A good relish is hard to beat. Here's a list of some hot-dog-friendly relish choices:

- Dilled Dog Relish (page 152)
- Classic Sweet Pickle Relish (page 154)
- Old-Time Hot Dog Relish (page 155)
- Classic Pepper Relish (page 173)
- Curried Summer Squash Relish (page 184)
- Green Tomato Pickle Relish (page 192)
- Busy Person's Zucchini Relish (page 196)
- Keeping the Harvest Piccalilli (page 197)
- Chow-Chow (page 198)
- Pennsylvania Chow-Chow (page 199)

Classic Sweet Pickle Relish

Makes 7 to 8 half-pints

What doesn't go well with a sweet pickle relish? It makes a great pairing with such homey favorites as hot dogs, barbecued meat on buns, grilled cheese, crackers and cheese, cold-cut sandwiches, and tuna fish salad. A spoonful or two added to Sweet Pickle Macaroni Salad (page 251) makes an all-American classic.

Ingredients

- 4 cups finely chopped cucumbers
- 2 cups finely chopped onions
- 1 green bell pepper, finely chopped
- 1 red bell pepper, finely chopped
- ¼ cup pickling or fine sea salt
- 2 cups cider vinegar
- 3 cups sugar
- 1 tablespoon celery seeds
- 1 tablespoon mustard seeds

1 Combine the cucumbers, onions, and green and red bell peppers in a large bowl. Sprinkle with the salt and toss well to mix. Cover with cold water. Let stand for at least 2 hours, and up to 6 hours. Drain well, pressing out the excess liquid.

2 Combine the cider vinegar, sugar, celery seeds, and mustard seeds in a saucepan and bring to a boil, stirring to dissolve the sugar. Add the vegetables and simmer for 10 minutes.

3 Pack into clean hot half-pint canning jars, leaving ½ inch headspace. Remove any air bubbles and seal.

4 Process in a boiling-water bath for 10 minutes, according to the directions on page 31. Let cool undisturbed for 12 hours. Store in a cool, dry place. Do not open for at least 6 weeks to allow the flavors to develop.

CUCUMBER RELISHES

Anything goes in a relish. If your cucumbers are somewhat overripe, just cut each in half lengthwise and scrape away the seeds before chopping. You can use either salad cucumbers or pickling cucumbers — or both — for a relish. The texture will be crunchier with pickling cucumbers because they have a greater ratio of skin to flesh, but the difference will be small.

Old-Time Hot Dog Relish

Makes 12 half-pints

Tomatoes, peaches, peppers, and onions, all mixed, sweetened with honey, and made tart with cider vinegar, give an interesting flavor profile to this old-fashioned relish.

Ingredients

- 10 large ripe tomatoes
- 9 peaches
- 2 red bell peppers, finely chopped
- 3 large onions, finely chopped
- 1½ cups cider vinegar
- 1½ cups honey
- 1 tablespoon pickling or fine sea salt
- ¼ cup mixed pickling spices, store-bought or homemade (page 18)

1 Bring a large saucepan of water to a boil. Blanch the tomatoes and peaches in the water for 30 seconds. Remove and plunge into a bowl of ice water. The skins will slip off easily. Finely chop the tomatoes and peaches and combine in a large saucepan.

2 Add the bell peppers, onions, cider vinegar, honey, and salt to the saucepan. Tie the pickling spices in a spice bag (see How to Make a Spice Bag, page 20) and add to the saucepan. Cook over medium heat for at least 2 hours, stirring occasionally, until the mixture thickens. Remove the spice bag.

3 Pack the mixture into clean hot half-pint canning jars, leaving ½ inch headspace. Remove any air bubbles and seal.

4 Process in a boiling-water bath for 15 minutes, according to the directions on page 31. Let cool undisturbed for 12 hours. Store in a cool, dry place.

Apple Chutney

Makes 6 half-pints

Major Grey's, the most well-known chutney in the United States, has a mango base, which makes a fine chutney. But apples are abundant here — and mangoes? Not so much. Apple chutney is a delicious condiment for curries and grilled meats or anywhere Major Grey's might be served.

Ingredients

4½ pounds apples, peeled, cored, and coarsely chopped

2 onions, finely chopped

2 green or red bell peppers, finely chopped

6 garlic cloves, minced

¾ cup firmly packed brown sugar

¾ cup cider vinegar

1 tablespoon mustard seeds

1½ teaspoons pickling or fine sea salt

¾ teaspoon freshly ground black pepper

¾ teaspoon ground ginger

1 Combine the apples, onions, bell peppers, garlic, brown sugar, cider vinegar, mustard seeds, salt, pepper, and ginger in a saucepan over medium heat. Bring to a simmer, and simmer for about 1 hour, stirring occasionally, until the apples break down and the chutney is thick.

2 Ladle the hot chutney into clean hot half-pint canning jars, leaving ½ inch headspace. Remove any air bubbles and seal.

3 Process in a boiling-water bath for 10 minutes, according to the directions on page 31. Let cool undisturbed for 12 hours. Store in a cool, dry place.

APPLES FOR CHUTNEYS

Any apple works for chutneys and relishes, though a good cooking apple, like Northern Spy or Golden, is best. But don't hesitate to make them with apples that are beyond their prime for eating out of hand. Most are forgiving recipes, and a good way to use up the end-of-the-season, bottom-of-the-barrel remains.

Figure that three medium-size apples weigh 1 pound.

Apple Raisin Chutney

Makes 6 half-pints

I am fortunate to live near one of the largest orchards of heirloom apple varieties in New England: Scott Farm in Dummerston, Vermont. Every week during apple season, the farm delivers crates of heirloom apples to the Middlebury Natural Foods Co-op, where I am a frequent shopper. I've fallen in love with many different varieties — Hudson's Golden Gem and Keepsake are particular favorites — but these apples come and go quickly. Each variety has its own season, and what I love one week may be replaced by a different variety the next. Chutney is what I make when these precious eating apples begin to soften. Pomegranate molasses adds depth of flavor to this chutney.

Ingredients

4½ pounds apples, peeled, cored, and chopped

1 cup raisins

2 onions, finely chopped

6 garlic cloves, minced

½ cup firmly packed brown sugar

¾ cup cider vinegar

2 tablespoons pomegranate molasses (see page 99)

1½ teaspoons pickling or fine sea salt

1 teaspoon ground ginger

½ teaspoon ground allspice

½ teaspoon freshly ground black pepper

1 Combine the apples, raisins, onions, garlic, brown sugar, cider vinegar, pomegranate molasses, salt, ginger, allspice, and pepper in a saucepan over medium heat. Bring to a simmer and simmer for about 1 hour, stirring occasionally, until the apples break down and the chutney is thick.

2 Ladle the hot chutney into clean hot half-pint canning jars, leaving ½ inch headspace. Remove any air bubbles and seal.

3 Process in a boiling-water bath for 10 minutes, according to the directions on page 31. Let cool undisturbed for 12 hours. Store in a cool, dry place.

AGING CHUTNEYS AND RELISHES

Most chutneys and many relishes are cooked long enough so they don't require additional aging in the jar. Feel free to use immediatly rather than wait the 6 weeks other briefly cooked relishes may require.

Apricot Date Chutney

Makes about 6 half-pints

Dates add exotic flavor to this honey-sweetened chutney.

Ingredients

2½ **pounds apricots**

10 **garlic cloves, minced**

1 **(1-inch) piece fresh ginger, peeled and minced, or 1-inch stack Pickled Ginger (page 229), minced**

1 **cup cider vinegar**

1 **cup honey**

½ **teaspoon pickling or fine sea salt**

¼ **teaspoon cayenne pepper, or to taste**

¼ **teaspoon ground cinnamon**

1 **cup chopped dates**

1 Blanch the apricots by immersing them in boiling water to cover for about 30 seconds, then plunging them in ice water to cool. Peel, remove the pits, and finely chop. A food processor does this job easily, but do not overprocess.

2 Combine the apricots, garlic, ginger, cider vinegar, honey, salt, cayenne, and cinnamon in a large saucepan. Bring to a boil, stirring to dissolve the honey. Decrease the heat and simmer, partially covered, for 30 minutes, stirring occasionally. Add the dates and continue to simmer for another 30 minutes, stirring frequently. This chutney scorches easily, so keep a close watch.

3 Ladle the hot chutney into clean hot half-pint canning jars, leaving ½ inch headspace. Remove any air bubbles and seal.

4 Process in a boiling-water bath for 10 minutes, according to the directions on page 31. Let cool undisturbed for 12 hours. Store in a cool, dry place.

Kitchen Notes

- Figure there are 8 to 12 apricots in a pound. Blanching the apricots makes them easier to peel. The skins should just slip off.
- If you have already dirtied the food processor to chop the apricots, it makes sense to use it to mince together the garlic and ginger.

Russian Beet Relish

Makes 8 pints

The combination of beets and cabbage with caraway flavoring is pretty typically Russian or eastern European. This makes a wonderful accompaniment to potato pancakes or a simple meal of baked potatoes.

Ingredients

- 10 **cups cubed cooked beets (page 93)**
- 4 **onions, diced**
- 10 **cups diced cabbage (about 4 pounds)**
- 3 **cups distilled white vinegar**
- 3 **cups sugar**
- 2 **tablespoons caraway seeds**
- 1 **tablespoon pickling or fine sea salt, or to taste**

1 Combine the beets, onions, and cabbage in a large saucepan. Add the white vinegar, sugar, caraway seeds, and salt. Bring to a boil, stirring to dissolve the sugar, and simmer for 10 minutes. Taste and add additional salt, if desired.

2 Ladle the hot relish into clean hot 1-pint canning jars, leaving about ½ inch headspace. Remove any air bubbles and seal.

3 Process in a boiling-water bath for 10 minutes, according to the directions on page 31. Let cool undisturbed for 12 hours. Store in a cool, dry place. Do not open for at least 6 weeks to allow the flavors to develop.

Kitchen Note

You will need about 3 pounds of raw beets for this recipe.

Tigress in a Pickle

If you've ever trolled the Internet for preserving recipes (and as a cookbook writer, I wince as I write this), you have undoubtedly come across Tigress, a dedicated blogger, food preserver, and builder of a community of canners.

Look for "Tigress in a Pickle," where Tigress's remarkable blog about pickling and preserving can be found. (Tigress in a Pickle represents her "savory" side; there is also a "sweet" side represented by Tigress in a Jam.)

Tigress is a perfect example of the sort of person who is pickling and preserving today. A part-time resident of Long Island City "downwind of Brooklyn," Tigress bought an old farmhouse in the Berkshires with her husband about six years ago. At the time she knew nothing about gardening, but her husband had gardened with his father for a few summers in his youth. That first year her husband grew tomatoes. The tomatoes were amazing, so the next year these part-time country dwellers expanded the garden.

"Now we have a huge garden and sustain ourselves all year with what we grow. I think preserving what we grew happened as a natural progression: How do you extend that season into what you eat all year?"

The blog happened "on a whim." At first, she says, "One of the reasons I did it was to keep track of what I was preserving. I just did it for myself. But quickly, quite quickly in fact, it started to gain a readership. I think it's the next step in the grow-your-own movement. Lots of people are trying to eat locally and trying to grow their own food. My blog sort of captured the zeitgeist."

With an avid readership, Tigress found the encouragement to expand her blogging. "When I started, I said to my husband, 'You know, if I get five people who like what I do, that's all that I need . . .'"

But the five people grew into many, many more when Tigress offered her first "Can Jam" challenge in 2010. So many more that she had to restrict the Can Jam participants to 130 people.

What's a Can Jam challenge? This is how the website described it: "Each month we'll focus on one fruit or vegetable to preserve. Recipes may include other fruits or veggies but the food of focus must be integral to the preserve, and the recipe must include hot water bath canning." The "produce of focus" is announced and the bloggers who have signed on to the challenge post their recipes by a deadline. At the end of the month,

Tigress presents a round-up of the recipes and directs the readers to the participating bloggers' recipes. It is a way of collecting recipes and ideas from a group of like-minded people who are doing like-minded things — making pickles with in-season produce. And of course, because of the nature of the canning blogosphere, the photographs are tantalizing, educational, and inspirational.

Out of the Can Jam challenge came a community of bloggers, "from fellow canning bloggers excited to share ideas and techniques, to those new to the blogosphere inspired to jump in the water for the first time just for the can jam. Now that is exciting!" Last year there were 60 people who participated in a full year of canning challenges (some didn't keep up with the challenge all year). Bloggers did not necessarily test each other's recipes, but Tigress did make sure that the recipes sounded safe and were done in accordance with USDA guidelines.

A community of people who meet via cyberspace is, of course, not at all like the canning bees of our great-grandmothers, where neighborhood women or members of an extended family might gather in one person's kitchen — preferably a summer kitchen with lots of screened windows open to the breezes — and "put up" a year's worth of fruits and veggies for families who put up or went hungry.

Do the bloggers ever meet face to face? It happens, as a matter of fact. Last summer there was a meet-up in the Hudson River Valley to pick strawberries. Other meet-ups have happened, and bloggers have exchanged jars of preserves. But for many, the connection via the website is enough, and really all they can fit into their busy lives.

"Being in a community and talking with others about preserving definitely pushes me out of my comfort zone. There were recipes I tried that I wouldn't have normally tried. I made a carrot marmalade that I never would have made, and we really loved it," Tigress explained.

"Recently I have been getting into fermenting. This summer I fermented like 75 pounds of cabbage. We are really trying to eat local and go through the winter with local vegetables. And we love sauerkraut. And kimchi, too. So it seemed like a good thing to do." And that, in fact, is exactly where the other locavores, bloggers, and picklers seem to be heading as well. Stay tuned for Tigress in a Crock?

To read more about Tigress, go to www.hungrytigress.com.

Red Cabbage and Apple Relish

Makes 3 quarts

You must make this relish, if for no other reason than its sheer good looks on the pantry shelf. This is more like a side dish served at room temperature than a relish to be dabbed on a hot dog or sandwich. Pork is the obvious match for the tangy cabbage and apples, but duck, chicken, and turkey are also naturals.

Ingredients

- 1 head red cabbage, very thinly sliced
- 2 tablespoons pickling or fine sea salt
- 1½ cups cider vinegar
- 1½ cups water
- 1½ cups sugar
- 2 teaspoons caraway seeds
- 1 teaspoon freshly ground black pepper
- 4 large tart apples, peeled, cored, and julienned

1 Combine the red cabbage and salt in a large bowl. With your hands, massage the salt into the cabbage until the cabbage looks wet, 1 to 2 minutes. Let stand for 3 hours.

2 With a potato masher or mallet, press on the cabbage to further break down the cell walls, a process that began with the salt. When the cabbage is completely limp, drain it. Taste. If it tastes too salty, rinse and then drain again.

3 Combine the cider vinegar, water, sugar, caraway seeds, and black pepper in a large saucepan over medium heat, stirring to dissolve the sugar. Add the cabbage and apples, stir well, and bring to a boil.

4 With a slotted spoon, pack the hot cabbage mixture into clean hot 1-quart canning jars. Add just enough of the remaining vinegar mixture to moisten the relish, leaving ½ inch headspace. Remove any air bubbles and seal.

5 Process in a boiling-water bath for 15 minutes, according to the directions on page 31. Let cool undisturbed for 12 hours. Store in a cool, dry place. Do not open for at least 6 weeks to allow the flavors to develop.

Kitchen Note

You can make this with green cabbage instead of red, but the relish won't have the lovely purple-red color.

Candied Carrot Relish

Makes 4 pints

Can't bear to compost overgrown cucumbers? This colorful, sweet relish uses grated cucumbers to add bulk, a perfect use for cucumbers that have gone by.

Ingredients

- **4 cups shredded or grated carrots**
- **3 cups peeled, seeded, and shredded or grated cucumbers**
- **1 small onion, diced**
- **1 red bell pepper, diced**
- **2 tablespoons pickling or fine sea salt**
- **1½ cups distilled white vinegar**
- **1½ cups sugar or honey**
- **¾ teaspoon mustard seeds**
- **½ teaspoon celery seeds**

1 Combine the carrots, cucumbers, onion, bell pepper, and salt in a large bowl. Toss well to mix. Let stand for at least 2 hours, and up to 6 hours. Drain well but do not rinse.

2 Combine the white vinegar, sugar, mustard seeds, and celery seeds in a saucepan and bring to a boil, stirring to dissolve the sugar. Add the vegetables and simmer for 15 minutes.

3 Pack the hot relish into clean hot 1-pint canning jars, leaving ½ inch headspace. Remove any air bubbles and seal.

4 Process in a boiling-water bath for 15 minutes, according to the directions on page 31. Do not disturb for 12 hours. Store in a cool, dry place. Do not open for at least 6 weeks to allow the flavors to develop.

Kitchen Note

Figure that 3 large carrots or 4 medium carrots will yield 4 cups grated carrots.

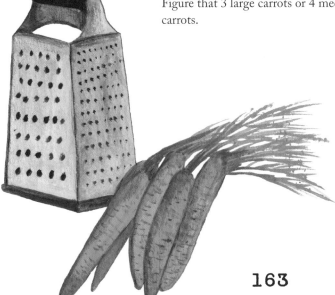

163

Sweet Honey Corn Relish

Makes 5 pints

This is a sweet one. Add the honey to taste, but don't adjust the vinegar — that's the preservative. Try this relish instead of chutney in Chutney-Cheese with Crackers (page 243).

Ingredients

- 8 cups raw corn kernels (from 10–12 ears)
- 2 onions, finely chopped
- 1 green bell pepper, finely chopped
- 1 red bell pepper, finely chopped
- 1–1½ cups honey
- 3¼ cups cider vinegar
- 1 teaspoon celery seeds
- 1 tablespoon pickling or fine sea salt
- ¼ teaspoon cayenne
- 1 tablespoon ClearJel (see page 151), or 2 tablespoons cornstarch

1 Combine the corn, onions, green and red bell peppers, 1 cup of the honey, 3 cups of the cider vinegar, celery seeds, salt, and cayenne in a large saucepan. Bring to a boil, stirring to dissolve the honey.

2 Stir together the ClearJel and remaining ¼ cup cider vinegar until smooth. Stir into the corn mixture and boil gently until thickened, about 5 minutes. Taste and add more honey, if desired.

3 Ladle the hot relish into clean hot 1-pint canning jars, leaving ½ inch headspace. Remove any air bubbles and seal.

4 Process in a boiling-water bath for 15 minutes, according to the direction on page 31. Let cool undisturbed for 12 hours. Store in a cool, dry place. Do not open for at least 6 weeks to allow the flavors to develop.

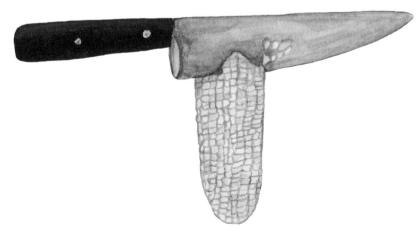

Chili Corn Relish

Makes 5 pints

Is your chili powder fresh? If not, throw it out and buy it fresh. A good chili powder elevates this recipe into an extraordinary relish. Use the relish as a salsa alternative — as a dip for chips, a topping for nachos, or a flavoring in burritos. You can also use it to spice up a ho-hum salsa with vibrant flavors and colors. Use it to make a tasty Chili Corn Bean Dip (page 247), or serve with crackers and cheese, or stuffed into tacos.

Ingredients

- 2 tablespoons olive or other vegetable oil
- 3 tablespoons chili powder
- 6 cups corn kernels (from 8–12 ears)
- 2 fresh hot green or red chiles, seeded (optional; see page 175) and finely chopped
- 1 bell pepper of any color, finely chopped
- 1 onion, finely chopped
- 2 garlic cloves, minced
- 3 cups cider vinegar
- 3 cups sugar, or to taste
- 1 teaspoon pickling or fine sea salt, or to taste
- 1 teaspoon freshly ground black pepper
- ½ cup chopped fresh cilantro

1 Heat the oil in a saucepan over medium-high heat. Add the chili powder and simmer until it smells fragrant, about 30 seconds. Add the corn, chiles, bell pepper, onion, and garlic and stir to coat with the chili powder. Add the cider vinegar, sugar, salt, and pepper. Bring to a boil, stirring to dissolve the sugar. Taste and adjust the sugar and salt. Remove from the heat and stir in the cilantro.

2 Ladle the hot relish into clean hot 1-pint canning jars, leaving ½ inch headspace. Remove any air bubbles and seal.

3 Process in a boiling-water bath for 15 minutes, according to the directions on page 31. Let cool undisturbed for 12 hours. Store in a cool, dry place. Do not open for at least 6 weeks to allow the flavor to develop.

CORN

To remove the kernels from an ear of corn, husk the corn and remove the silks. Stand the ear on a cutting board and, using a paring knife, cut downward to slice off a few rows of kernels from the ear. Rotate the cob and continue.

Kitchen Notes

- You can play with the heat by using hotter chiles. Substituting a few habaneros for jalapeños, for example, will make your relish *very* hot.
- For the best-looking relish, make sure the pieces of the chopped vegetables are no bigger than the corn kernels.

Savory Cranberry-Apple Relish

Makes 4 to 5 half-pints

If you are used to the traditional sweet cranberry sauce, this relish may come as a shock. Tangy-sweet and savory with onion and rosemary, this relish will transform a turkey sandwich into a cause for celebration. It also makes a fine addition to Cranberry Chicken Salad (page 270). Or serve with crackers and goat cheese.

Ingredients

- 4 cups fresh or frozen cranberries (12 ounces)
- 2 apples, peeled, cored, and finely chopped
- 2 onions, peeled and finely chopped
- 3 cups firmly packed brown sugar
- 2 teaspoons pickling or fine sea salt
- 1 (1-inch) piece fresh ginger, peeled and minced, or 1-inch stack Pickled Ginger (page 229), minced
- 1 teaspoon freshly ground black pepper
- 1 teaspoon ground cinnamon
- pinch of dried rosemary

1 Combine the cranberries, apples, onions, brown sugar, salt, ginger, pepper, cinnamon, and rosemary in a large saucepan. Bring to a boil over medium heat, stirring frequently. Decrease the heat and simmer, stirring often, until all the cranberries have popped and the mixture is thick and jamlike, about 40 minutes.

2 Ladle the hot relish into clean hot half-pint canning jars, leaving ½ inch headspace. Remove any air bubbles and seal.

3 Process in a boiling-water bath for 15 minutes, according to the directions on page 31. Let cool undisturbed for 12 hours. Store in a cool, dry place.

Kitchen Note

Unlike many relishes, this relish can be served as soon as it is made.

CRANBERRIES

Cranberries are unusual because they can be frozen without any processing and remain unchanged in texture. So when fresh cranberries are available, stock up on extra. Just put the cranberries in a plastic bag (if they aren't sold in bags) and freeze.

Traditional Cranberry Relish

Makes 4 to 5 half-pints

This is a holiday classic. The apples provide an abundance of pectin to make the relish jell.

Ingredients

- 4 **cups fresh or frozen cranberries (12 ounces)**
- 1 **apple, peeled, cored, and very finely chopped**
- 1⅓ **cups honey**
- ½ **cup water**
- 1 **tablespoon bottled lemon juice**

1 Combine the cranberries, apple, honey, water, and lemon juice in a large saucepan. Bring to a boil over medium heat, stirring frequently. Decrease the heat and simmer, stirring often, until all the cranberries have popped and the mixture is thick and jamlike, about 40 minutes.

2 Ladle the hot relish into clean hot half-pint canning jars, leaving ½ inch headspace. Remove any air bubbles and seal.

3 Process in a boiling-water bath for 15 minutes, according to the directions on page 31. Let cool undisturbed for 12 hours. Store in a cool, dry place.

Kitchen Notes

- If you prefer a jellied cranberry relish with a smooth texture, strain the cooked mixture through a food mill. Return the strained pulp to the saucepan and bring to a boil. Boil for 2 minutes, then ladle into jars.
- If you like, double the recipe and process in pint jars. Processing time remains the same.
- Unlike many relishes, this one can be served as soon as it is made.

Horseradish Relish

Makes 1 pint

Very fresh horseradish should be served with a warning. Grating the root releases a substance called sinigrin, which, when decomposed by the action of enzymes, releases a substance not unlike the mustard gas used in World War I. The volatile oil dissipates fairly quickly, so keep the lid on the jar, make only a little horseradish at a time, and don't expose it to heat.

Ingredients

1 horseradish root (about 12 ounces)

4–6 tablespoons distilled white vinegar

4 tablespoons water

1 Peel the root and cut it into 1-inch pieces, then chop it very finely in a food processer.

2 Through the feed tube, add 4 tablespoons white vinegar and the water, and process until mixed. Loosen the top of the processor and allow the fumes to dissipate for about 30 seconds — otherwise be prepared for an intense sensation when the fumes reach your sinuses. Scrape down the sides of the mixing bowl and check the texture of the relish. If it seems dry, add the additional vinegar, a little at a time.

3 Quickly pack the horseradish into a clean jar and seal tightly. Store in the refrigerator. To maintain the flavor, expose the horseradish to as little air as possible.

Kitchen Notes

- If you grow your own horseradish, harvest the roots when the plant is dormant in the late fall or early spring. If you must buy your horseradish, look for it in supermarkets in the spring. Choose roots that are firm and have no mold or soft or green spots. Avoid older roots, which will look shriveled and dry.
- Store horseradish root unwashed in a plastic bag in the vegetable drawer of the refrigerator, where it will keep for months.
- You can grate the root by hand and stir in the vinegar and water, without the aid of the food processor, but the fumes are nearly deadly!

Homemade Mustard

Makes 3 half-pints

I collected this recipe from Olwen Woodier, author of three cookbooks, including the *Apple Cookbook*, which won the R.T. French Co. Best Cookbook Tastemaker Award. Ironically, Woodier prefers her own mustard to French's.

Ingredients

- 2 ounces mustard seeds (½ cup plus 2 tablespoons)
- 1 cup white wine, or more if needed
- ½ cup wine vinegar, cider vinegar, malt vinegar, or distilled white vinegar
- ½ cup water
- 2 tablespoons honey
- ½ teaspoon ground allspice
- ½ teaspoon pickling or fine sea salt

1 Put the mustard seeds in a small bowl, cover with the wine, vinegar, and water, and let soak overnight.

2 Transfer the seeds and liquid to a blender or food processor. Add the honey, allspice, and salt. Blend until the mixture is thick and smooth. If the mustard is too thick, add more wine, vinegar, or water, 1 tablespoon at a time, until the mixture has a pleasing texture. Give the mixture a final blend and pour into sterilized hot half-pint canning jars. Store in the refrigerator. It will keep at least 6 months.

Kitchen Notes

- During blending, you can add 1 tablespoon of your favorite dried herb (such as tarragon, lemon thyme, or oregano), ¼–½ cup drained green peppercorns, or ½ cup fresh basil leaves.
- The vinegar you choose will affect the flavor of the mustard. Mustard made with distilled white vinegar will be quite sharp; malt vinegar and wine vinegar produce a mellower mustard.
- Maple syrup can replace the honey.

Rosemary Onion Confit

Makes 3 pints

This sweet onion relish is the perfect accompaniment to meats, particularly pork roasts. Use the confit with goat cheese to top Goat Cheese Crostini (page 246) or crackers. It is also fine with crackers and cheddar cheese. Turn it into a quickly made tart (substitute it for the tomato relish in Tomato-Mozzarella Tart, page 265). You can also slide it under the skin of a chicken before roasting.

Ingredients

¼ cup extra-virgin olive oil

3 pounds onions, chopped

1 cup cider vinegar or wine vinegar

¾ cup sugar

1 tablespoon rosemary

1 tablespoon soy sauce, or to taste

freshly ground black pepper

1 Heat the oil in a large saucepan over medium-high heat. Add the onions, decrease the heat to low, and stir to coat the onions with the oil. Cook, stirring occasionally, until the onions are brown and meltingly tender, about 30 minutes.

2 Stir in the cider vinegar, sugar, rosemary, soy sauce, and pepper and simmer for 5 minutes.

3 Pack the onion mixture into clean hot 1-pint canning jars, leaving ½ inch headspace. Remove any air bubbles and seal.

4 Process in a boiling-water bath for 10 minutes, according to the directions on page 31. Let cool undisturbed for 12 hours. Store in a cool, dry place. Do not open for at least 6 weeks to allow the flavors to develop.

Peach Ginger Chutney

Makes 6 half-pints

The lovely golden hue of this chutney is part of its appeal, which is why I avoided dark spices, such as cinnamon. A food processor makes this easy to whip together. If you are using the food processor for chopping the peaches, you might as well use it for the onion and ginger as well.

Ingredients

- 3 pounds peaches
- 1 onion, finely chopped
- 1 cup honey
- ½ cup white wine vinegar
- 1 tablespoon minced peeled fresh ginger or Pickled Ginger (page 229)
- ½ teaspoon pickling or fine sea salt
- ½ teaspoon ground turmeric
- ¼ teaspoon ground coriander
- ⅛ teaspoon cayenne pepper

1 Blanch the peaches in boiling water to cover for 30 seconds. Peel, remove the pits, and finely chop. A food processor does this job nicely. Pulse; do not purée.

2 Combine the peaches, onion, honey, white wine vinegar, ginger, salt, turmeric, coriander, and cayenne in a large saucepan. Bring to a simmer and cook for about 1 hour, stirring occasionally. The chutney will thicken and reduce.

3 Ladle the hot chutney into clean hot half-pint canning jars, leaving ½ inch headspace. Remove any air bubbles and seal.

4 Process in a boiling-water bath for 10 minutes, according to the directions on page 31. Let cool undisturbed for 12 hours. Store in a cool, dry place.

Kitchen Note

You can double or triple the recipe, but don't increase the onion because its flavor intensifies over time.

171

Ginger Pear Chutney

Makes 10 half-pints

"Connie's Pear Chutney": I don't know who Connie was, but I do know that when I asked friends about their favorite recipes from my *Pickles and Relishes*, this chutney was mentioned frequently.

Ingredients

- 10 **cups peeled, cored, and sliced firm ripe pears (about 5 pounds)**
- ½ **green bell pepper, finely chopped**
- 1½ **cups raisins**
- 1 **cup chopped crystallized ginger**
- 4 **cups sugar**
- 3 **cups cider vinegar**
- 1 **teaspoon pickling or fine sea salt**
- ½ **teaspoon allspice berries**
- ½ **teaspoon whole cloves**
- 3 **cinnamon sticks**

1. Combine the pears, bell pepper, raisins, crystallized ginger, sugar, cider vinegar, and salt in a large saucepan. Tie the allspice, cloves, and cinnamon in a spice bag (see How to Make a Spice Bag, page 20) and add to the mixture. Bring the mixture to a boil over medium heat, stirring to dissolve the sugar. Decrease the heat and simmer until the pears are tender and the mixture is thick, about 1 hour, stirring occasionally. The chutney will thicken and become jamlike.

2. Remove the spice bag. Ladle the chutney into clean hot half-pint canning jars, leaving ½ inch headspace. Remove any air bubbles and seal.

3. Process in a boiling-water bath for 10 minutes, according to the directions on page 31. Let cool undisturbed for 12 hours. Store in a cool, dry place.

Kitchen Notes

- Crystallized ginger gives an important crunch and sweetness to the chutney; don't substitute another form of ginger. Crystallized ginger is found in the spice department of most grocery stores.

- Harvesting or finding perfect pears is the challenge for all pear recipes. Because pears ripen from the inside out, they will be mushy on the inside if left on the tree until fully ripe on the outside. So pear growers pick the pears when "mature," but not ripe. Then they subject them to cold temperatures, after which they will ripen on your counter. To tell if a pear is ready for eating, press near the stem with your thumb; there should be some amount of give to the area. Then rush to make this chutney — a ripe pear becomes overripe very quickly.

Classic Pepper Relish

Makes 6 pints

The uses for pepper relish are seemingly endless. There are few sandwiches that don't benefit from pepper relish, but it is especially good with hamburgers and grilled cheese. Use it to season a meatloaf or enliven macaroni and cheese or spaghetti sauce. If you have some on hand, you will find ways to enjoy it!

Ingredients

- 12 **red bell peppers, finely chopped**
- 12 **green bell peppers, finely chopped**
- 12 **onions, finely chopped**
- 2 **cups distilled white vinegar**
- 2 **cups sugar**
- 1 **tablespoon pickling or fine sea salt**

1 Bring a kettle of water to a boil. Combine the red and green peppers and onions in a large bowl. Cover with boiling water and let stand for 5 minutes. Drain.

2 Combine the vegetables, white vinegar, sugar, and salt in a large saucepan. Bring to a boil, stirring to dissolve the sugar, and boil for 5 minutes.

3 Ladle into clean hot 1-pint canning jars, leaving ½ inch headspace. Remove any air bubbles and seal.

4 Process in a boiling-water bath for 10 minutes, according to the directions on page 31. Let cool undisturbed for 12 hours. Store in a cool, dry place. Do not open for at least 6 weeks to allow the flavors to develop.

Kitchen Notes

- To give this recipe a little spunk, add a hot chile or two.
- To delay canning until the weather cools off, freeze bell peppers without blanching: Wash the peppers and dry thoroughly. Cut in half, remove the seeds and core, and tray-freeze. Put the frozen peppers into freezer bags; they'll keep for several months. To make this relish, defrost in a colander, chop finely, and proceed to step 2; it is not necessary to cover them with boiling water.

Smoky Red Hot Sauce

Makes 1 pint

Chipotles add a whisper of smoke to this otherwise classic red chile sauce. This ages well but has too many uses to last.

Ingredients

- water
- 3 **chipotle chiles**
- 1½ **cups distilled white vinegar**
- ¾ **pound fresh red jalapeños (12–18), seeded and chopped**
- 1½ **teaspoons pickling or fine sea salt**

1 Bring a kettle of water to a boil. Pour boiling water over the chiles and set aside to soak for at least 30 minutes, and up to 6 hours.

2 Combine the chipotles and 1½ cups of the soaking water with the white vinegar, jalapeños, and salt in a small saucepan and bring to a boil. Simmer for 30 minutes.

3 Process until smooth in a blender or food processor.

4 Pour into a clean 1-pint canning jar. Store in the refrigerator. The sauce is ready to use immediately but will improve in flavor with age — if you can wait. Stir or shake before using.

Kitchen Notes

- When you pour off the chipotle soaking water, avoid any grit that has sunk to the bottom of the bowl.
- This recipe can be multiplied, but don't make more than you can use in 3–4 months.

HOW HOT IS IT?

The Scoville scale is a measurement of the spicy heat of chiles. Named after its creator, an American pharmacist by the name of Wilbur Scoville, Scoville heat units (SHUs) indicate the amount of capsaicin present in a typical chile. (Capsaicin is the chemical compound that is responsible for the spicy flavor of chiles.)

Bell peppers have 0 Scoville heat units. Here are heat ratings for commonly used chiles. Proceed accordingly.

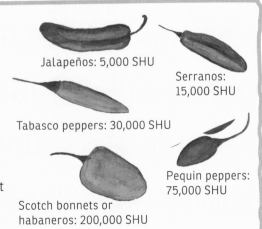

Jalapeños: 5,000 SHU

Serranos: 15,000 SHU

Tabasco peppers: 30,000 SHU

Pequin peppers: 75,000 SHU

Scotch bonnets or habaneros: 200,000 SHU

Green Chile Sauce

Makes 1 pint

Green chile sauces just aren't that beautiful to behold, unless your favorite color happens to be olive green. But, oh! The flavor more than makes up for the dull color.

Ingredients

- 1½ **cups cider vinegar**
- 1½ **cups water**
- ¾ **pound green jalapeños (12–18), seeded and chopped**
- 1½ **teaspoons pickling or fine sea salt**
- 3 **garlic cloves**
- 1 **teaspoon dried oregano**

1 Combine the cider vinegar, water, jalapeños, salt, garlic, and oregano in a small saucepan and bring to a boil. Simmer for 30 minutes.

2 Process until smooth in a blender or food processor.

3 Return to the saucepan and bring to a boil. Boil for 5 minutes, stirring frequently to avoid scorching.

4 Pour into a clean 1-pint canning jar, leaving ½ inch headspace. Remove any air bubbles and seal.

5 Process in a boiling-water bath for 10 minutes, according to the directions on page 31. Let cool undisturbed for 12 hours. Store in a cool, dry place.

Kitchen Notes

- After pureeing, the sauce is returned to a boil to cook off the air that the blender introduced. If you skip this step, you run the risk that the jar will explode in the canner.
- Red jalapeños can be used instead of green jalapeños to make a more attractive sauce.
- If you don't want to bother canning the sauce, store it in the refrigerator.
- This recipe can be multiplied by the amount of chilies you want to preserve.

CHILE PEPPERS

The heat of a chile pepper is a function of its variety, but you can also affect the heat of the final dish by removing or not removing the seeds before chopping. To seed a chile, slice it in half vertically. Use the tip of a small spoon, knife, or vegetable peeler to scrape out the seeds and membrane if you like; that's where most of the heat is found.

Five-Spice Plum Chutney

Makes 5 half-pints

Five-spice powder, available wherever Asian foods are sold, is usually made up of equal parts ground cinnamon, cloves, fennel seeds, star anise, and Szechuan peppercorns, a combination that is unmistakably exotic and appealing. This chutney makes a great dipping sauce for egg rolls.

Ingredients

- 6 pounds Italian prune plums
- 2 onions, finely chopped
- 4 garlic cloves, minced
- 1 cup cider vinegar
- ¼ cup honey
- 2 teaspoons Chinese five-spice powder
- ½ teaspoon cayenne pepper
- ½ teaspoon pickling or fine sea salt

1 Plunge the plums into boiling water for 1 minute to loosen the skins, then plunge into ice water. Peel and pit the plums.

2 Combine the plums, onions, garlic, cider vinegar, honey, five-spice powder, cayenne, and salt in a large saucepan. Bring to a boil, decrease the heat, and simmer until the mixture becomes a smooth sauce, about 1 hour. As the chutney cooks, stir frequently to avoid scorching and break the plums up with the spoon.

3 Ladle the hot chutney into clean hot half-pint canning jars, leaving ½ inch headspace. Remove any air bubbles and seal.

4 Process in a boiling-water bath for 10 minutes, according to the directions on page 31. Let cool undisturbed for 12 hours. Store in a cool, dry place.

Kitchen Note

Italian prune plums may also be called European plums or Stanley plums. They have dusky purple skins and green flesh. These plums are less juicy than Japanese plums and are better for cooking and baking.

Sweet-Tart Rhubarb Chutney

Makes 7 half-pints

The preserving season begins with rhubarb. This recipe allows the flavor of the rhubarb to remain distinct in a sweet, savory, tart relish. It is delicious served with curries and cold sliced cheeses and meats. My favorite way to enjoy this chutney is in a turkey sandwich, with chutney on one slice of bread and mayo on the other.

Ingredients

- 2½ pounds fresh rhubarb stems, sliced about 1 inch thick (about 8 cups)
- 1 large onion, diced
- ½ cup dried tart cherries or cranberries
- 1 cup honey
- ½ cup cider vinegar
- 1 tablespoon minced peeled fresh ginger or Pickled Ginger (page 229)
- 2 garlic cloves, minced
- ½ teaspoon ground cinnamon
- ¼ teaspoon ground cumin
- ¼ teaspoon pickling or fine sea salt

1 Combine the rhubarb, onion, cherries, honey, vinegar, ginger, garlic, cinnamon, cumin, and salt in a large saucepan. Bring to a simmer and simmer for 30 minutes, until the rhubarb is tender and the mixture thickens slightly, stirring occasionally.

2 Ladle the hot chutney into clean hot half-pint canning jars, leaving ½ inch headspace. Remove any air bubbles and seal.

3 Process in a boiling-water bath for 10 minutes, according to the directions on page 31. Let cool undisturbed for 12 hours. Store in a cool, dry place.

Kitchen Note

You can double or triple the recipe, but don't increase the amounts of onion or garlic because their flavors intensify over time.

Helen Nearing's Rhubarb Chutney

Makes 5 pints

Helen and Scott Nearing were heroes of the back-to-the-land movement of the 1960s and 1970s. From their farm in Vermont, they wrote about their experience living what they termed "the good life," which included gardening, preserving, and eating simply. Helen's pickle recipe was quite simple: Put cucumbers in a sterilized crock and cover with cider vinegar. Use as needed. This recipe is more complex — and more flavorful.

Ingredients

- 4 **pounds rhubarb, cut into small pieces**
- 1 **pound pitted dates**
- 5 **cups firmly packed brown sugar**
- 2 **cups cider vinegar**
- 1 **tablespoon ground cinnamon**
- 1 **tablespoon ground cloves**

1   Combine the rhubarb, dates, sugar, vinegar, cinnamon, and cloves in a saucepan and bring to a boil, stirring to dissolve the sugar. Decrease the heat and simmer for 2 hours, stirring frequently to avoid scorching.

2   The chutney will keep well in the refrigerator, or you can process it. To process, pack the chutney into clean hot 1-pint canning jars, leaving ½ inch headspace. Remove any air bubbles and seal.

3   Process in a boiling-water bath for 10 minutes, according to the directions on page 31. Let cool undisturbed for 12 hours. Store in a cool, dry place.

Mixed Fruit Chutney

Makes 11 half-pints

This flavorful chutney features red ripe tomatoes, apples, raisins, and dried apricots, as well as onions and garlic. The ginger brings all the flavors together.

Ingredients

- **12** ripe tomatoes, peeled (see page 189) and chopped
- **5** large apples, peeled and chopped
- **1** large onion, diced
- **2** garlic cloves, minced
- **1½** cups raisins
- **1** cup diced dried apricots
- **1** cup cider vinegar
- **⅓** cup finely diced crystallized ginger
- **2** teaspoons pickling or fine sea salt
- **1** teaspoon ground cinnamon
- pinch of cayenne pepper

1 Combine the tomatoes, apples, onion, cloves, raisins, apricots, vinegar, ginger, salt, cinnamon, and cayenne in a large saucepan. Bring to a boil, decrease the heat, and simmer until thick, about 1½ hours, stirring frequently.

2 Pack the mixture into clean hot half-pint canning jars, leaving ½ inch headspace. Remove any air bubbles and seal.

3 Process in a boiling-water bath for 15 minutes, according to the directions on page 31. Let cool undisturbed for 12 hours. Store in a cool, dry place.

Tomatillo Salsa

Makes 3 pints

Sometimes called Mexican green tomatoes, tomatillos are not tomatoes at all, though they are in the same nightshade family as tomatoes and eggplant. If you let them ripen to yellow, they are quite sweet, but they are generally picked and used green. They make a lovely green salsa, nicely complementing red tomato-based salsas. This salsa is flavored with pimentón, ground smoked paprika. It adds a hint of smoke to the salsa, contributing to the complexity of the flavor. Before serving, stir in some fresh chopped cilantro to brighten the flavor, and use this salsa any way you would serve a red salsa.

Ingredients

- 2½ pounds tomatillos
- 3 green jalapeños
- 1 large onion, quartered
- 4 garlic cloves
- ¾ cup bottled lime juice or lemon juice
- 1 tablespoon sugar, or to taste
- 2 teaspoons pickling or fine sea salt, or to taste
- 1 teaspoon cumin seeds
- ¼ teaspoon pimentón, or to taste (optional)

1 Remove the husks from the tomatillos and wash to remove their sticky coating. Chop into quarters. (You should have about 7 cups.)

2 Roast the jalapeños over the open flame of a gas burner or under a broiler, turning until charred all over, about 5 minutes. Place in a paper or plastic bag or covered container and allow the chiles to steam for 10 minutes. This makes the skins easier to remove.

3 While the chiles steam, put the tomatillos in the food processor and pulse until finely chopped. Transfer to a large saucepan. Put the onion and garlic in the food processor (don't bother to wash it out) and pulse until finely chopped. Add to the tomatillos along with the lime juice, sugar, salt, cumin seeds, and pimentón, if using. Place the saucepan over medium heat.

4 Peel the jalapeños (but do not rinse), then cut them open to remove the seeds. Chop the jalapeños and add to the saucepan. Increase the heat to medium-high and bring to a boil, stirring occasionally. Taste and adjust the amount of salt, sugar, or pimentón. The cumin flavor will develop over time, but the flavor of the salsa should be fairly balanced.

5 Ladle the hot salsa into clean hot 1-pint canning jars, leaving ½ inch headspace. Remove any air bubbles and seal.

6 Process in a boiling-water bath for 15 minutes, according to the directions on page 31. Let cool undisturbed for 12 hours. Store in a cool, dry place. Do not open for at least 6 weeks to allow the flavor to develop.

Kitchen Notes

- You can substitute ground chipotle powder for the pimentón, but you may want to use fewer jalapeños, unless you like a really hot salsa.
- You can substitute ground cumin for cumin seeds (use about ½ teaspoon), but it will color the salsa.
- I recommend bottled lime or lemon juice because both have consistent levels of acidity, necessary for safe preserving.
- The consistency of the salsa will vary depending on the ripeness of the tomatillos. Sometimes the salsa will appear watery, with floating fruit. If that happens, mix well before serving from the jar with a slotted spoon.

Tomato Ketchup

Makes 8 pints

If you are looking for ketchup that tastes like a store-bought version, this one's for you. The secret is using corn syrup as a sweetener — unfortunately, that's the only way you can get that store-bought flavor. If you don't want to mimic the supermarket brands, then use white or brown sugar, maple syrup, or honey instead.

Ingredients

- **24 cups quartered ripe tomatoes (12 pounds; cut into wedges if large)**
- **4 onions, chopped**
- **3 cups cider vinegar**
- **12 ounces tomato paste**
- **1 cup light corn syrup**
- **2 teaspoons Tabasco sauce**
- **2 teaspoons fennel seeds**
- **2 teaspoons pickling or fine sea salt**
- **2 teaspoons freshly ground black pepper**
- **1 teaspoon celery seeds**
- **1 teaspoon mustard seeds**
- **½ teaspoon ground allspice**

1 Combine the tomatoes, onions, and cider vinegar in a large saucepan. Bring to a boil, cover, and continue to boil gently until the tomatoes are quite soft, 15 to 20 minutes.

2 Purée the tomato mixture in a blender or food processor; you will have to do this in a few batches. Return the mixture to the saucepan and add the tomato paste, corn syrup, Tabasco, fennel seeds, salt, pepper, celery seeds, mustard seeds, and allspice. Simmer over low heat, uncovered, stirring occasionally, until the mixture is reduced by half and is quite thick, 6 to 8 hours. Do not allow the mixture to scorch.

3 Ladle the hot ketchup into clean hot 1-pint canning jars, leaving ⅛ inch headspace. Remove any air bubbles and seal.

4 Process in a boiling-water bath for 15 minutes, according to the directions on page 31. Let cool undisturbed for 12 hours. Store in a cool, dry place.

Kitchen Note

Watch for scorching and stir more frequently as the mixture thickens.

Classic Homemade Tomato Ketchup

Makes 5 half-pints

No store-bought flavor here, just old-fashioned goodness. This is what ketchup used to taste like, before Heinz stepped in and retrained our palates.

Ingredients

12 **cups chopped ripe plum tomatoes (6 pounds)**

1 **large onion, chopped**

1 **red bell pepper, diced**

1¼ **cups cider vinegar**

2 **teaspoons celery seeds**

1½ **teaspoons mustard seeds**

2 **cinnamon sticks**

½ **cup honey or firmly packed brown sugar**

1 **tablespoon pickling or fine sea salt**

1 Combine the tomatoes, onion, bell pepper, and cider vinegar in a large saucepan. Bring to a boil, decrease the heat, and simmer for 30 minutes, until soft.

2 Transfer the mixture to a blender in batches and purée until smooth. Return to the saucepan.

3 Tie together the celery seeds, mustard seeds, and cinnamon sticks in a spice bag (see How to Make a Spice Bag, page 20). Add the spice bag to the saucepan, along with the honey and salt. Simmer for 20 to 30 minutes, until the ketchup has the desired consistency, stirring frequently to avoid scorching. Remove and discard the spice bag.

4 Ladle the hot ketchup into clean hot half-pint canning jars, leaving ⅛ inch headspace. Remove any air bubbles and seal.

5 Process in a boiling-water bath for 15 minutes, according to the directions on page 31. Let cool undisturbed for 12 hours. Store in a cool, dry place.

Curried Summer Squash Relish

Makes 8 pints

The curved shape of most yellow summer squash makes it a challenge to pickle as slices or spears. Chop it up in a relish and the problem is solved. This relish is great with crackers and cheese as an appetizer, or as a condiment with chicken, fish, or meat.

Ingredients

- 4 pounds yellow summer squash, seeded and finely chopped
- 4 red bell peppers, finely chopped
- 2 onions, finely chopped
- 4 garlic cloves, minced
- 1 (1-inch) piece fresh ginger, peeled and minced, or 1-inch stack Pickled Ginger (page 229), minced
- 3 cups firmly packed brown sugar
- 3 cups cider vinegar
- 3 tablespoons curry powder
- 2 teaspoons mixed pickling spices, store-bought or homemade (page 18)
- ¼ cup ClearJel (page 151) or ½ cup cornstarch
- ½ cup water
- salt and freshly ground black pepper
- cayenne (optional)

1 Combine the vegetables, garlic, ginger, brown sugar, cider vinegar, curry powder, and mixed pickling spices in a large saucepan. Bring to a boil, stirring to dissolve the sugar.

2 Make a paste with the Clearjel and water. Briskly stir the solution into the boiling relish. Boil until the syrup appears almost clear and the mixture has thickened, about 5 minutes. Season to taste with salt and pepper. Add the cayenne to taste, if using.

3 Pack the relish into clean hot 1-pint canning jars, leaving ½ inch headspace. Remove any air bubbles and seal.

4 Process in a boiling-water bath for 10 minutes, according to the directions on page 31. Let cool undisturbed for 12 hours. Store in a cool, dry place. Allow 6 weeks for the full flavor to develop.

Kitchen Notes

- Working in batches in a food processor, chop all the vegetables using the pulsing action. You might as well mince the garlic and ginger in the food processor while you are at it.
- You can substitute any variety of zucchini or summer squash for the yellow squash, though yellow squash will have the best appearance.
- If the squash seeds are very small, seeding is not necessary.

Simple Salsa

Makes about 4 pints

Very little fussing is required for this salsa, so it is ideal to make during the harvest season. It can be a hot one, depending on the variety of chiles you use. Use a mild chile or substitute bell peppers for some of the chiles if you prefer. While the tomatoes cook down, you can prepare the onions, garlic, and chiles in a food processor, using the pulsing action to chop without pureeing.

Ingredients

24 **cups quartered ripe tomatoes (12 pounds; cut into wedges if large)**

2 **cups distilled white or cider vinegar**

2 **onions, finely chopped**

2 **garlic cloves, minced**

1–1¼ **cups finely chopped fresh chiles or a mixture of chiles and bell peppers (seeding optional)**

pickling or fine sea salt

1. Combine the tomatoes and vinegar in a large saucepan and bring to a boil. Decrease the heat and simmer until the tomatoes are very soft, stirring occasionally, about 45 minutes.

2. When the tomatoes are very soft, process them through a food mill or push through a strainer to remove the seeds and skins.

3. Return the tomatoes to the saucepan, and add the onions, garlic, and chiles. Simmer until the salsa has reduced to a thick sauce, about 1 hour, stirring occasionally. Season with salt to taste.

4. Ladle into clean hot 1-pint canning jars, leaving ½ inch headspace. Process in a boiling-water bath for 15 minutes, according to the directions on page 31. Let cool undisturbed for 12 hours. Store in a cool, dry place.

TOMATO YIELDS

When making tomato sauces, salsas, and chutneys, your yield will vary depending on the juiciness of the tomatoes. Plum tomatoes tend to yield more than salad tomatoes because they have a higher flesh-to-juice ratio.

Chipotle Salsa

Makes about 4 pints

Chipotle chiles (smoke-dried jalapeños) add a lick of smoke and fire to this otherwise simple salsa.

Ingredients

24 cups quartered ripe tomatoes (12 pounds; cut into wedges if large)

2 cups distilled white vinegar

8 garlic cloves, peeled and left whole

4 chipotle chiles

2 onions, minced

1 cup minced fresh green chiles

1 cup minced bell pepper of any color

pickling or fine sea salt

1 Combine the tomatoes, white vinegar, garlic, and chipotles in a large saucepan and bring to a boil. Decrease the heat and simmer until the tomatoes are very soft, stirring occasionally, about 45 minutes.

2 Process the tomato mixture through a food mill, discarding the seeds and skins.

3 Return the strained mixture to the saucepan and add the onions, fresh chiles, and bell pepper. Simmer until the salsa has reduced to a nice thick sauce, about 1 hour, stirring occasionally. Season to taste with salt.

4 Ladle the hot salsa into clean hot 1-pint canning jars, leaving ½ inch headspace. Remove any air bubbles and seal.

5 Process in a boiling water bath for 15 minutes, according to the directions on page 31. Let cool undisturbed for 12 hours. Store in a cool, dry place.

Kitchen Note

For a milder salsa, remove the seeds of the chipotle and fresh chiles before adding to the salsa.

Barbecue Sauce

Makes about 5 pints

A good tomato-based barbecue sauce is a must-have recipe. This one is classic in flavor, though it does not have the ultra-smooth texture of bottled sauces. The pimentón, a smoked ground paprika, adds a subtle touch of smoke.

Ingredients

16 cups quartered tomatoes (8 pounds; cut into wedges if large)

1½ cups cider vinegar

3 large onions, finely chopped

2 red or green bell peppers, finely chopped

2 garlic cloves, minced

1 tablespoon molasses

1 tablespoon soy sauce

1 cup firmly packed brown sugar

¼ cup chili powder

1 teaspoon freshly ground black pepper

2 tablespoons pimentón

1 tablespoon dry mustard powder

1 tablespoon pickling or fine sea salt, or more to taste

1 Combine the tomatoes and cider vinegar in a large saucepan and bring to a boil. Decrease the heat and simmer until the tomatoes are very soft, stirring occasionally, about 45 minutes.

2 Process the tomato mixture through a food mill, discarding the seeds and skins.

3 Return the strained mixture to the saucepan and add the onions, bell peppers, garlic, molasses, soy sauce, brown sugar, chili powder, black pepper, pimentón, mustard powder, and salt. Simmer until the mixture has reduced to a nice thick sauce, about 3 hours, stirring occasionally. Taste and adjust the seasoning.

4 Ladle the hot sauce into clean hot 1-pint canning jars, leaving ½ inch headspace. Remove any air bubbles and seal.

5 Process in a boiling-water bath for 15 minutes, according to the directions on page 31. Let cool undisturbed for 12 hours. Store in a cool, dry place.

Kitchen Notes

• You can substitute ground chipotle for the pimentón. If you do that, you may want to reduce the amount of chili powder, unless you like your sauce spicy-hot.

• If you want a smooth sauce, cook the onions and peppers with the tomatoes and run through the food mill. Your yield will be reduced significantly.

Betty Jacobs's Red Tomato Chutney

Makes 7 pints

Betty E. M. Jacobs and her husband started Canada's first commercial herb farm in 1965 on southern Vancouver Island. Their experience running this farm for eight years, plus a lifetime of interest in herbs, led to Betty's 1981 book, *Growing & Using Herbs Successfully*, still a classic in its field. When I collected this recipe from Betty in 1983, she told me that the recipe came from *The A B C of Canning, Preserving, Smoking, Drying, Pickling*, a 25-cent booklet she bought in 1952. The booklet, by the way, had no author, publisher, or printer to credit for this delicious recipe.

Ingredients

- 6 pounds ripe tomatoes (about 24), peeled (see opposite) and finely chopped
- 6 pounds tart green apples (about 12), peeled, cored, and finely chopped
- 2 pounds onions (about 6), finely chopped
- ½ pound red bell peppers (about 3), seeded and finely chopped
- ½ pound green bell peppers (about 3), seeded and finely chopped
- 1 cup finely chopped celery
- 5 cups cider vinegar or malt vinegar
- 2½ cups sugar
- ¼ cup pickling or fine sea salt
- 1 pound golden raisins

1 Combine the tomatoes, apples, onions, red and green bell peppers, celery, vinegar, sugar, and salt in a large saucepan. Bring to a boil, stirring to dissolve the sugar. Decrease the heat and simmer until the mixture thickens, stirring frequently, about 1½ hours.

2 Add the raisins and continue to simmer for 20 to 30 minutes, until the mixture reaches a desired consistency. Stir frequently to prevent scorching.

3 Pack the mixture into clean hot 1-pint canning jars, leaving ½ inch headspace. Remove any air bubbles and seal.

4 Process in a boiling-water bath for 15 minutes, according to the directions on page 31. Let cool undisturbed for 12 hours. Store in a cool, dry place.

Sweet Chili Sauce

Makes 4 to 5 pints

American chili sauce is pretty similar to ketchup. It is usually sweeter and often spicier. I collected this recipe from Jo Frohbieter-Mueller.

Ingredients

- 16 cups small tomatoes, peeled and chopped
- 1¾ cups distilled white vinegar
- 2 cups sugar
- 1 cup finely chopped onions
- 1½ cups finely chopped celery
- ¾ cup finely chopped bell pepper of any color
- 2¼ teaspoons pickling or fine sea salt
- 1½ teaspoons ground cinnamon
- 1½ teaspoons ground ginger
- 1 teaspoon mustard seeds

1 Combine the tomatoes, white vinegar, sugar, onions, celery, bell pepper, salt, cinnamon, ginger, and mustard seeds in a large saucepan. Bring to a boil, stirring to dissolve the sugar. Decrease the heat and simmer for 2 hours, until the sauce cooks down and thickens. Stir frequently to prevent scorching.

2 Pack the mixture into clean hot 1-pint canning jars, leaving ½ inch headspace. Remove any air bubbles and seal.

3 Process in a boiling-water bath for 15 minutes, according to the directions on page 31. Let cool undisturbed for 12 hours. Store in a cool, dry place.

PEELING TOMATOES

To peel tomatoes, dip them in boiling water for about 30 seconds, then plunge them into ice water to stop the cooking. The skins should slip off easily.

Italian Tomato Relish

Makes about 5 pints

Looking for a cure for the wintertime sandwich blues? You think something is missing from your sandwiches when tomato season ends? Not anymore. This relish gives a terrific traveling-in-Italy twist to a salami or ham sandwich and makes a tasty instant topping for crostini or for simply cooked fish and chicken breasts.

Ingredients

- 4 pounds plum tomatoes
- ¼ cup extra-virgin olive oil
- 1 onion, diced
- 1 green bell pepper, diced
- 1½ cups white wine vinegar
- ½ cup white wine
- 2 tablespoons balsamic vinegar
- 2 tablespoons chopped fresh oregano
- 2–3 tablespoons sugar
- 2 teaspoons pickling or fine sea salt, or to taste
- 1 head garlic, cloves, separated, peeled, and minced
- 5 large sprigs fresh basil

1 Dip the tomatoes in boiling water for about 30 seconds. Remove, peel, and dice. You should have 9 cups.

2 Heat the olive oil in a large saucepan over medium-high heat. Add the onion and bell pepper and sauté until softened, about 4 minutes. Add the tomatoes, wine vinegar, wine, balsamic vinegar, oregano, 2 tablespoons sugar, and salt. Bring to a boil, stirring occasionally, and simmer for 5 to 10 minutes. Remove from the heat and stir in the garlic. Taste and adjust the sugar and salt, if needed.

3 Pack 1 sprig basil into each clean hot 1-pint canning jar. Pack in the tomato mixture, leaving ½ inch headspace. Remove any air bubbles and seal.

4 Process in a boiling-water bath for 15 minutes, according to the directions on page 31. Let cool undisturbed for 12 hours. Do not open for at least 6 weeks to allow the flavors to develop.

Kitchen Notes

- I like a fairly strong garlic presence in this relish. If you would like the garlic tamed, add it with the tomatoes so it has a chance to cook and mellow. If you are very garlic averse, you can also reduce the amount you use to a few cloves.

- When you dice the tomatoes, keep in mind that you want pieces that are small enough to rest nicely on a cracker or crostini, but large enough to retain their character.

- Italian Tomato Relish can be served with cheese and crackers, made into Tomato-Mozzarella Tart (page 265), or used to dress Tortellini Pasta Salad (page 253). You'll undoubtedly find other uses for it as well.

Green Tomato Pickle Relish

Makes about 12 pints

When life (or an early frost) hands you green tomatoes, make relish.

Ingredients

- 4 cups finely chopped green tomatoes
- 2 onions, finely chopped
- 4 green bell peppers, finely chopped
- 2 red bell peppers, finely chopped
- ½ cup pickling or fine sea salt
- 3 cups distilled white vinegar
- 1 cup water
- 2 cups sugar
- 1 tablespoon celery seeds
- 1 teaspoon mixed pickling spices, store-bought or homemade (page 18)
- 2 cinnamon sticks

1 Combine the green tomatoes, onions, and green and red bell peppers in a large bowl. Sprinkle with the salt and toss to mix. Let stand overnight.

2 Drain the vegetables well. Transfer to a large saucepan and add the white vinegar, water, sugar, and celery seeds. Tie the mixed pickling spices and cinnamon sticks in a spice bag (see How to Make a Spice Bag, page 20) and add to the saucepan. Bring to a boil over medium heat, stirring occasionally. Decrease the heat and simmer for 30 minutes. Remove the spice bag and discard.

3 Pack the hot relish into clean hot 1-pint canning jars, leaving ½ inch headspace. Remove any air bubbles and seal.

4 Process in a boiling-water bath for 25 minutes, according to the directions on page 31. Let cool undisturbed for 12 hours. Store in a cool, dry place.

Keeping the Harvest
Green Tomato Mincemeat

Makes 6 pints

I won't mince my words: In the world of cooking, to mince is to finely chop. Minced beef, minced pork, and so on, in England, is the same as what we Americans call ground beef. Sometime in medieval England, "mincemeat" became a mixture of dried fruits, sweetener, and spices, often with meat or suet (beef fat) in it. These days, mincemeat is often vegetarian. Apples form the bulk of most mixtures, though green tomatoes and even beets are not unheard of.

Ingredients

- 8 **cups coarsely chopped green tomatoes**
- 1 **tablespoon pickling or fine sea salt**
- 1 **orange**
- 5 **pounds apples**
- 1 **pound raisins**
- 3½ **cups firmly packed brown sugar**
- ½ **cup cider vinegar**
- 2 **teaspoons ground cinnamon**
- 1 **teaspoon ground cloves**
- 1 **teaspoon freshly grated nutmeg**
- ½ **teaspoon ground ginger**
- ¼ **teaspoon pickling or fine sea salt**

1 Grind the tomatoes in a meat grinder or finely chop in a food processor using the pulsing action. Sprinkle with the salt and let stand for at least 2 hours, and up to 6 hours.

2 Bring a kettle of water to a boil. Drain the green tomatoes, cover them with boiling water, and let stand for 5 minutes. Drain again.

3 Finely grate the zest from the orange; peel and chop the fruit. Peel and core the apples, then finely chop by hand or in the food processor.

4 Combine the green tomatoes, orange zest and fruit, and apples in a large saucepan. Add the raisins, brown sugar, cider vinegar, cinnamon, cloves, nutmeg, ginger, and salt. Bring to a boil over medium heat and simmer until tender, about 2 hours, stirring frequently.

5 Pack the mixture into clean hot 1-pint canning jars, leaving ½ inch headspace. Remove any air bubbles and seal.

6 Process in a boiling-water bath for 25 minutes, according to the directions on page 31. Let cool undisturbed for 12 hours. Store in a cool, dry place.

Kitchen Notes

- Just about anything you can do with apple pie filling, you can do with mincemeat. Use as a pie or tart filling, a turnover filling, or a strudel filling.

- If you prefer, you can freeze mincemeat instead of canning it.

Janet Ballentyne's Green Tomato Mincemeat

Makes 10 pints

I worked with Janet Ballentyne in 1982, when she developed a cookbook's worth of recipes using red and green tomatoes. This is one of hers; I have adapted it slightly.

Ingredients

8 cups finely chopped green tomatoes

1–1½ cups apple cider

8 cups finely chopped apples (do not peel)

1½ pounds raisins

1 pound chopped dates

2 cups honey

1⅓ cups cider vinegar

2 tablespoons finely grated orange zest

2 tablespoons ground cinnamon

2 teaspoons ground cloves

1 teaspoon ground allspice

½ teaspoon freshly ground black pepper

⅔ cup vegetable oil

1 Drain the tomatoes for 10 minutes in a colander set over a measuring cup. Discard the juice and replace with an equal amount of apple cider.

2 Combine the green tomato mixture, apples, raisins, dates, honey, cider vinegar, orange zest, cinnamon, cloves, allspice, and black pepper in a large saucepan. Bring to a boil, decrease the heat, and simmer until thick, about 2 hours, stirring frequently.

3 Stir in the oil.

4 Ladle the mixture into clean hot 1-pint canning jars, leaving ½ inch headspace. Remove any air bubbles and seal.

5 Process in a boiling-water bath for 25 minutes, according to the directions on page 31. Let cool undisturbed for 12 hours. Store in a cool, dry place.

Kitchen Note

The oil is a replacement for the traditional beef suet. It adds a measure of richness to the recipe.

Old-Fashioned Green Tomato Mincemeat with Suet

Makes 8 to 10 pints

Old-fashioned mincemeat recipes typically included ground meat. Then the meat was dropped but the beef fat remained to give the mincemeat a rich flavor and mouthfeel. This version retains the suet, which can be obtained from any butcher; just ask.

Ingredients

- 8 cups finely chopped green tomatoes, drained
- 3 pounds apples, cored and chopped (do not peel)
- 2 pounds raisins, washed and drained
- 3 cups sugar
- 1 cup cider vinegar
- 1 cup strong brewed coffee
- 1 cup finely chopped suet
- 1 cup apple jelly or cider
- 2 teaspoons ground cinnamon
- 1 teaspoon freshly grated nutmeg
- 1 teaspoon pickling or fine sea salt
- ¾ teaspoon ground cloves

1 Drain the green tomatoes in a colander for 10 minutes.

2 Combine the apples, raisins, sugar, cider vinegar, coffee, suet, apple jelly, cinnamon, nutmeg, salt, and cloves in a large saucepan. Add the tomatoes. Bring to a boil, decrease the heat, and simmer until thick, about 1½ hours, stirring occasionally.

3 Ladle the mixture into clean hot 1-pint canning jars, leaving ½ inch headspace. Remove any air bubbles and seal.

4 Process in a boiling-water bath for 25 minutes, according to the directions on page 31. Let cool undisturbed for 12 hours. Store in a cool, dry place.

Busy Person's Zucchini Relish

Makes 7 pints

Zucchini harvest filling your refrigerator? Here's a recipe to turn the crisis into an opportunity for swapping, gift-giving, or topping lots of hot dogs. Put your food processor to work on all the chopping.

Ingredients

- 10 **cups finely chopped zucchini**
- 4 **cups finely chopped onions**
- 1 **green bell pepper, finely chopped**
- 1 **red bell pepper, finely chopped**
- 5 **tablespoons pickling or fine sea salt**
- 1 **tablespoon cornstarch**
- 2½ **cups distilled white vinegar**
- 4½ **cups sugar**
- 1 **large hot red or green chile (cayenne is recommended), seeded and finely chopped**
- 1 **tablespoon freshly grated nutmeg**
- 1 **tablespoon dry mustard powder**
- 1 **tablespoon ground turmeric**
- 2 **teaspoons celery salt**
- ½ **teaspoon freshly ground black pepper**

1 Combine the zucchini, onions, and green and red bell peppers in a large bowl. Sprinkle with the salt and toss to mix well. Let stand overnight.

2 Drain the vegetables. Rinse thoroughly with cold tap water. Drain again. Transfer the vegetables to a large saucepan.

3 Dissolve the cornstarch in the white vinegar and add it to the vegetables, along with the sugar, chile, nutmeg, mustard powder, turmeric, celery salt, and black pepper, and stir well. Bring to a boil, stirring to dissolve the sugar, then decrease the heat. Simmer for 30 to 45 minutes, until thick, stirring occasionally.

4 Pack the hot relish into clean hot 1-pint canning jars, leaving ½ inch headspace. Remove any air bubbles and seal.

5 Process in a boiling-water bath for 10 minutes, according to the directions on page 31. Let cool undisturbed for 12 hours. Store in a cool, dry place.

Keeping the Harvest Piccalilli

Makes 6 pints

Piccalilli is a wonderful name for a relish that has fans on both sides of the Atlantic, with no one able to explain where the name comes from. It probably derives from the word "pickle," and it has been applied to relish recipes since at least 1845, when the first recipe appeared in print. British piccalillis are highly spiced and possibly influenced by Indian cuisine. American piccalillis often contain green tomatoes, as does this relish, a classic version. Piccalilli makes a fine hot dog relish.

Ingredients

- 8 cups finely chopped green tomatoes
- 3 green bell peppers, finely chopped
- 3 red bell peppers, finely chopped
- 10 small onions, finely chopped
- 2 tablespoons pickling or fine sea salt, or more to taste
- 3 cups cider vinegar
- 1¾ cups sugar
- ¼ cup mustard seeds
- 1 teaspoon celery seeds
- ½ teaspoon ground allspice
- ½ teaspoon ground cinnamon

1 Combine the green tomatoes, green and red bell peppers, and onions in a large colander. Add the salt and toss to mix well. Let drain for at least 2 hours, and up to 6 hours. Press on the mixture to remove any excess liquid and transfer to a large saucepan.

2 Add 1½ cups of the cider vinegar and bring to a boil. Boil for 30 minutes, stirring often. Drain, discarding the liquid.

3 Add the remaining 1½ cups cider vinegar, sugar, mustard seeds, celery seeds, allspice, and cinnamon to the vegetables. Bring to a simmer. Taste and add salt if needed.

4 Pack the mixture into clean hot 1-pint canning jars, leaving ½ inch headspace. Remove any air bubbles and seal.

5 Process in a boiling-water bath for 15 minutes, according to the directions on page 31. Let cool undisturbed for 12 hours. Store in a cool, dry place. Do not open for at least 6 weeks to allow the flavors to develop.

Kitchen Note

A food processor makes the chopping easy, but you want a chopped mixture, not a purée. So chop the vegetables individually and use the pulsing action.

Chow-Chow

Makes 6 to 8 pints

There's really no distinction between piccalillis and chow-chows: both are relishes made with mixed vegetables, though some food historians claim that chow-chows are made with mustard. It's hard to be sure, though, since the venerable British brand Crosse & Blackwell (established in 1706) sells a "chow chow piccalilli mustard & pickle relish," which "is a traditional English relish perfected by a famous chef centuries ago."

Ingredients

- 16 green tomatoes, finely chopped
- 1 head green cabbage, finely chopped
- 6 red bell peppers, finely chopped
- 6 green bell peppers, finely chopped
- 6 onions, finely chopped
- 6 tablespoons pickling or fine sea salt
- 2 tablespoons mustard seeds
- 1 tablespoon celery seeds
- 1 tablespoon mixed pickled spices, store-bought or homemade (page 18)
- 2 tablespoons yellow ballpark mustard
- 6 cups distilled white vinegar
- 2½ cups sugar
- 1½ teaspoons ground turmeric
- 1 teaspoon ground ginger

1 Combine the green tomatoes, cabbage, red and green bell peppers, and onions in a large bowl. Sprinkle with the salt and mix well. Let stand overnight.

2 The next day, drain well.

3 Combine the mustard seeds, celery seeds, and mixed pickling spices in a spice bag (see How to Make a Spice Bag, page 20). Put the yellow mustard in a large saucepan. Stir in the white vinegar, sugar, turmeric, and ginger. Add the spice bag. Bring to a boil, decrease the heat, and simmer for 2 minutes. Add the drained vegetables and simmer for 10 minutes. Remove the spice bag.

4 Pack the mixture into clean hot 1-pint canning jars, leaving ½ inch headspace. Remove any air bubbles and seal.

5 Process in a boiling-water bath for 15 minutes, according to the directions on page 31. Let cool undisturbed for 12 hours. Store in a cool, dry place. Do not open for at least 6 weeks to allow the flavors to develop.

Pennsylvania Chow-Chow

Makes about 5 pints

So many recipes are handed down on worn index cards, it's hard to trace their origins. This one was collected by Janet Ballentyne, and I've adapted it slightly. Was it really developed in Pennsylvania? I don't know, but the curry powder is an interesting twist on an old favorite.

Ingredients

- 10 cups finely chopped green tomatoes
- 6 cups finely chopped onions
- 1½ cups finely chopped red or green bell peppers
- ¼ cup pickling or fine sea salt
- 2⅔ cups cider vinegar
- 1 cup sugar
- 1 cup honey
- 2 tablespoons ClearJel (see page 151) or ¼ cup cornstarch
- ½ teaspoon curry powder
- ½ teaspoon dry mustard powder
- ½ teaspoon ground turmeric

1 Combine the green tomatoes, onions, and bell peppers in a large bowl. Sprinkle the salt over the vegetables and mix well. Let stand overnight.

2 The next day, drain the vegetables and transfer them to a large saucepan. Stir in 2⅓ cups of the cider vinegar, the sugar, and the honey and bring to a boil, stirring to dissolve the sugar and honey. Decrease the heat and simmer for 1 hour, stirring occasionally.

3 Combine the ClearJel, curry powder, mustard powder, and turmeric in a small bowl. Stir in the remaining ⅓ cup cider vinegar to make a smooth paste. Stir this mixture into the chow-chow and continue cooking until the mixture becomes quite thick, about 15 minutes.

4 Ladle the mixture into clean hot 1-pint canning jars, leaving ½ inch headspace. Remove any air bubbles and seal.

5 Process in a boiling-water bath for 15 minutes, according to the directions on page 31. Let cool undisturbed for 12 hours. Store in a cool, dry place. Do not open for at least 6 weeks to allow the flavors to develop.

Homemade Branston-Style Pickle Relish

Makes about 7 half-pints

Made from chopped vegetables, and distinctively tangy from malt vinegar and fruity sweet from dates, this chutney-like relish is unlike most American pickle relishes. Branston is a brand name, and competitors may call their versions "sweet pickle." To many in the UK and the rest of the Commonwealth, a Branston pickle is simply called "pickle," as in cheese and pickle — the perfect sandwich.

Ingredients

- 1 small head cauliflower, broken into florets
- 2 large carrots
- 1 small rutabaga, peeled
- 2 onions
- 4 garlic cloves
- 2 apples, peeled and cored
- 1¼ cups pitted dates
- 2 cups malt vinegar
- 1 cup firmly packed brown sugar
- ½ cup ketchup, store-bought or homemade (page 182 and 183)
- ½ cup Worcestershire sauce
- 1 tablespoon soy sauce
- 2 teaspoons ground allspice
- 1 teaspoon pickling or fine sea salt
- ½ teaspoon dry mustard powder
- ¼ teaspoon cayenne pepper

1 Boil the cauliflower in a large pot of salted water until soft but not mushy, about 10 minutes. Finely chop. Reserve 1 cup of the cauliflower and put the remainder into a large saucepan.

2 While the cauliflower cooks, finely chop the carrots and rutabaga in a food processor, using the pulsing action. Add to the cauliflower in the saucepan. Without washing the food processor, finely chop the onions, garlic, and apples together, again using the pulsing action. Add to the chopped vegetables. Again, without washing the food processor, finely chop the dates and add to the saucepan.

3 Add the malt vinegar, brown sugar, ketchup, Worcestershire sauce, soy sauce, allspice, salt, mustard powder, and cayenne to the saucepan. Mix well and bring to a boil over high heat. Decrease the heat and simmer until the vegetables are cooked through, about 2 hours, stirring occasionally. The mixture will be thick; take care to avoid scorching.

4 Purée about half the mixture in a food processor. Return to the saucepan with the reserved cauliflower. Return to a boil, stirring frequently.

5 Pack the mixture into clean hot half-pint canning jars, leaving ½ inch headspace. Remove any air bubbles.

6 Process in a boiling-water bath for 15 minutes, according to the directions on page 31. Let cool undisturbed for 12 hours. Store in a cool, dry place.

Kitchen Notes

- Do not make the mistake of undercooking the cauliflower. If the cauliflower is overcooked, it will harmlessly melt into the relish and you won't be able to pick out the individual pieces. But if the cauliflower is undercooked, it will give the relish an unpleasantly gritty texture — something to be avoided at all costs.
- The vegetables can be chopped without the aid of the food processor, but why would you want to bother?

LET'S TALK PICKLES!

Certain combinations of words that include "pickle" can cause a search engine to bring you to unsavory porn sites. All the more reason to appreciate the "Pickle Club," a website devoted to sharing links with news articles about pickles, a calendar of pickle events (mostly in the New York City area), videos, recipes, and pickle vendors. The site is maintained by people who "find pickles fascinating." They seek to "learn more about everything pickled, including how this process relates to people, history, religion, and culture. We also want to provide a resource for members to learn and interact with the pickle community on a local, national, and global level." To view the website yourself, go to www.thepickleclub.com.

Chapter 6

Refrigerator & Freezer Pickles

Refrigerator Quick Dills • Quick Refrigerated Dill Chips • Japanese Cucumber Pickles • Freezer Dills • Freezer Bread and Butters • Ginger-Garlic Freezer Pickles • Freezer Curry Chips • Quick Curtido • Freezer Cabbage Relish • Freezer Ginger-Garlic Cabbage Relish • Overnight Pickled Cauliflower • Pickled Whole Chiles • Chinese Sweet Pickled Daikon • Gingery Quick Pickled Daikon and Carrot • Chinese Spicy-Sweet Pickled Daikon and Carrot • Vietnamese-Style Pickled Daikon and Carrot • Soy Sauce Daikon and Carrot Pickles • Pickled Garlic Cloves • Pickled Ginger • Pub-Style Pickled Onions • Overnight Orange Pickles • Freezer Tomato Salsa • Freezer Bread and Butter Zucchini Chips • Freezer Mixed Pickles • Dill Pickled Eggs

Back in the days before modern refrigeration, people had ingenious methods of keeping foods cool, including harvesting ice from frozen ponds to refrigerate "ice boxes" and underground pits. On New England farms, springhouses were built directly over running water streams. Crocks of food were put in the running water, which stayed at a constant temperature below 50°F.

Some of the refrigerated pickles assembled here are traditional recipes that may not have been refrigerated when they were developed. Refrigerating these quick pickles extends their life. After a while, a pickle that isn't stored in the refrigerator will be fine to eat, but its texture will soften.

The line between a marinated vegetable and a refrigerated pickle can be very thin. I propose that a marinated vegetable contains oil and vinegar, while a pickle contains just vinegar, though there are exceptions. Freezer pickles, on the other hand, are quite distinct; the technique is a simple and fast way to preserve vegetables that, when defrosted, are ready to eat. The flavor is less vinegary and fresher than that of the standard pickle, and the texture marginally softer.

Most of the freezer pickles require a brief bath in a salt brine to eliminate excess water and improve texture. This step should never be skipped, or the defrosted pickles will turn out to be mush. The type of salt you use does not matter here, but the pickles were tested with a finely ground sea salt with the same texture as table salt. The cucumbers must be sliced paper-thin if they are to go into the freezer. A thick slice will yield a mushy pickle.

The pickles are all vinegar-cured and not canned. Unlike the recipes in chapters 3 and 4, these recipes are designed for eating quickly and don't need to sit in a jar for 6 weeks to develop full flavor. The recipes yield relatively small quantities of pickles but are designed to be multiplied if you have large quantities of vegetables to deal with and space for storage in the refrigerator or freezer.

When packing pickles for the freezer, don't forget to leave room for expansion; it's a drag to have sticky pickle juice frozen on the freezer shelves. There are no ideal containers for the freezer; your choice is basically plastic or glass, and glass is breakable. Heavy-duty freezer bags work fine. Once I've defrosted the pickles I transfer them into glass jars and store in the refrigerator.

The recipes in this chapter start with cucumbers and then are organized alphabetically by main vegetable, followed by mixed vegetable recipes. The chapter ends with an odd-ball recipe for pickled eggs. I tried my first pickled egg in the course of writing this book, and I loved it! It isn't a vegetable, like the rest of the recipes, but it *is* a pickle.

Refrigerator Quick Dills

Makes 1 quart

Artisan pickle makers are selling these pickles at farmers' markets and natural food stores. Why not make your own? These are easy and delicious and take only about 10 minutes to make, start to finish. Waiting 3 days for them to "pickle"? That's the hardest part.

Ingredients

- 2 garlic cloves, chopped
- 2 sprigs fresh dill, chopped
- ½ teaspoon mixed pickling spices, store-bought or homemade (page 18)
- ½ teaspoon black peppercorns
- 5–6 small pickling cucumbers, cut into spears
- ½ cup distilled white vinegar
- 1 tablespoon pickling or fine sea salt
- water

1 Put the garlic, dill, mixed pickling spices, and peppercorns into a 1-quart container. Pack in the cucumber spears; the fit should be tight.

2 Combine the white vinegar and salt in a small microwave container and heat for 1 minute, or until the salt dissolves. Pour over the cucumbers. Add water to cover. Seal the top.

3 Let stand for 24 hours.

4 Refrigerate for at least 3 days and up to 2 to 3 months. The pickles will continue to develop flavor and change color and texture. They reach their peak of flavor at about 1 month but are completely enjoyable before then.

Kitchen Note

At 3 days, the cucumbers are crisp and mildly pickled. At about 1 week, the dill flavor becomes more pronounced. I think the pickles are at their peak at 1 month, but you'll probably eat them up before then. After a month, the pickles begin to soften and show their age, though they are still fine to eat.

Quick Refrigerated Dill Chips

Makes about 1 quart

These quick pickles are a step before classic deli "half-sour" dills. They are rather mild, but flavor intensifies as long as the supply lasts — which in my house is only up to a week (if I'm lucky).

Ingredients

- ½ cup distilled white vinegar
- 2 garlic cloves, very thinly sliced
- 1 tablespoon dill seeds
- 2 teaspoons sugar
- 1 teaspoon black peppercorns
- 1 teaspoon pickling or fine sea salt
- 6 cups very thinly sliced cucumbers
- ½ sweet onion, such as Vidalia, thinly sliced

1 Combine the white vinegar, garlic, dill seeds, sugar, peppercorns, and salt in a small saucepan or microwave container and heat just enough to completely dissolve the sugar. Let cool to room temperature.

2 Combine the cucumbers and onion with the vinegar mixture and toss gently. The cucumbers will seem dry, but the salt will draw out moisture from the cucumbers to create more brine.

3 Cover and refrigerate for at least 1 day before serving. The cucumbers can be stored for at least a week in the refrigerator.

ILOVEPICKLES.ORG

Life have you down? I always get a laugh when I go to the Pickle Packer's website. Years ago, I wrote a book about making pickles and contacted the organization for information. They graciously sent me the information I sought, as well as a key chain with a pickle attached. I still use the key chain. And I visit the site from time to time to see what great new merchandise they have to offer. Who wouldn't want to arrive at the beach with an inflated pickle float? Or go dancing wearing a pair of earrings that look like pickle chips?

Japanese Cucumber Pickles

Makes about 1 quart

More like marinated cucumbers than pickles, these delicate, subtly flavored cucumbers are the perfect accompaniment to grilled foods. I keep a batch going in the refrigerator through most of the summer.

Ingredients

½ cup rice vinegar

2 teaspoons sugar

1 teaspoon pickling or fine sea salt

6 cups very thinly sliced cucumbers

1 mild red onion, thinly sliced

1 red or green fresh chile, seeded (see page 175) and thinly sliced

1 Combine the rice vinegar, sugar, and salt in a small saucepan or microwave container and heat just enough to completely dissolve the sugar. Let cool to room temperature.

2 Combine the cucumbers, onion, and chile with the vinegar mixture and toss gently. The cucumbers will seem dry, but the salt will draw out moisture from the cucumbers to create more brine.

3 Cover and refrigerate for at least 30 minutes before serving. The cucumbers can be stored for at least a week in the refrigerator.

Kitchen Note

A red onion looks pretty in this pickle, but any mild sweet onion, such as Vidalia, works.

Freezer Dills

Makes about 3 cups

Freezer pickles taste like a cross between a true pickle and a marinated cucumber. This recipe makes a sweet, subtly flavored pickle.

Ingredients

- 3½ cups very thinly sliced cucumbers
- 2 garlic cloves, thinly sliced
- 1 tablespoon pickling or fine sea salt
- 1 cup distilled white vinegar
- ¼ cup sugar
- 1 sprig fresh dill
- 1 teaspoon dill seeds
- 1 bay leaf

1 Combine the cucumbers, garlic, and salt in a large bowl. Cover with ice water and set aside for at least 2 hours, and up to 6 hours. Then drain, rinse, and drain the cucumbers again.

2 Combine the white vinegar and sugar in a small saucepan over low heat. Heat just enough to dissolve the sugar.

3 Pour the vinegar mixture over the drained cucumbers and toss well to coat.

4 Pack the fresh dill, dill seeds, and bay leaf into a freezer container. Pack in the cucumbers and vinegar mixture, leaving at least 1 inch headspace. Close tightly and freeze.

5 Defrost in the refrigerator for at least 8 hours before serving.

PICKLE CAPITAL OF THE UNITED STATES

In Mount Olive, North Carolina, the air is always scented with a faint aroma of vinegar brine. The day begins at 6:50 AM when the Mt. Olive factory horn sounds a blast, signaling the beginning of the workday. Mount Olive is a small town with a population of about 5,000 people, most of whom are employed or were employed, if only for a summer, at the pickle factory, which turns some 130 million pounds of fresh produce into 90 million jars of pickles and condiments each year. The Mt. Olive Pickle Company is the #1 selling pickle brand in the southeastern United States and the #2 seller across the nation.

The Mt. Olive Pickle Company story is a classic American success story. The company, located at the corner of Cucumber and Vine in Mount Olive, was founded in 1926 by Lebanese immigrant Shickrey Baddour and George Moore, a former sailor who had worked in a pickle plant. Originally, the plan was to buy cucumbers from local growers and brine them, with the intention of selling the the brined vegetables to pickle producers. Turned out, there wasn't much of a demand for brined vegetables, so the two began to make pickles.

In 1986, the Mt. Olive Pickle Company co-founded the North Carolina Pickle Festival. These days, on the third weekend in April every year, more than 35,000 visitors descend on the small town of Mount Olive to celebrate all things pickle. Activities include a 5K Cucumber Patch Run and a 75-mile Tour de Pickle bike race (winners receive jars of pickles), as well as music, pig and duck races, petting zoos, carnival rides, and vendors. A recent addition is the very popular Pickle Packing Production Challenge, with an assembly line set up to measure how fast contestants can pack a pickle jar.

The local schools get into the act in advance of the festival, challenging students to create pickle art and pickle poetry for the festival.

Amber Game, a fourth grader at the Grantham School, wrote my favorite poem in 2010:

> Pickle, pickle in a jar
> Can't wait to get you in my car
> Take you home with gentle care
> Eat one alone or in a pair
> Oh how I love to hear that crunch
> Can't hardly wait to munch, munch, munch
> The taste of you is oh so yummy
> All you have to do is ask my tummy.

Can't make it to the pickle festival? Celebrate New Year's Eve in Mount Olive by watching a neon green, glowing 3-foot pickle make a 45-foot plunge down the company's flagpole and into a redwood pickle tank at the stroke of 7 PM, which is actually midnight Greenwich Mean Time.

People go to bed early in this small town.

Freezer Bread and Butters

Makes 4 cups

The seasonings are the same as in a traditional bread and butter pickle, but the flavor is fresher and brighter. The recipe is designed to be multiplied if you have more cucumbers than you know what to do with. These pickles make a terrific addition to a sandwich.

Ingredients

- 4 cups very thinly sliced cucumbers
- 1 onion, very thinly sliced
- 2 teaspoons pickling or fine sea salt
- 1¼ cups distilled white vinegar
- ½ cup sugar
- ½ teaspoon ground turmeric
- ¼ teaspoon celery seeds
- ¼ teaspoon freshly ground black pepper
- ⅛ teaspoon dry mustard powder

1 Combine the cucumbers, onion, and salt in a colander. Cover with ice water and let stand for at least 2 hours, and up to 6 hours. Drain well.

2 Meanwhile, combine the white vinegar and sugar in a small saucepan over low heat and stir until the sugar is dissolved. Stir in the turmeric, celery seeds, black pepper, and mustard powder. Let cool to room temperature.

3 Pack the cucumbers into four 1-cup freezer containers or zippered freezer bags, leaving at least 1 inch headspace. Pour in the vinegar mixture; it will not cover the cucumbers. Mix well. Then freeze.

4 Defrost in the refrigerator for at least 8 hours before serving.

Kitchen Note

Multiply this recipe to pickle as many cucumbers as you have on hand, but 1-cup freezer containers are advised.

Ginger-Garlic Freezer Pickles

Makes 4 cups

The perfect accompaniment to stir-fries, which don't require elaborate side dishes.

Ingredients

- 3 cups cucumbers, very thinly sliced
- 1 onion, thinly sliced
- 1 carrot, grated
- 3 garlic cloves, thinly sliced
- 1 (1-inch) piece fresh ginger, very thinly sliced, or 1-inch stack Pickled Ginger (page 229)
- 1 tablespoon pickling or fine sea salt, or to taste
- 1 cup distilled white vinegar
- ½ cup sugar

1 Combine the cucumbers, onion, carrot, garlic, ginger, and salt in a large bowl. Cover with ice water and let stand for at least 2 hours, and up to 6 hours. Then drain, rinse, and drain again. The cucumber should taste pleasantly salty. If not, add salt to taste.

2 Meanwhile, combine the white vinegar and sugar in a small saucepan over low heat. Heat just enough to dissolve the sugar, stirring. Let cool to room temperature.

3 Pour the vinegar solution over the drained vegetables. Pack the mixture into freezer containers, leaving at least 1 inch headspace, and freeze.

4 Defrost in the refrigerator for at least 8 hours before serving.

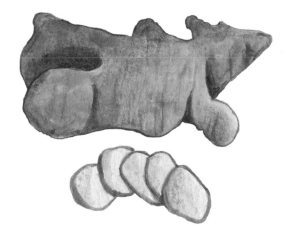

Freezer Curry Chips

Makes 3 cups

Wonderful! Unexpected! Delicious! These curry chips taste more "pickled" than your average freezer pickle. They make a great snacking pickle.

Ingredients

3 cups thinly sliced cucumbers

1 small onion, thinly sliced

1 tablespoon pickling or fine sea salt

1 cup rice vinegar

½ cup sugar

1 teaspoon curry powder

2 garlic cloves

2 thin slices fresh ginger or Pickled Ginger (page 229)

1 cardamom pod

1   Combine the cucumbers, onion, and salt in a large bowl. Cover with ice water and let stand for at least 2 hours, and up to 6 hours. Drain well.

2   Meanwhile, combine the rice vinegar, sugar, and curry powder in a small saucepan over low heat and stir until the sugar is dissolved. Stir in the garlic, ginger, and cardamom. Let cool to room temperature.

3   Pack the cucumbers into a freezer container or zippered freezer bag, leaving at least 1 inch headspace. Pour in the vinegar mixture; it will not cover the cucumbers. Mix well, then freeze.

4   Defrost in the refrigerator for at least 8 hours before serving.

Quick Curtido

Makes about 8 cups

A lightly fermented cabbage salad, curtido is commonly served with pupusas, which are stuffed pancakes made from masa harina. Curtido is called the Latin American sauerkraut, but that doesn't do it justice. It's a fiesta of flavors, a very special cabbage salad you are going to love to have on hand. It is perfect for picnics, and since it contains no mayonnaise, there is no worry of spoilage, as there is with many cabbage salads. This version uses vinegar instead of natural fermentation. There are two versions that rely on natural fermentation in chapter 2.

Ingredients

- 1 small head cabbage, very thinly sliced or grated (about 6 cups)
- 2 carrots, coarsely grated
- ½ red onion, very thinly sliced
- ½ cup chopped fresh cilantro
- 1 fresh red or green jalapeño, minced
- 1 teaspoon dried oregano
- 1 cup pineapple vinegar, coconut vinegar, or cider vinegar
- 2 tablespoons water
- 2 teaspoons pickling or fine sea salt
- freshly ground black pepper

1 Combine the cabbage, carrots, onion, cilantro, jalapeño, oregano, pineapple vinegar, water, salt, and black pepper to taste. Cover and refrigerate overnight.

2 Serve directly from the refrigerator or let it come to room temperature first.

Kitchen Note

Pineapple vinegar is traditional but hard to find. Coconut vinegar is a pleasing alternative and perhaps a little easier to find. Really, any light, fruit-based vinegar (but not raspberry) will work.

Dehydrated Pickles

"Stop the presses!" I told my editor at Storey Publishing. Pickling is such an ancient art that it is rare to uncover a new approach to the subject, but Kathy Harrison had just opened my eyes to an intriguing new pickling technique. So despite the fact that the manuscript was "done," I found myself with more to say.

I had just spent a terrific weekend at a Mother Earth News Fair, doing cooking demos and spending time with lots of like-minded people — about 13,000 in all. One of those like-minded individuals was Kathy Harrison, possibly one of the most generous people on the planet. Harrison, the author of *Just in Case, Another Place at the Table,* and *One Small Boat,* is a national spokesperson for both foster parenting and family preparedness and has appeared on the *Today Show,* the *Oprah Winfrey Show,* and National Public Radio. She lives with her family in western Massachusetts, where she cans and preserves most of the food her family eats.

When we started to talk about pickling, she confessed that last summer, "I was so

Kathy Harrison

overwhelmed with cucumbers. I was busy anyhow and so sick of pickling. So I tried to dehydrate cucumber slices. I thought about rehydrating them and serving then with a nice dilly sauce. And then I thought, why rehydrate in water? Why not rehydrate in brine?"

Harrison used to put up about 250 jars of pickles every summer. "I pickle carrots, string beans, cauliflower, and cucumbers. But the cucumbers are a pain because they come on so fast. You do load after load after load." Since discovering this shortcut, she has cut back on the number of jars of cucumbers she cans. "I still put up a lot, but in the heat of the summer, this is what I am going to be doing from now on."

Harrison explained the method. "I start by slicing my cucumbers about ¼ inch thick. I don't like to use large cucumbers; I want them fleshier rather than seedier." She noted that when she cut the chips thicker than ¼ inch, the pickles were "a bit more rubbery than I wanted."

"Then I don't do a thing to them. No salt or anything. I just put them in the dehydrator and dry them. They take a while. I want them dry and crispy, not leathery and floppy. Then I put them in a jar with a FoodSaver lid and suck out all the air. Those chips will last a good year.

"When I want pickles, I'll make up a hot brine. Just a small amount, not the whole recipe. Then I bring it to a boil. I pour the spices into the jar, then fill the jar about two-thirds full with the cucumber chips. I add the hot brine, then loosely cover the jar and tuck it away in the fridge."

The brine is vinegar-based, said Harrison. "Usually vinegar, salt, water, and spice. I use my regular recipes. If I want a bread and butter pickle, it will have sugar as well.

"The next day I have pickles. They are real crisp, without any alum or lime. It saves me the canning kettle time at a time of the year when the canning kettle is being used for so much.

"I got a pickle recipe this year. It called for a lot of orange. I didn't love the pickle. If I had done a giant batch, we'd be stuck eating it. But with this method, I only made one jar."

As we were speaking, Harrison got an idea. She regularly dries cauliflower but she has never tried to pickle dried cauliflower. "Cauliflower gets all brown and shriveled when it's dried, but then it rehydrates beautifully. I'll bet I can pickle it this way!" And she was off.

Freezer Cabbage Relish

Makes 6 pints

No root cellar? **Not fond of sauerkraut? This recipe is another good way to** preserve cabbage.

Ingredients

- **1 head cabbage, shredded (14–16 cups)**
- **2 carrots, shredded**
- **1 onion, thinly sliced**
- **1 green bell pepper, thinly sliced**
- **1 tablespoon pickling or fine sea salt**
- **½ cup sugar**
- **2 teaspoons dry mustard powder**
- **2 cups cider vinegar**

1 Combine the cabbage, carrots, onion, green pepper, and salt. Mix well and set aside for at least 2 hours, and up to 6 hours.

2 Mix together the sugar and mustard powder in a small saucepan. Stir in the cider vinegar and heat gently until all is dissolved. Let cool to room temperature.

3 Taste the vegetables. If they are too salty, rinse and drain briefly. (I usually do not rinse them.)

4 Pour the vinegar mixture over the drained vegetables. Pack the mixture into freezer containers, leaving at least 1 inch headspace, and freeze.

5 Defrost in the refrigerator for at least 8 hours before serving.

Freezer Ginger-Garlic Cabbage Relish

Makes 3 cups

It is surprising how crunchy and fresh-tasting this cabbage relish is. A handy condiment to have on hand for dinners that feature stir-fries, it also makes an excellent addition to an Asian-inspired wrap.

Ingredients

- 1 small head cabbage, shredded (about 6 cups)
- 2 carrots, shredded
- 1 onion, thinly sliced
- 1 tablespoon pickling or fine sea salt
- ¾ cup rice vinegar
- 3 tablespoons sugar
- ½ teaspoon Chinese chili paste with garlic
- 4 garlic cloves, minced
- 1 (1-inch) piece fresh ginger, peeled and minced, or 1-inch stack Pickled Ginger (page 229), minced

1   Combine the cabbage, carrots, onion, and salt. Mix well and set aside for at least 2 hours, and up to 6 hours.

2   Mix together the rice vinegar, sugar, chili paste, garlic, and ginger in a small saucepan over low heat. Heat, stirring, until the sugar dissolves. Let cool to room temperature.

3   Taste the vegetables. If they are too salty, rinse and drain briefly. (I usually do not rinse them.)

4   Pour the vinegar mixture over the drained vegetables. Pack the mixture into freezer containers, leaving at least 1 inch headspace, and freeze.

5   Defrost in the refrigerator for at least 8 hours before serving.

Kitchen Note

Because this is powerfully flavored, a little goes a long way, so I like to pack it into containers that hold no more than 1 cup.

Overnight Pickled Cauliflower

Makes 1 quart

The red wine vinegar adds a surprisingly fruity flavor to the cauliflower. Enjoy the pickles on an antipasto platter or serve as a crunchy surprise in a salad.

Ingredients

about 4 cups cauliflower florets

1 small onion, sliced

1¼ cups red wine vinegar

1 cup water

¼ cup sugar

1 teaspoon pickling or fine sea salt

2 garlic cloves

1 bay leaf

1 sprig fresh basil, or 1 teaspoon dried

1 Bring a large pot of salted water to a boil. Add the cauliflower and blanch for 3 minutes. Drain well. Toss with the onion and set aside.

2 Combine the red wine vinegar, water, sugar, and salt in a saucepan. Bring just to a boil, stirring to dissolve the sugar.

3 Pack the garlic, bay leaf, and basil into a clean 1-quart container. Pack in the cauliflower. Pour in the hot vinegar mixture. Seal and refrigerate overnight.

Pickled Whole Chiles

Makes 1 quart

This is the easiest way to preserve chiles, short of stringing them up to dry in the sun (which isn't an option in cool, rainy fall climates). For most of us, these peppers are too hot and too strongly flavored to be eaten out of hand. Sliced thinly and seeded, if desired, the pickled peppers can be added to a variety of Tex-Mex dishes, including nachos and taco salads.

Ingredients

- **4 cups whole jalapeños or similar fresh hot chiles**
- **2¾ cups distilled white vinegar, plus more as needed**
- **1 teaspoon pickling or fine sea salt**
- **about ¼ cup extra-virgin olive oil**

1. Cut a tiny slit in each chile. Pack into a clean 1-quart canning jar.

2. Heat the white vinegar in a saucepan almost to boiling. Pour the hot vinegar over the chiles. Cap by covering with a two-piece canning lid. Do not tighten the screw band.

3. Let the jar stand for 1 to 2 weeks at a constant temperature of about 65°F, until the chiles taste pickled.

4. Pour off the vinegar. Add fresh vinegar to fill the jar about three-quarters full. Add the salt and top with the olive oil.

5. Store the pickles in the refrigerator for up to 3 months.

Farm-Grown Ferments

There's a pickle maker where I live in Ripton, Vermont. Her name is Kate Corrigan, and she makes and sells sauerkraut, curtido, and kimchi at area farmers' markets. To make her pickles, she mostly uses organic vegetables that she grows at North Branch Farm and Gardens, which she runs with her partner, Sebastian Miska.

What you have to understand about Ripton is that it is a tiny hamlet in the Green Mountains, mostly in what the USDA calls Plant Hardiness Zone 3. In Zone 3 (think Juneau, Alaska), the frost-free date is Memorial Day. The growing season is about 140 days, *if* we are lucky. First frost comes with the full moon in September, be it early in the month or late. In other words, it isn't an easy climate — which is why we have so few farms here. Indeed, Corrigan and Miska's North Branch Farm and Gardens is one of a handful of farms in this mountain village in this mostly rural state.

Sebastian Miska and Kate Corrigan

North Branch Farm and Gardens is a recently begun effort. Miska bought the 22-acre parcel about five years ago; Corrigan joined him about six months later. Both are in their late twenties. Together they raise about a dozen pigs a year, plus many more ducks and chickens, for both meat and eggs. They also tend a garden of about an acre. Corrigan used to juggle full-time work with farming but now is focusing on the farm. Miska has a landscaping business. It's not easy making a full-time living on a small farm.

Pickle making is new, something Corrigan started in 2010 to generate foot traffic at their market booths, make good use of their cabbage crop, and sell a product no one else was making. Sales took off immediately.

The three pickles she offers are naturally fermented, all with a cabbage base. Salt is the only preservative. Sauerkraut is, of course, of European origins; kimchi comes from Korea; and curtido is from Central America. Vermonters who haven't traveled much are unfamiliar with it. "Almost everyone who tries it, likes it," Corrigan observes. "But I weed out people who aren't likely to be happy with it. I say, 'If you don't like sauerkraut, you won't like this.' I protect people, protect myself."

Her curtido is far more popular than either her kimchi or sauerkraut. After one taste, I understand why. Curtido is called the Latin American sauerkraut. In addition to cabbage, it usually contains onion, carrot, oregano, and chiles. The oregano provides a haunting flavor; the carrots and onion are faintly sweet. It is quite unlike the sauerkraut to which it is compared. Corrigan tells me that one of her customers tells her it is exactly like the curtido he enjoyed in a Salvadoran restaurant. Another commented that curtido is found in bars in Southern California, where it is served to encourage more beer drinking. Not being a beer drinker myself, I found myself thinking of a German Riesling or a French Gewürztraminer.

Corrigan has a weekly production schedule. She makes her pickles in 2-quart canning jars. Her recipes are not precise — so much salt to one head of cabbage, and the weight of the cabbages vary. She notes that one small head of cabbage will fill the bowl of her Cuisinart food processor, so that's her basic measure. After combining the ingredients, she stuffs the mixture into sterilized 2-quart canning jars and lets the fermentation process happen on the kitchen counter. "I taste often. And when the ferments taste right, I put them in the refrigerator."

Her sauerkraut is sometimes flavored with caraway, sometimes with juniper berries. She's also tried cumin seeds, which customers seemed to like.

The pickles are never subjected to any heat, which would soften the texture and destroy the valuable enzymes that are present in lacto-fermented products. "When someone wants to buy some pickles at the market, I just scoop it out of my big jars and put it into a clean pint jar." She sells the pint jars for seven dollars.

This past year, demand was so great, Corrigan ran out of her own cabbage and had to purchase more from another organic farm. The challenge for her second year in business is to grow enough of her own ingredients to cover demand and branch out to a few more markets. But, at least for now, she'll continue working with her small 2-quart canning jar batches. "It really works. I've had success with it, so I'm reluctant to change my equipment."

As they say, nothing succeeds like success.

To learn more about North Branch Farm and Gardens, visit www.greenmountaingrown.com.

Chinese Sweet Pickled Daikon

Makes 1 pint

Gingery sweet, these pickled daikons could last for about a month in the refrigerator, but probably won't.

Ingredients

- ¾ pound daikon radish (about 12 inches), peeled and thinly sliced (about 2 cups)
- 2 teaspoons pickling or fine sea salt
- 3 tablespoons sugar
- ¾ cup water
- 2 tablespoons distilled white vinegar
- 6 thin slices peeled fresh ginger or Pickled Ginger (page 229)
- 1 garlic clove, sliced

1 Combine the daikon with the salt in a bowl and mix well. Cover with ice water and let sit for at least 2 hours, and up to 6 hours.

2 Dissolve the sugar in water by heating for a few seconds in a microwave and stirring vigorously. Add the white vinegar and let cool to room temperature.

3 Drain the daikon and pack into a clean 1-pint canning jar along with the ginger and garlic. Pour in the vinegar mixture. Seal. Refrigerate overnight. The pickles will be ready to eat the next day. After 3 days, discard the garlic so it doesn't overwhelm the flavor.

DAIKON RADISHES

- The daikon radish appears in many Asian-style pickle recipes. It's a terrific, all-purpose winter vegetable that makes a fine pickle.

- Daikon radish probably didn't originate in Japan, but we know it by its Japanese name. "Dai" means large and "kon" means root. These are indeed large roots, ranging in size from 6 inches to 3 feet, depending on the variety. The variety that we see in the United States is usually a 1-foot-long radish that is 2 to 3 inches in diameter. It is often sold in 4- to 6-inch pieces, so it is hard to be certain of its variety.

- The large radish stores well, far better than the typical red salad radish. In fact, the daikon radish is more like a turnip and will keep in a moist root cellar for up to 4 months. If you grow your own you have the additional advantage of the daikon leaves, which can be sautéed or stir-fried like mustard greens.

- When you buy daikon, look for firm roots with smooth, unblemished skin. Daikons that are about 2 inches in diameter are perfect because they have a milder flavor. Really young, thin daikon can be tasteless and really fat daikon can be old, bitter, or woody in texture. Keep uncut daikon in a plastic bag in the refrigerator. After cutting the root, wrap it in plastic wrap.

Gingery Quick Pickled Daikon and Carrot

Makes 1 quart

Daikon is a long-keeping radish found wherever Asian vegetables are sold. It is usually about 1½ inches in diameter and grows over a foot in length. Often the produce manager cuts the daikon into more manageable lengths. This is a nice pickle to have on hand to accompany Chinese or Japanese dishes.

Ingredients

- 1 **pound daikon (about 16 inches in length), peeled and cut into matchsticks**
- 1 **carrot, cut into matchsticks**
- 1 **tablespoon pickling or fine sea salt**
- 1 **cup distilled white vinegar**
- 1 **cup water**
- ½ **cup sugar**
- 3 **thin slices peeled fresh ginger or Pickled Ginger (page 229)**
- 2 **garlic cloves, peeled and halved**

1 Combine the daikon, carrot, and salt in a bowl and mix well. Cover with ice water and let sit for at least 2 hours, and up to 6 hours.

2 Combine the white vinegar, water, sugar, ginger, and garlic in a small saucepan. Bring to a boil, stirring to dissolve the sugar. Remove from the heat and allow it to cool to room temperature.

3 Drain the vegetables and pack into a clean 1-quart canning jar. Pour the cooled vinegar mixture into the jar to cover the vegetables. Refrigerate for at least 12 hours, and preferably 1 day. The pickles will keep for several weeks.

Kitchen Notes

- Red radishes, salad turnips, or kohlrabi can replace some or all of the daikon.
- Carrots are pretty but can be replaced with more radish. Or make this with only carrots.

Chinese Spicy-Sweet Pickled Daikon and Carrot

Makes about 1 quart

In the nearest Chinatown (Montreal's), I fell in love with a sweet pickle. I found it in the refrigerator case of a Chinese deli where barbecued ducks and pork were the star attractions. The label read "daikon, carrots, vinegar, sugar, and salt," but clearly there was more going in the flavor. Countless attempts to re-create the pickle proved useless, but somewhere along the way, I took a delicious left turn and came up with this recipe.

Ingredients

- ½ **pound daikon radish (about 8 inches), peeled and cut into matchsticks**
- 1 **large carrot, cut into matchsticks**
- 2 **teaspoons salt**
- 1 **cup water**
- ½ **cup sugar**
- ⅓ **cup mirin (sweet Japanese rice wine)**
- ⅓ **cup rice vinegar**
- ¼ **cup distilled white vinegar**
- 6 **thin slices peeled fresh ginger or Pickled Ginger (page 229)**
- 1 **garlic clove, sliced**
- 1 **dried red chile (optional)**

1 Combine the daikon and carrot with the salt in a bowl and mix well. Cover with ice water and let sit for at least 2 hours, and up to 6 hours.

2 Combine the water and sugar in a small saucepan and heat, stirring, until the sugar completely dissolves. Remove from the heat and stir in the mirin, rice vinegar, white vinegar, ginger, and garlic. Let cool to room temperature.

3 Drain the vegetables and pack into a clean 1-quart canning jar. Strain the brine, discarding the ginger and garlic, and pour in. Add the dried chile, if desired. Seal. Refrigerate and allow to cure for at least 1 week before eating.

Kitchen Notes

- The pickles will keep for about 1 month in the refrigerator.
- If you like, make it with all daikon radish.
- Using one chile adds subtle heat; my son says more would be better, but he always says that. . . .

Vietnamese-Style Pickled Daikon and Carrot

Makes 1 quart

Daikon radishes and carrots make an interesting pickle mix because they have both crunch and beautiful flavor. The fish sauce gives these pickles a distinctive taste.

Ingredients

- ½ **pound carrots, cut into matchsticks**
- ½ **pound daikon radish (8–9 inches in length), peeled and cut into matchsticks**
- 2 **teaspoons pickling or fine sea salt**
- 1 **cup Vietnamese or Thai fish sauce**
- 1 **cup distilled white vinegar**
- ¾ **cup sugar**
- 3 **garlic cloves, minced**
- ¼ **teaspoon red pepper flakes**

1 Combine the carrots and daikon radish with the salt in a bowl and mix well. Cover with ice water and let sit for at least 2 hours, and up to 6 hours.

2 Combine the fish sauce, white vinegar, sugar, garlic, and red pepper in a small saucepan over low heat. Stir until the sugar dissolves. Let cool to room temperature.

3 Drain the vegetables and pack into a clean 1-quart canning jar. Pour in the vinegar mixture. Seal. Refrigerate overnight. The pickles will be ready to eat the next day but will reach a peak of a flavor after about 1 week; they will keep for at least a month in the refrigerator.

Soy Sauce Daikon and Carrot Pickles

Makes 1 quart

The soy sauce colors the vegetables a muted brown. Not the most attractive color, perhaps. But what they lack in beauty, they make up in flavor.

Ingredients

- ½ pound daikon radish (8–9 inches in length), peeled and cut into matchsticks
- ½ pound carrots, cut into matchsticks
- 2 teaspoons pickling or fine sea salt
- ¼ cup rice vinegar
- ¼ cup soy sauce
- 2 tablespoons Chinese rice wine or dry sherry
- 1 tablespoon Chinese black vinegar
- 1 teaspoon brown sugar
- 4 inches kombu, cut into little pieces with kitchen scissors

1 Combine the daikon radish, carrots, and salt in a bowl. Cover with ice water and set aside for 2 hours, and up to 6 hours.

2 Meanwhile, combine the rice vinegar, soy sauce, rice wine, Chinese black vinegar, brown sugar, and kombu in a small saucepan. Bring to a boil. Remove from the heat and let cool to room temperature.

3 Drain the vegetables and rinse well. Pat dry. Transfer to a 1-quart canning jar. Pour in the vinegar mixture. Cover and refrigerate. The pickles will be ready to eat the next day but will reach a peak of flavor after about 1 week; they will keep for about 1 month in the refrigerator.

Kitchen Notes

- Kombu is dried kelp (seaweed), used for flavoring. You can omit it if you can't find it, but it does add a richness to the flavor.
- Chinese black vinegar is available wherever Chinese foods are sold. Often made from rice (but sometimes from other grains), it is thicker, sweeter, and more complex in flavor than regular rice vinegar, in much the same way that balsamic vinegar is thicker, sweeter, and more complex than red wine vinegar. Chinese black vinegar may be labeled Chinkiang vinegar. A reasonable substitute would be 1 part soy sauce, 1 part Worcestershire sauce, and 1 part rice vinegar.

Pickled Garlic Cloves

Makes 1 half-pint

The pickling process mellows the garlic considerably. It makes a tasty pickle, something to munch on with drinks or put atop cheese and crackers. I don't process this pickle because the processing softens the texture of the cloves too much.

Ingredients

- 4 **heads garlic**
- 1½ **cups distilled white vinegar**
- ½ **cup sugar**
- 1 **teaspoon pickling or fine sea salt**
- 1 **teaspoon dill seeds**

1 Peel the garlic by putting the heads into a bowl and covering them with boiling water. Let stand for 3 minutes. Drain, break the heads into cloves, and peel them, cutting off the hard root end of each clove.

2 Combine the white vinegar, sugar, and salt in a saucepan. Bring to a boil, stirring until the sugar dissolves. Drop the garlic into the mixture and simmer, uncovered, for about 10 minutes, stirring occasionally, just until the garlic is tender but still crunchy. Remove from the heat; let cool.

3 Pour the garlic and vinegar into the sterilized canning jar. Add the dill seeds. Cover and store in a tightly covered jar in the refrigerator. The garlic is ready to enjoy in 3 days and will keep for 6 months or longer.

Kitchen Note

Although you can multiply the recipe as many times as you want and pickled garlic keeps well in the refrigerator, garlic bulbs, when stored in a cool, dry spot, do not need preservation like other vegetables.

Pickled Ginger

Makes 1 pint

Young, green-tipped ginger is ideal for this, but use what is available to you. Young ginger will be much more tender and will turn a pleasing pink in the jar. Older ginger will become pinkish and may be slightly fibrous, but it is still very acceptable. A mandoline will do the best job of slicing the ginger; you really do want it paper-thin.

Ingredients

- ½ pound fresh ginger, peeled and sliced paper-thin
- 1 teaspoon pickling or fine sea salt
- 1 cup rice vinegar
- ⅔ cup sugar

1   Combine the ginger and salt in a colander, mix well, and let drain for about 1 hour. Dry the ginger with paper towels and pack into a clean 1-pint canning jar.

2   Mix together the rice vinegar and sugar in a small saucepan and bring to a boil, stirring to dissolve the sugar. Pour the hot vinegar mixture over the ginger slices. Let cool to room temperature.

3   Cover the jar and store in the refrigerator. The pickled ginger will be ready in about 1 week and will last indefinitely.

Kitchen Notes

- Pickled ginger is fine to use in place of regular ginger root in most dishes. It makes a great addition to dipping sauces and salad dressings.
- It is probably safer to store the ginger in the refrigerator, but I keep mine in a cupboard with the soy sauce and other shelf-stable condiments.
- The vinegar becomes nicely infused with ginger and can be used in any dish calling for rice vinegar.

Pub-Style Pickled Onions

Makes about 1 quart

When malt vinegar appears in a recipe, you can be pretty sure the recipe is of British origin. Well, the word "pub" in the title is also a dead giveaway. As the onions age, the oniony flavor diminishes and the vinegar and spices begin to dominate.

Ingredients

- 1¼ pounds very small boiling onions (about 4½ cups)
- ¼ cup pickling or fine sea salt
- 1¼ cups malt vinegar
- ¼ cup water
- ½ cup firmly packed brown sugar
- 1 teaspoon allspice berries
- 1 teaspoon mixed pickling spices, store-bought or homemade (page 18)
- 1 teaspoon black peppercorns

1 Bring a large kettle of water to a boil. Put the onions in a bowl and cover with boiling water to make peeling easier; let stand for 5 to 10 minutes. Meanwhile, pour 1 cup boiling water into another bowl. Add the salt and stir to dissolve. Add enough cold water to make a brine that will cover the onions (about 3 cups). Peel the onions and add to the brine. Weight the onions with a plate that fits inside the bowl so they are submerged in the brine (otherwise they will float). Let them stand for 12 hours.

2 Combine the malt vinegar, ¼ cup water, and brown sugar in a saucepan and bring to a boil, stirring to dissolve the sugar. Let the liquid cool.

3 Drain the onions. Pack the allspice, mixed pickling spices, and peppercorns into a clean 1-quart canning jar. Pack in the onions. Cover with the cooled vinegar mixture. Seal the jar.

4 Refrigerate for at least 1 month before eating the onions; longer is better. They will keep for at least 6 months.

Kitchen Notes

- The smaller the onion, the quicker they will taste fully pickled.
- Technically, pickler onions are less than 1 inch in diameter; pearls are between ¾ inch and 1 inch; creamers are between 1 inch and 1¼ inches; and boilers range from 1¼ inches to 1⅞ inches. In most supermarkets, small onions are called boiling or pearl onions. If there are differences in flavor, they are difficult to discern.
- The pickled onions are delicious in Pickled Onion and Potato Salad (page 259).

Overnight Orange Pickles

Makes 1 quart

Tangy sweet oranges flavored with cilantro and a touch of heat make a wonderful accompaniment to any Asian dish. The pickled oranges will keep for up to 1 week in the refrigerator.

Ingredients

- ½ cup rice vinegar
- ¼ cup sugar
- 1 tablespoon Vietnamese or Thai fish sauce
- ½ teaspoon crushed red pepper flakes
- 5 or 6 oranges
- ¼ cup chopped fresh cilantro

1 Combine the rice vinegar, sugar, fish sauce, and red pepper in a saucepan over medium heat, stirring until the sugar dissolves. Pour into a 1-quart canning jar or deep glass or ceramic bowl.

2 Very finely grate the zest from one of the oranges, and add the zest to the vinegar mixture. Juice two of the oranges and add the juice to the vinegar mixture. Peel and section the remaining oranges, and add them to the jar, along with the cilantro.

3 Cover the jar and gently shake the mixture to be sure the oranges are mixed into the liquid. If using a bowl, gently stir; cover the bowl. Refrigerate overnight, shaking or stirring occasionally.

4 Drain the oranges and reserve the liquid. Arrange the oranges in a shallow bowl, drizzle them with some of the reserved liquid, and serve.

Kitchen Notes

To section an orange, use a small, sharp knife to remove both the peel and white membrane covering the fruit inside. Working over a bowl, cut each orange segment free from the membranes on either side. This is a fussy step, but necessary to enable the flavors to penetrate the orange flesh.

Freezer Tomato Salsa

Makes about 1 quart

Freezing is absolutely the easiest way to preserve a salsa. Mix together the raw ingredients and pop it in the freezer. Nothing could be simpler. And the results are outstanding: freezer salsas taste like fresh, uncooked salsas. The only drawback is that you lose half the volume you started with. Hence, the 1 quart (4 cups) noted as the yield above becomes 1 pint (2 cups) to serve. Freezing breaks down the cell walls of the vegetables, making the salsa watery. The only way to overcome this is to drain the defrosted salsa in a colander set over a bowl. Return to the salsa only as much of the watery liquid as is needed to make the salsa moist. This salsa is brightly flavored and mild. To make it hotter, increase the number of chiles or substitute a hotter variety.

Ingredients

6 large ripe plum tomatoes or medium salad tomatoes, peeled (see page 189) and finely chopped

½ small onion, finely chopped

1 or 2 fresh red or green jalapeños, seeded (optional; see page 175)

½ green or red bell pepper, finely chopped

2 tablespoons finely chopped fresh cilantro, plus more as needed

juice of 1 lime (about 2 tablespoons), plus more as needed

salt and freshly ground black pepper

1 Mix together the tomatoes, onion, jalapeños, bell pepper, cilantro, and lime juice. Add salt and pepper to taste. Some flavor will be lost in the freezer, so use a bold hand.

2 Freeze in an airtight plastic bag or container.

3 Defrost in a colander set over a bowl at room temperature. Transfer the salsa to a small bowl. Return enough of the collected liquid to give the salsa a pleasing texture. Taste and adjust the seasoning, adding additional cilantro, lime juice, salt, or pepper to brighten the flavors.

Kitchen Notes

- A handful of chopped fresh cilantro added to the defrosted salsa will brighten up the flavors.
- The salsa liquid you do not return to the defrosted salsa can be reserved for soup stock.

Freezer Bread and Butter Zucchini Chips

Makes about 4 cups

It turns out that zucchini can be used to make freezer pickles just as easily as cucumbers. For best results, select young zucchini. Use the monster overgrown zucchini for relishes or other recipes.

Ingredients

- 4 cups thinly sliced small zucchini
- 1 onion, thinly sliced
- 1½ teaspoons pickling or fine sea salt
- 1¼ cups distilled white vinegar
- ½ cup sugar
- 1 teaspoon ground turmeric
- ½ teaspoon celery seeds
- ¼ teaspoon freshly ground black pepper

1 In a large bowl, combine the zucchini, onion, and salt. Toss to mix and set aside for at least 2 hours, and up to 6 hours. Drain, but do not rinse.

2 Combine the white vinegar, sugar, turmeric, celery seeds, and black pepper in a saucepan. Heat just enough to dissolve the sugar. Pour over the zucchini mixture. Toss to mix.

3 Pack the mixture into freezer containers, leaving about 1 inch headspace. Freeze.

4 Defrost in the refrigerator for at least 8 hours before serving.

Kitchen Note

Use a food processor or mandoline for even slices. The thinner the slices, the better the final results.

Freezer Mixed Pickles

Makes 4 cups

The secret to freezing unblanched vegetables, such as carrots and green peppers, is to have them sliced or grated very finely. Then the loss in texture isn't noticeable.

Ingredients

- 4 cups very thinly sliced cucumbers
- 1 small onion, sliced
- ½ green bell pepper, very thinly sliced
- 1 carrot, grated
- 1 tablespoon pickling or fine sea salt
- 1 cup distilled white vinegar
- ½ cup sugar
- 1 teaspoon celery seeds

1 Combine the cucumbers, onion, bell pepper, carrot, and salt in a large bowl. Mix well and cover with ice water. Let stand for 2 hours, and up to 6 hours. Drain well. Taste a cucumber. If it tastes too salty, rinse and drain again.

2 Combine the white vinegar, sugar, and celery seeds in a small saucepan over low heat. Heat, stirring, just until the sugar dissolves. Cool to room temperature.

3 Pour the vinegar mixture over the drained vegetables. Pack the mixture into freezer containers, leaving at least 1 inch headspace, and freeze.

4 Defrost in the refrigerator for at least 8 hours before serving.

Dill Pickled Eggs

Makes 1 quart

Those who keep chickens know it is easy to accumulate too many eggs. Pickled eggs are the obvious solution to the problem of excess. They have long been a popular bar snack. The Brits make theirs with malt vinegar, which dyes the eggs a tan color. Pennsylvania Dutch cooks add a few slices of cooked beets to the brine to dye the eggs pink. This version keeps the eggs white and flavors them with dill. Having never dared to sample a pickled egg that sat unrefrigerated on a bar counter, I was *very* surprised by how much I like these eggs! High in protein, convenient, delicious — how did I live so long without them?

Ingredients

- ½ cup water
- 2 teaspoons pickling or fine sea salt
- 1 cup distilled white vinegar
- 6 sprigs fresh dill or 1 dill head or 1 tablespoon dill seeds
- 2 garlic cloves
- ½ teaspoon black peppercorns
- ½ teaspoon mixed pickling spices, store-bought or homemade (page 18)
- ½ teaspoon mustard seeds
- 9–12 eggs, hard-cooked and peeled

1 Heat together the water and salt, stirring to dissolve the salt. Add the white vinegar and let cool to room temperature.

2 Pack the dill, garlic, peppercorns, mixed pickling spices, and mustard seeds into a clean 1-quart canning jar. Pack in the eggs. Pour in the vinegar mixture. Refrigerate immediately.

3 The eggs are ready to enjoy in 1 to 2 weeks. Use the eggs within 3 to 4 months for best quality. The longer the eggs stay in the brine, the more rubbery the texture becomes.

Kitchen Note

Peeling farm-fresh boiled eggs can be difficult. This method, developed by the Georgia Egg Commission, helps. Make a pinhole in the large end of each raw egg, place eggs in a single layer in a saucepan, and cover with cold water. Cover saucepan and bring to a boil. Remove from heat, keeping the cover on, and let sit for 15 to 18 minutes, depending on the size of the eggs. Move eggs with a slotted spoon from hot water to a bowl of ice water and let sit for 1 minute. In the meantime, return pan of hot water to simmering. Return eggs to the simmering water for 10 seconds to allow the shells but not the rest of the eggs to expand. Peel immediately by cracking the shells all over. Roll each egg gently between your hands to loosen the shell. Peel, starting at the large end of the egg, under cold running water.

Chapter 7

Recipes for Enjoying Homemade Pickles

Pickle Shot • The Sheesham and Lotus • Fried Pickles • Chutney-Cheese with Crackers • Goat Cheese Crostini • Chili Corn Bean Dip • Thousand Island Dressing • Pickled Pepper Spinach Salad • Dilly Mustard Coleslaw • Sweet Pickle Macaroni Salad • Kimchi Rice Salad with Tofu • Tortellini Pasta Salad with Italian Tomato Relish • Creamy Dilled Smoked Fish Pasta Salad • Dilled Potato and Egg Salad • Pickled German Potato Salad • Hot German Potato Salad with Sauerkraut • Pickled Onion and Potato Salad • Kimchi Fried Rice • Kimchi Noodle Bowl • Pickled Pepper Pasta with Goat Cheese • Tomato-Mozzarella Tart • Zuurkoolstamppot • Shrimp Congee • Kimchi Fish Stew • Fish Tacos • Cranberry Chicken Salad • Pulled Chicken Barbecue • Kimchi Chicken Stir-Fry • Roasted and Braised Duck with Sauerkraut and Root Vegetables • Spice-Crusted Pork Tenderloin with Chutney • Szechuan Green Beans • Pork Chops with Red Cabbage and Apple Relish • Roast Pork with Sauerkraut • Oven-Baked Barbecued Ribs • Choucroute Garnie • Korean Bulgogi Tacos with Kimchi • German Chocolate Sauerkraut Cake • Peanut Butter–Chocolate Chip Sauerkraut Cake

You have a pantry loaded with jars of pickles. The refrigerator is burdened with too many half-filled jars of pickles. Now what?

I've heard about a lot of crazy pickle combinations in my day: pickle juice snow cones, pickle-flavored popcorn, even pickle cupcakes. So the temptation was strong to go wild with this chapter. Still, I restrained myself to a couple of bar drinks and a couple of desserts made with sauerkraut, a combination I was introduced to by my mother in the 1960s.

The recipes in this chapter make good use of pickles. Some pickles spice up bland American classics like macaroni salad, some present new American classics like Korean tacos, and some feature pickles as they are served in the cuisines from which they arose. And, of course, there is a recipe for fried pickles.

An especially rich store of traditional recipes use naturally fermented pickles, such as sauerkraut and kimchi.

Sauerkraut finds its way into recipes all across eastern Europe and through Austria, Germany, and northern France. And kimchi is just one of the salt-cured pickles enjoyed by people throughout Asia. Szechuan cuisine has many recipes that use pickled greens as an accent flavoring. I find these flavors addictive, and once I get going, I find it hard to stop.

Most of the recipes are designed to utilize a variety of different pickles. For example, any of the three kimchi versions in the book work with the kimchi recipes in this chapter.

The recipes in this chapter are organized like a traditional cookbook, beginning with starters and snacks and ending with a few cakes that make use of sauerkraut. Besides providing fun, sauerkraut in cakes actually serves a purpose: the sauerkraut adds moisture-holding fiber to the cake. Cakes made with sauerkraut stay moist and tasty longer than your average butter cake. Plus the cakes provide a great way to use up sauerkraut that has gotten a little funky or a little soft. And in case you were worrying, let me assure you that the sauerkraut is rinsed until its flavor is gone.

DID YOU PACK THE SAUERKRAUT?

Captain James Cook of England was the first to explore the Antarctic in the late eighteenth century. The bad news for him was that his wooden ship couldn't penetrate the thick slushy ice and he never did find land. The good news? He was the first captain to prevent scurvy among sailors by providing daily rations of sauerkraut (and limes).

AND A HAPPY NEW YEAR!

Although the very word "pickle" conjures up Jewish kosher half-sour dills to many pickle lovers, to others the pickle belongs on the Christmas tree. Legend has it that German families would hide a glass pickle ornament on the Christmas tree after the children were in bed. The next morning, the first to find the pickle ornament would get an extra gift. That legend probably isn't true, though it is promoted heavily by sellers of pickle ornaments.

A similar legend involves a Civil War soldier of German descent who was captured by the Confederates and confined to the notorious Andersonville prison, where he nearly starved to death. But a kind-hearted (?) jailer was convinced to give the poor man a pickle to eat. Thus nourished, the soldier survived and created the custom of hiding a small glass pickle ornament in the family Christmas tree. Its finder on Christmas morning would benefit from a year of good luck.

The story of the soldier has the ring of truth to me. I always feel lucky when I have good homemade pickles to eat.

While researching this book, I came across *America Eats!*, a book that originated from a 1935 WPA project that sent out-of-work writers to explore regional American cuisine, focusing on church suppers, harvest festivals, state fairs, political rallies, lodge suppers, and any gathering where food took center stage. In one piece, a Mrs. Mabel G. Hall of Maine wrote about the pride a farmwife takes in her well-stocked cellar. "It is the favored guest who is invited by the housewife to inspect the farmhouse cellar; no other member of the family may either issue the invitation or conduct the tour." The piece goes on to explain the etiquette of the tour, and the expected appreciation the visitor should express.

I take the most pride in the spring when my pantry shelves are empty. When all the pickles and preserves that I put by are gone, those empty shelves mean that what I canned was appreciated and used up. No dusty jars are left, signaling a batch of something too good to throw out, not good enough to serve. All of my pickles were appreciated and enjoyed.

I could probably create a whole cookbook based on recipes that use pickled and preserved foods. This chapter may be just the beginning — but for now, it is the end of some well-spent time in the kitchen.

Pickle Shot

Serves 1

Full disclosure: I did not come up with the idea of this drink (it probably belongs to the bartenders at Bushwick Country Club in Brooklyn, where McClure's Pickles stores their stock in the basement). Nor have I tasted this drink (I don't like whiskey). But I have served it in my home to the following comments: "Wow! That's good!" "Yes! High five!" "I'm shocked." "I never would have guessed." "Best whiskey combo I've ever had." "I thought there'd be a war in my mouth, but instead it's this perfect warm glow." Here's to the glow.

Ingredients

- 1½ fluid ounces (1 shot) Jameson's whiskey
- 1½ fluid ounces (1 shot) pickle brine from naturally fermented dill pickles (full sour or half sour), pages 48–51

Present the shots in separate glasses, side by side. Drink the whiskey first, immediately followed by the pickle juice.

Kitchen Notes

- There are 2 tablespoons in a fluid ounce.
- Only the brine of fermented pickles is recommended here. A vinegar brine would be too harsh.

The Sheesham and Lotus

Serves 1

The world is filled with people passionate about good food and drink (like me), as well as people passionate about music (like my husband). When our worlds collide, it is great fun. Those worlds collided when old-timey roots musicians Sheesham and Lotus played at the Ripton Community Coffeehouse, a once-a-month concert series my husband and I run with a group of friends. Sheesham and Lotus play fiddle tunes, hokum blues songs, and ragtime string music on fiddle, banjo, and an array of homemade musical curiosities. One night after a concert, we got to talking about pickles as I pulled jar after jar of tests from the refrigerator. Sheesham left with a half-finished jar of curtido that he fell in love with, and I had a new recipe for this book.

Ingredients

- 3 fluid ounces (2 shots) pickle brine from naturally fermented dill pickles (full sour or half sour), pages 48–51
- 1½ fluid ounces (1 shot) bourbon
- ice
- water (optional)

Pour the pickle brine and then the bourbon into a glass filled with ice. Add a splash of water, if desired. Drink at once.

Kitchen Notes

- Some people prefer the drink with 1 part brine to 1 part bourbon. Experiment.
- Again, only the brine of naturally fermented pickles is recommended here.
- Visit www.sheeshamandlotus.com to learn more about their music.

Fried Pickles

Serves 4

The thing you have to remember about fried pickles is that they can only be as good as your pickles. Soggy pickles going in, soggy pickles coming out. I have a preference for breaded fried pickles, though you do see them batter-dipped (not here). And I prefer chunks or thick slices over spears because they have a better crunch ratio, and I don't think the breaded bit clings well to the top of a spear. Also, when you bite into a spear you run the risk of a hot pickle juice burn on the chin. Popping a bite-size chunk in your mouth is less risky. It's the custom to serve ranch dressing with fried pickles, but I think this whole ranch dressing thing has gone too far, with ranch dressing served even with pizza. I will go on the record: My fried pickles don't need dressing.

Ingredients

- 36 (¾-inch) pieces dill pickles (about 8 whole pickles)
- oil for deep-frying
- ¾ cup buttermilk
- ½ cup all-purpose white flour
- ½ cup finely ground yellow cornmeal

1 Pat the pickle pieces dry with paper towels. Heat 2 inches of oil in a tall saucepan for deep-frying to 375°F.

2 Pour the buttermilk into a shallow dish. Combine the flour and cornmeal in a paper bag or bowl and mix well.

3 Add about half of the pickles to the buttermilk and stir to coat well. Using a slotted spoon, transfer to the flour mixture. Shake or toss to coat well. Lift out of the flour mixture and shake off any excess. Slip the pickles into the hot oil.

4 Fry for about 3 minutes, until golden. Remove from the hot oil and drain on paper towels. Repeat with the remaining pickles, dipping first in the buttermilk, then tossing in the flour mixture, and frying until golden. Drain on paper towels.

5 Serve hot.

Kitchen Notes

- It is important that the cornmeal be very finely ground, otherwise the coating will be too gritty.
- A wash of egg and milk can replace the buttermilk.
- If you don't have whole pickles, use spears or halves, cut into ¾-inch pieces.

Chutney-Cheese with Crackers

Serves 6 to 12

The secret to good party food? Low-stress recipes and pretty serving dishes. If you have chutney in your cupboard, it doesn't get any lower in stress than this preparation.

Ingredients

- 1 (8-ounce) log soft, fresh goat cheese
- 1 cup any chutney from chapter 5
- 8 ounces large whole-grain crackers

Set the goat cheese in the center of a large platter. Spoon the chutney over the top, allowing it to drip over the sides. Surround with crackers and serve.

Kitchen Notes

- The chutney can be replaced with a relish. With the goat cheese, I prefer a relish with a sweet flavor profile, such as Italian Tomato Relish (page 190), Sweet Honey Corn Relish (page 164), Savory Cranberry-Apple Relish (page 166), or the very versatile Rosemary Onion Confit (page 170).
- Don't like goat cheese? Try this combination with a ripe Brie or Camembert instead.

Preserving the Foodways of New York

Perhaps no one has done more to encourage and embrace the new wave of pickle makers than Nancy Ralph, founder of the New York Food Museum.

The New York Food Museum is not located in a physical space. Instead, according to its website, it originates exhibits "to encourage people to think about the food they eat. Programs inspire people to remember and learn about the sources of their food, from home gardens to deep-sea fishing. We want our audience to reconnect with the people who plant, grow, harvest, raise, catch, and find their foods; who cook, serve, and clean up their meals; who invent and purvey the products they buy. This connection will add to public understanding, appreciation, and remembrance of the importance of food and nutrition as an indispensable part of our society. Issues of labor, class, religion, race, and gender, of food security and distribution, of ecology and land use, all come into play and each program consciously addresses many of these issues. Free exhibits and events pay tribute to the people that make New York's food culture one of the most fascinating and influential in the world."

In September of 2001, the museum inaugurated the First Annual New York City International Pickle Day, now an annual event with tens of thousands of visitors. Pickle Day is a celebration of a favorite food common to many cultures, with the richness of variety the different traditions provide. The festival originated at the epicenter of New York's pickling neighborhood in the Lower East Side, on Orchard Street between Houston and Stanton.

"The original idea behind the festival," explained Ralph, "was to celebrate the history of the pickle." The Lower East Side was once lined with immigrant pushcart entrepreneurs selling the foods of their homelands. Eventually the pushcarts gave way to storefronts, but only the kosher dill pickle business was long-lasting. As recently as the 1990s, there were still at least five pickle vendors in the area, selling pickles from barrels on the street. Today only Guss' remains (see page 49).

"We wanted to explore the culinary traditions of New York City as it relates to pickles. Scratch the surface, and you find a multicultural network of picklers. The festival has featured Haitian pickles; Lebanese pickles; Russian pickles; Polish, Indian, Sri Lankan pickles; kimchi. Quite a wide spectrum."

The festival has grown every year. "There are a lot of up-and-coming picklers out there. . . . We

New York City Pickle Festival

Chinese salted turnip was "surprisingly earthy and fairly mild." A Scotch bonnet and beet combination she remembered as "very fiery."

Ralph's pickle eating days might be over, except for the occasional pickle in a sandwich. "I used to like them okay. But now I can't eat them. I overdosed on them in the third year of the festival." She still likes to make pickles, with carrots and scallions.

When asked what she has learned about pickling that has surprised her, she responded, "Sandor Katz's whole take on pickling [see page 38] has been most surprising. His fermented roots, his parsnip-turnip pickle. He says, 'Just make it. And, if it doesn't taste good, don't eat it.' Pretty simple and straightforward."

You can learn more about the New York Food Museum at www.nyfoodmuseum.org.

started out thinking about the history of pickles, but [pickling] is more of a living tradition. Pickling is improvisational in nature. It's not so much fusion but working with the ingredients that are extraordinary."

Naturally Ralph has tasted a wide range of pickles. She has particularly fond memories of Russian pickled watermelon. "Not the rind. The watermelon. It's a little salty and a little sweet."

Goat Cheese Crostini

Serves 4

One of the reasons to make pickle relishes is to have ingredients on hand to make something special. Crostini, toasts topped with an intensely flavored spread, are delicious with either an Italian-style tomato relish or an onion confit. Serve as a light lunch or appetizer.

Ingredients

- 8 slices dense country bread
- 2 garlic cloves, halved
- 4 ounces soft goat cheese
- 1 (½-pint) jar Italian Tomato Relish (page 190) or Rosemary Onion Confit (page 170)

1 Preheat the broiler.

2 Arrange the bread in a single layer on a baking sheet. Toast under the broiler until golden brown on both sides, 1 to 2 minutes per side. Remove from the broiler and rub on both sides with the garlic cloves. The garlic will disintegrate into the bread.

3 Divide the goat cheese evenly among the toasts and spread with a knife. Top each toast with 1 tablespoon of the relish and serve.

Chili Corn Bean Dip

Serves 8

Seven-layer bean dip is a Tex-Mex standard, and there is no one right way to make it; you don't even have to have seven layers. This is my variation on the classic, with Chili Corn Relish (page 165) replacing the more traditional salsa.

Ingredients

- 2 tablespoons extra-virgin olive oil
- 2 cups refried beans, store-bought or homemade
- 3–4 tablespoons water (optional)
- salt
- 1 cup shredded Monterey Jack or cheddar cheese
- 1 avocado, peeled and chopped
- 1 cup Chili Corn Relish (page 164)
- 1 cup sour cream
- 1 (3.5-ounce) can sliced ripe black olives, drained
- 1 large or 2 small scallions, white and tender green parts, chopped
- ¼ cup chopped fresh cilantro
- corn tortilla chips, to serve

1 Heat the olive oil over medium heat in a small saucepan. Add the beans and a few tablespoons of water, if needed for a creamy consistency, and heat. Add salt to taste.

2 When the beans are hot and bubbly, spoon them into a wide, shallow serving bowl or pie pan. Immediately sprinkle on the cheese so that the heat from the beans helps melt the cheese. Layer on the chopped avocado, then the corn relish. Spoon on the sour cream. Top with the olives. Mix together the scallions and cilantro and sprinkle on top to garnish.

3 Serve immediately with the chips.

Kitchen Notes

Regard the ingredients as suggestions only. You can replace the beans with chili made from ground meat. Guacamole can replace the chopped avocados. Salsa (see chapter 5) can replace the corn relish. Chopped fresh tomatoes can be added. Mexican crema, crème fraîche, or even soft goat cheese can replace the sour cream. Shredded lettuce also makes a fine addition.

Thousand Island Dressing

Makes about ¾ cup

In this variation on Russian dressing, the relish or chopped pickles swim in the dressing like a thousand islands in a large ocean. Or something like that. It is an old-fashioned dressing, necessary to a Reuben sandwich and absolutely perfect on a wedge of iceberg lettuce.

Ingredients

- ½ cup mayonnaise
- ¼ cup ketchup, store-bought or homemade (see Tomato Ketchup, page 182, and Classic Homemade Tomato Ketchup, page 183)
- 2 tablespoons Dilled Dog Relish (page 152) or 2 tablespoons finely chopped cucumber pickle (any in chapter 2, 3, 4, or 6)
- 1 tablespoon finely chopped onion (optional)
- 1 dash Classic Hot Pepper Sauce (page 69) or Tabasco sauce
- salt and freshly ground black pepper

Mix the mayonnaise, ketchup, relish, onion (if using), and hot sauce together in a small bowl. Season with salt and pepper.

Pickled Pepper Spinach Salad

Serves 4 to 6

When spring-fresh spinach appears in your garden or local markets, and you haven't yet finished with all your canned goodies, this is a great salad to pull out.

Ingredients

- 8 ounces bocconocini (fresh small mozzarella balls, available at specialty stores or Italian markets) or fresh mozzarella, quartered and sliced
- 1 cup diced Roasted Pickled Peppers (page 110)
- 1 (1-inch) slice red onion, diced, or 2 scallions, white and tender green parts, thinly sliced
- ¼ cup extra-virgin olive oil
- 2 tablespoons pickle juice from jar, or to taste
- salt and freshly ground black pepper
- 9 ounces baby spinach

1   In a large salad bowl, combine the mozzarella, pickled peppers, onion, olive oil, and pickle juice. Season with salt and pepper and toss gently. Taste and add more pickle juice, if needed. Let sit for at least 30 minutes, and up to 3 hours.

2   Add the spinach and toss gently. Serve immediately.

Kitchen Note

If you like, substitute other greens for the spinach. Romaine hearts are particularly good here.

Dilly Mustard Coleslaw

Serves 6 to 8

This is my mother's coleslaw, with some major tweaks. The addition of pickles gives it a certain *je ne sais quoi*. (I usually don't effuse in French over humdrum dishes such as coleslaw, but I really love this salad.) I think it is the perfect accompaniment to barbecue.

Ingredients

- **1 small head green cabbage, shredded (4–6 cups)**
- **2 carrots, grated**
- **¼ cup minced onion**
- **½ cup minced dill pickles (see chapters 2, 3, and 4), or ½ cup drained Dilled Dog Relish (page 152)**
- **1 cup mayonnaise**
- **3 tablespoons yellow ballpark mustard**
- **salt and freshly ground black pepper**

1 In a large bowl, combine the cabbage, carrots, onion, and pickles. Mix well.

2 In a small bowl, combine the mayonnaise and mustard and mix until well combined. Spoon over the cabbage mixture and mix until well combined. Add salt and pepper to taste.

3 Cover and refrigerate for up at least 1 hour, and up to 8 hours, before serving.

Kitchen Note

The standing time is important in this recipe. Give it some time to develop flavor before serving.

Sweet Pickle Macaroni Salad

Serves 6 to 8

Before there was pasta salad, there was macaroni salad. And before there was a global supermarket, there were pickles to spice up bland American cooking. Classic bread and butter pickles make the classic American macaroni salad — a picnic favorite.

Ingredients

1 pound elbow macaroni

1 cup finely chopped Classic Bread and Butters (page 80), Vermont Maple Sweet Pickles (page 82), Keeping the Harvest Bread and Butter Pickles (page 125), or any other sweet pickles (see chapters 3 and 4)

2 celery ribs, chopped

1 carrot, grated

½ small red onion, finely chopped

¾ cup mayonnaise

6 tablespoons pickle juice from jar, plus more to taste

salt and freshly ground black pepper

1 Cook the macaroni in plenty of boiling salted water until thoroughly cooked (the macaroni should be cooked a tad beyond al dente). Drain well, rinse under cold water to cool, and drain well.

2 In a large bowl, mix together the macaroni, pickles, celery, carrot, and onion. Add the mayonnaise and pickle juice and mix until well combined. Add salt (it may not need very much) and lots of black pepper. Taste and adjust the seasoning, adding more pickle juice if desired.

3 Chill for 30 minutes before serving.

Kitchen Notes

- One heaped cup of pickle slices should yield 1 cup chopped.
- Leftovers should be stored in an airtight container in the refrigerator. To brighten the flavor of leftover macaroni salad, add a tablespoon or two of pickle juice from the jar.

Kimchi Rice Salad with Tofu

Serves 4 to 6

This is a ridiculously healthy, beautiful, and delicious main-dish salad: high in protein and fiber, low in fat.

Ingredients

- 1 **pound firm tofu**
- 2 **tablespoons mirin (sweet Japanese rice wine)**
- 2 **tablespoons soy sauce**
- 1 **tablespoon toasted sesame oil**
- 2 **cups cooked brown or white rice**
- 1 **carrot, finely diced**
- 2 **scallions, white and tender green parts, chopped**
- 1 **cup fresh or frozen peas**
- 1½ **cups Kimchi (page 58), Napa Cabbage and Carrot Kimchi (page 60), or Mild Kimchi (page 61)**
- **soy sauce or salt**
- 1 **sheet nori, cut into ribbons about 2 inches long and ⅛ inch wide**

1 Wrap the tofu in a clean kitchen towel or paper towel. Place on a plate or cutting board and weight down with another board or heavy plate with a weight (such as a filled juice can). This will force out excess moisture from the tofu. Leave to drain for about 30 minutes.

2 Dice the drained tofu.

3 Combine the mirin, soy sauce, and sesame oil in a large salad bowl. Add the tofu and let marinate for about 30 minutes.

4 Add the rice, carrot, scallions, peas, and kimchi. Toss well. Taste and add soy sauce or salt, if desired. Serve garnished with shredded nori.

Kitchen Note

Feel free to substitute other vegetables for the ones chosen here.

Tortellini Pasta Salad
with Italian Tomato Relish

Serves 4 to 6

Thanks to the tomato relish, this main-dish salad practically makes itself. The flavors of summer are captured in the relish and perfectly complement the cheese-stuffed pasta.

Ingredients

- 20 ounces fresh or frozen cheese-stuffed tortellini
- 3 tablespoons extra-virgin olive oil
- 1 cup Italian Tomato Relish (page 190)
- ½ cup brined black olives

1 Cook the pasta according to the package directions. Drain and rinse briefly under cold running water.

2 Transfer the pasta to a large bowl and add the olive oil. Toss to coat. Add the tomato relish and olives and toss again. The pasta is best served immediately, but it will hold up for a while on a buffet table.

Kitchen Note

You can vary the flavor by adding a tablespoon or two of capers or a handful of caperberries.

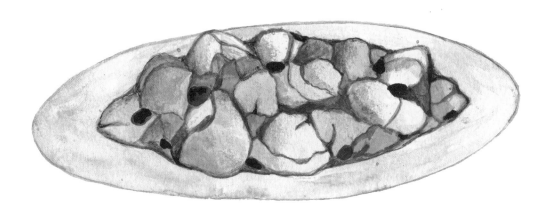

Creamy Dilled Smoked Fish Pasta Salad

Serves 6 to 8

Eating seasonably sometimes means substituting frozen and pickled foods for out-of-season fresh vegetables. And that is where this colorful pasta salad comes in. Made with pink smoked salmon and frozen green peas and yellow corn, this salad is a fiesta in a bowl. Any dill pickle will work, so think beyond the cucumber.

Ingredients

- 1 pound shell pasta
- 2 tablespoons extra-virgin olive oil
- 4 ounces smoked salmon, chopped
- 1 cup frozen peas, defrosted
- 1 cup frozen corn, defrosted
- ½ cup chopped dill pickles (from chapter 2, 3, or 4) or ½ cup drained Dilled Dog Relish (page 152)
- 4 thin slices red onion, chopped
- ¼ cup chopped fresh dill
- ½ cup buttermilk, plus more to taste
- ½ cup sour cream
- ¼ cup pickle juice from jar, plus more to taste
- salt and freshly ground black pepper

1 Cook the pasta in a large pot of boiling salted water until just done. Drain and rinse thoroughly to cool. Put in a large mixing bowl and toss with the olive oil.

2 Add the salmon, peas, corn, pickles, onion, and dill and mix well. Mix together the buttermilk, sour cream, and pickle juice; add to the salad and toss again. Season to taste with salt (it may not need any) and plenty of pepper. If the fish is overwhelmingly smoky, some extra buttermilk will tame the flavor.

Kitchen Note

Buttermilk is an underutilized ingredient. It is rich and creamy, yet low in fat, and makes an excellent base for salad dressing. Additional buttermilk can be drizzled over leftovers to restore the fresh flavor and creamy texture of the salad.

Dilled Potato and Egg Salad

Serves 6 to 8

Winter or summer, it's always time for potato salad to take to potlucks and to accompany cold cuts and casual suppers of hot dogs or hamburgers. Of course, potato salad needs little bits of crunchy vegetables to play against the soft potato/egg/mayonnaise mixture. That's where the crunchy pickle bits come in.

Ingredients

- 2½ **pounds waxy potatoes**
- 3 **hard-cooked eggs, peeled and chopped**
- ½ **small onion, finely chopped or grated**
- 1 **cup finely chopped dill pickles (from chapter 2, 3, or 4), or 1 cup drained Dilled Dog Relish (page 152)**
- 1 **cup finely chopped Spiced Carrot Sticks (page 65) or 1 fresh carrot, grated**
- 1 **cup mayonnaise**
- 1 **tablespoon yellow ballpark mustard**
- **salt and freshly ground black pepper**
- **paprika or dried dill, to garnish**

1 Put the potatoes in a large saucepan and fill with enough cold water to cover the potatoes by 1 inch. Bring to a simmer over medium-high heat and simmer until the potatoes are tender, 15 to 30 minutes, depending on the size of the potatoes. Drain well and let cool.

2 When the potatoes are cool enough to handle, peel and slice them into ½-inch cubes.

3 Combine the potatoes, eggs, onion, pickles, and carrots in a large mixing bowl. Add the mayonnaise and mustard and mix well. Add salt and pepper to taste. How much salt you will need depends on how salty the dill pickles are and whether you are using pickled or fresh carrot. Chill well, for at least 4 hours or overnight. (The flavor of the salad improves after several hours.)

4 Just before serving, taste and adjust the seasoning. Sprinkle paprika on top to garnish.

Kitchen Note

Any dill pickles or pickle relish can be used in this salad, so don't limit yourself to cucumber pickles.

Pickled German Potato Salad

Serves 4 to 6

The pickles add the crunch in this otherwise classic potato salad. Waxy potatoes are necessary because they keep their shape in a salad. It is important not to overcook the potatoes since there isn't a creamy dressing to disguise the appearance of broken-down potatoes.

Ingredients

2½ **pounds waxy potatoes, scrubbed, halved, and sliced ¼ inch thick**

salt

6 **ounces bacon, diced**

1 **shallot, minced**

2 **tablespoons extra-virgin olive oil**

5 **tablespoons white wine vinegar or red wine vinegar**

1 **teaspoon sugar**

1 **cup dill pickles (from chapter 2, 3, or 4), finely chopped, or 1 cup drained Dilled Dog Relish (page 152)**

freshly ground black pepper

1   Cover the potatoes with cold water in a medium saucepan and add about 1 tablespoon salt. Bring to a boil, decrease the heat, and simmer until the potatoes are just tender, 5 to 10 minutes. Reserve ¼ cup of the cooking liquid and drain. Transfer the potatoes to a large mixing bowl and keep warm.

2   Meanwhile, in a large skillet, cook the bacon over medium heat until brown and crisp, about 4 minutes. Remove the bacon with a slotted spoon and transfer to the bowl with the potatoes. Drain off all but 3 tablespoons of the bacon grease.

3   Add the shallot to the skillet and cook until slightly softened, about 3 minutes. Stir in the reserved cooking liquid, oil, vinegar, and sugar. Bring to a boil. Pour the mixture over the potatoes and toss to coat. Add the pickles and salt and pepper to taste. Serve immediately.

SERVING SAUERKRAUT

Before serving sauerkraut, drain it and rinse it if it is too salty for your palate. Do the same before cooking with it and you will then have a vegetable that is perfect for combining with meat, especially smoked or cured meat. If you are looking for vegetarian recipes using sauerkraut, think potatoes. There is a popular Minnesota hotdish (casserole to Easterners) that combines potatoes, cheese, and sauerkraut, topped with green beans. Sauerkraut makes a fine substitute for leeks in a creamy potato soup. And then there is the gold standard: grilled cheese with sauerkraut, with or without Thousand Island dressing (hold the tempeh please!).

Hot German Potato Salad with Sauerkraut

Serves 4 to 6

Sauerkraut and potatoes are a natural combination, as this variation on German potato salad demonstrates.

Ingredients

- 1 **cup Sauerkraut (page 56), drained**
- 2½ **pounds thin-skinned potatoes, scrubbed, halved, and sliced ¼ inch thick**
- **salt**
- 4 **ounces bacon, diced**
- 1 **shallot, minced**
- 2 **tablespoons extra-virgin olive oil**
- 5 **tablespoons cider vinegar, plus more to taste**
- 1 **tablespoon brown sugar**
- **freshly ground black pepper**

1 Taste the sauerkraut and rinse under warm water if it is too salty. Drain well.

2 Cover the potatoes with cold water in a medium saucepan and add about 1 tablespoon salt. Bring to a boil, decrease the heat, and simmer until the potatoes are tender, 5 to 10 minutes. Reserve ¼ cup of the cooking liquid and drain. Transfer the potatoes to a large mixing bowl and keep warm.

3 Meanwhile, in a large skillet, cook the bacon over medium heat until brown and crisp, about 4 minutes. Remove the bacon with a slotted spoon and transfer to the bowl with the potatoes. Drain off all but 3 tablespoons of the bacon drippings.

4 Add the shallot to the skillet and cook until slightly softened, about 3 minutes. Stir in the reserved cooking liquid, oil, cider vinegar, and brown sugar. Bring to a boil. Pour the mixture over the potatoes and toss to coat. Add the sauerkraut and toss to mix. Taste and add more vinegar and salt, if needed (both the bacon and sauerkraut may be salty), and pepper to taste. Serve immediately.

Pickled Onion and Potato Salad

Serves 4

We get into ruts with our potato salads, but many combinations of ingredients make tasty salads. In this version, a French-style potato salad dressed with vinaigrette is given a twist with pickled onions.

Ingredients

1½ **pounds waxy potatoes**

1 **cup Pub-Style Pickled Onions (page 230), finely chopped**

2 **celery stalks, finely chopped**

5 **tablespoons strained pickle juice from jar**

¼ **teaspoon Dijon mustard**

¼ **cup extra-virgin olive oil**

salt and freshly ground black pepper

1 Put the potatoes in a saucepan and fill with enough cold water to cover the potatoes by 1 inch. Bring to a simmer over medium-high heat and simmer until the potatoes are tender, 15 to 30 minutes, depending on the size of the potatoes. Drain well and let cool.

2 When the potatoes are cool enough to handle, peel and slice them into ½-inch cubes.

3 Combine the potatoes, pickled onions, and celery in a large bowl.

4 To make the dressing, whisk together the pickle juice and mustard. Slowly add the oil, whisking until fully incorporated. Pour over the salad and toss gently to coat. Season to taste with salt and pepper.

5 Before serving, check for seasoning and toss again. Serve at room temperature.

Kitchen Notes

- Strain the pickle juice to eliminate the whole spices.
- For a completely different take on the salad, choose a different pickle, such as a bean, cauliflower, or cucumber pickle.

Kimchi Fried Rice

Serves 4

Kimchi bokumbap is the Korean name for this fried rice, which uses kimchi for both the vegetables and the flavoring. The dish can include meat — Spam is a popular choice! — but this version is vegetarian, with eggs supplying the protein. To make it a heartier meal, allow two eggs per serving.

Ingredients

1 tablespoon plus 1 teaspoon peanut or other vegetable oil

2 garlic cloves, minced

1 (1-inch) piece fresh ginger, peeled and minced, or 1-inch stack Pickled Ginger (page 229), minced

2 cups Kimchi (page 58), Napa Cabbage and Carrot Kimchi (page 60), or Mild Kimchi (page 61), chopped

4 large scallions, white and tender green parts, chopped

1 tablespoon sugar

6 cups cooked rice, preferably short-grain white

3 tablespoons soy sauce, or to taste

¼ cup kimchi liquid from jar

salt and freshly ground black pepper

4–8 eggs

toasted sesame oil

chopped fresh cilantro

1 Heat a large wok over high heat. Swirl in 1 tablespoon of the oil and allow it to heat. Add the garlic and ginger and stir-fry until fragrant, about 30 seconds. Add the kimchi, scallions, and sugar and stir-fry until the kimchi becomes a little crisp and browned, about 5 minutes.

2 Add the rice, soy sauce, and kimchi liquid. Stir-fry to thoroughly mix and heat the rice through, about 5 minutes. Season to taste with salt and pepper. Decrease the heat to low to keep the rice warm.

3 In a separate nonstick skillet, heat the remaining 1 teaspoon oil over medium-low heat. Crack each egg and add to the skillet. When the whites are cooked but the yolks are still runny, remove from the heat.

4 To serve, mound the rice in serving bowls. Drizzle each serving with sesame oil and sprinkle with cilantro. Top each serving with an egg (or two) and serve immediately.

Kitchen Notes

- When your kimchi begins to get old and tastes a little funky, it can be cooked to mellow the flavor, as in this dish.
- The eggs can be cooked over easy, if that is your preference. Also, you can beat the eggs, flavor with a little soy and sesame oil, and cook as you would a rolled omelet. Cut the omelet into shreds to serve on top of the rice.

Kimchi Noodle Bowl

Serves 4 to 6

It is hard to imagine a more comforting, more healthful bowl of soup on a cold night. With the kimchi already made, this soup is ready in the time it takes to boil the noodles. YouTube features a number of how-to videos showing how to add kimchi to packaged ramen noodles. Trust me when I say that this soup is way better.

Ingredients

8 cups chicken broth or neutral-tasting vegetable broth

2 tablespoons Chinese rice wine or dry sherry

1 tablespoon soy sauce, or to taste

1 (1-inch) piece fresh ginger, peeled and minced, or 1-inch stack Pickled Ginger (page 229), minced

3 garlic cloves, minced

3 scallions, white and tender green parts, finely chopped

¾ pound Chinese egg noodles, udon noodles, or thin spaghetti

1 pound firm or silken tofu, cubed

4–6 cups chopped Kimchi (page 58), Napa Cabbage and Carrot Kimchi (page 60), or Mild Kimchi (page 61), drained

toasted sesame oil

chopped fresh cilantro

Classic Hot Pepper Sauce (page 69) or Sriracha sauce

1 Combine the broth, rice wine, soy sauce, ginger, garlic, and scallions in a large saucepan. Simmer for 25 minutes.

2 Meanwhile, bring a large pot of salted water to a boil. Add the noodles and cook until just barely tender. Drain well and return the noodles to the pot to keep warm.

3 Add the tofu and kimchi to the broth and simmer for 2 minutes. Taste and add soy sauce as needed. It may not need any, depending on how hot and salty your kimchi tastes.

4 To serve, place a nest of noodles in each bowl. Ladle the soup over the noodles, drizzle with sesame oil, sprinkle with cilantro, and serve hot, passing the hot sauce at the table.

Kitchen Notes

- Much depends on the flavor of the soup after the kimchi has been added. So taste carefully and adjust the seasoning as needed.
- Cilantro is essential for bringing the flavors together.
- Like the previous recipe, this can be made with kimchi that is beginning to show its age.

Pickled Pepper Pasta
with Goat Cheese

Serves 4 to 6

With pickled peppers in the pantry and goat cheese in the fridge, this simple, beautiful dish can be readied in minutes.

Ingredients

- **1 pound rotini or other short pasta**
- **6 ounces soft, fresh goat cheese, crumbled**
- **1 cup sliced Roasted Pickled Peppers (page 110)**
- **2 garlic cloves, minced**
- **¼ cup dry white wine**
- **1 cup frozen peas**
- **salt and freshly ground black pepper**

1 Cook the pasta in plenty of salted boiling water until just al dente. Drain, reserving 1 cup of the pasta cooking water. Return the pasta to the pot.

2 Stir the goat cheese, pickled peppers, garlic, wine, and peas into the pasta. Place the pot over low heat and cook, stirring, until the goat cheese melts and becomes creamy, 1 to 2 minutes.

3 Add enough of the reserved cooking water to make a sauce of a pleasing consistency. Add salt sparingly and pepper generously, and serve as soon as the peas have heated through, 3 to 4 minutes.

Tomato-Mozzarella Tart

Serves 4 as a main course, or 8 to 12 as an appetizer

Between the frozen puff pastry and last summer's Italian
Tomato Relish, this tart is quickly assembled and delicious to eat.

Ingredients

1 (17.3-ounce) box frozen
puff pastry, thawed

1 egg, lightly beaten

1 cup Italian Tomato
Relish (page 190)

8 ounces fresh mozzarella,
thinly sliced

1   Preheat the oven to 400°F. Line a baking sheet with parchment paper.

2   Set the pastry sheets side by side on the baking sheet and pinch together the edges to form a rectangle about 8½ inches by 16 inches. Fold over the edges to form a crust. Prick the pastry with the tines of a fork at ½-inch intervals. Brush the egg over the crust.

3   Bake for 15 minutes, until golden.

4   Spoon the relish over the inside of the tart. Arrange the cheese on top. Return to the oven to bake until the cheese is melted, about 10 minutes.

5   Cut into rectangles and serve hot or at room temperature.

Kitchen Note

If you prefer, substitute crumbled soft, fresh goat cheese for the sliced mozzarella and/or Rosemary Onion Confit (page 170) for the relish.

Zuurkoolstamppot

Serves 4

From Holland comes this classic dish of sauerkraut, **mashed with potatoes and flavored with bacon. In many respects it is similar to the Irish dish colcannon, potatoes mashed with sautéed cabbage.**

Ingredients

2½ **pounds baking or russet potatoes, peeled and cut into large pieces**

2 **garlic cloves (optional)**

salt

6 **ounces high-quality thick-cut bacon, diced**

1 **quart Sauerkraut (page 56), drained**

½ **cup milk**

freshly ground black pepper

1 Put the potatoes and garlic, if using, in a saucepan and cover with water. Salt generously, cover, and bring to a boil over high heat. Decrease the heat and boil gently until completely tender, 15 to 20 minutes.

2 Meanwhile, cook the bacon in a large skillet over medium heat until crisp, about 4 minutes, stirring frequently. Remove the bacon with a slotted spoon and drain on paper towels. Drain off all but 2 tablespoons of the bacon drippings.

3 Add the sauerkraut to the remaining bacon drippings and cook over medium heat until heated through, stirring occasionally, about 5 minutes. Keep warm.

4 When the potatoes are completely tender, drain well. Mash the potatoes with a potato masher, press through a ricer, or whip in a stand mixer until you have a light texture. Beat in the milk. Stir the potatoes into the sauerkraut along with the bacon pieces. Season to taste generously with pepper; it shouldn't need any salt.

5 Transfer to a serving dish and serve hot.

Kitchen Notes

- I always add garlic to my mashed potatoes; it gives them a hint of buttery flavor.
- Traditionally, this "Dutch farmer" dish would be served with a smoked beef sausage known as rookwurst. I think it is fine to serve as a main dish for four, without the sausage, or as side dish for six to eight.

Shrimp Congee

Serves 4

Millions of people in Asia start their day with congee (or jook, as it is also known), so aren't you curious about this velvety rice porridge? It is enjoyed in both sweet and savory versions, and I love it. Top it with any pickled vegetable, including kimchi. This takes a little over 2 hours to cook, but it can be made in advance and reheated; a microwave does the job very handily. Serve it for breakfast, lunch, dinner, or whenever you are in need of a bowl of comfort.

Ingredients

- ¾ cup uncooked short-grain rice
- 2 garlic cloves, minced
- 1 (½-inch) piece fresh ginger, peeled and minced, or ½-inch stack Pickled Ginger (page 229), minced
- ½ pound shrimp, peeled and chopped
- 6 scallions, white and tender green parts, chopped
- soy sauce
- toasted sesame oil
- pickled vegetables, to serve (see Kitchen Notes)

1 Bring 8 cups water to a boil in a tall saucepan. Add the rice, decrease the heat to medium, and simmer, uncovered, for 40 minutes.

2 Stir in the garlic and ginger. Decrease the heat to low, cover, and cook for another 1¼ hours, or until the rice is very thick and creamy. Stir occasionally.

3 Stir in the shrimp and scallions and continue to cook until the shrimp is opaque and pink, about 5 minutes.

4 Serve, passing the soy sauce, sesame oil, and pickled vegetables at the table.

Kitchen Notes

- There are many pickled vegetables that make a fine topping for this dish, including kimchi (pages 58, 60, and 61), Fermented Asian-Style Turnips and Carrots (page 64), Korean-Style Pickled Garlic (page 66), Pickled Mustard Greens (page 68), Ginger-Garlic Freezer Pickles (page 211), Freezer Ginger-Garlic Cabbage Relish (page 217), Chinese Sweet Pickled Daikon (page 222), Gingery Quick Pickled Daikon and Carrot (page 224), Chinese Spicy-Sweet Pickled Daikon and Carrot (page 225), Vietnamese-Style Pickled Daikon and Carrot (page 226), and Soy Sauce Daikon and Carrot Pickles (page 227).

- The shrimp can be omitted or replaced with a different meat or chicken, raw or cooked. If adding raw chopped meat, adjust the timing as needed.

Kimchi Fish Stew

Serves 6

My brother spends a month fishing on Lake Champlain every summer and fills my freezer with delicious freshwater perch. This is one of the dishes I make with my bounty — a delicious bowl of wintertime comfort, which cooks in less than a half hour. Use any firm white fish you can catch or buy.

Ingredients

¼ **pound pork belly or salt pork, diced**

1½ **pounds firm white fish, cut into a few pieces if large**

2 **cups Kimchi (page 58), Napa Cabbage and Carrot Kimchi (page 60), or Mild Kimchi (page 61)**

1 **cup chicken broth**

2 **tablespoons Chinese rice wine or dry sherry**

1 **tablespoon soy sauce, or to taste**

8 **ounces firm tofu, cubed**

2 **cups bean sprouts, rinsed and drained**

4 **large scallions, white and tender green parts, chopped**

hot cooked white rice

Classic Hot Pepper Sauce (page 69) or Sriracha sauce

1 Brown the pork in a large saucepan over medium heat until the pork renders its fat and becomes crisp, about 8 minutes. Remove the pork with a slotted spoon and set aside on paper towels to drain.

2 Add the fish to the saucepan and sauté for 2 minutes, until all the pieces are coated in the fat. Add the kimchi, broth, rice wine, and soy sauce and simmer for 10 minutes, until the fish is cooked and the kimchi is heated through. Stir in the pork, tofu, bean sprouts, and scallions and cook until the bean sprouts wilt, 1 to 2 minutes.

3 Serve hot over rice, passing the hot sauce at the table.

Kitchen Note

You can use older, strongly flavored kimchi for this dish.

Fish Tacos

Serves 6

Fish tacos were invented in the summery climes of Southern California, but the idea can be adapted to the winter kitchen. For the topping, use either a Tex-Mex-inspired chili corn relish or a Salvadoran pickled cabbage relish, and cook the fish in a skillet rather than on the grill. The sour cream sauce defines the fish taco, in my opinion, and should not be omitted. Fresh corn tortillas are the preferred wrap, but flour wrappers do fine, especially where good fresh corn tortillas aren't available.

Ingredients

FISH AND MARINADE

3 tablespoons extra-virgin olive oil

2 tablespoons fresh lime juice

1½ pounds fresh mahimahi or other white fish fillet

SOUR CREAM SAUCE

1 cup sour cream

½ cup mayonnaise

2 tablespoons fresh lime juice

1 teaspoon (packed) finely grated lime zest

pinch of salt

dash of Classic Hot Pepper Sauce (page 69) or other red hot pepper sauce

TORTILLAS AND GARNISHES

18 small flour or corn tortillas

Chili Corn Relish (page 165), Curtido (page 62), Curtido with Cilantro (page 63), or Quick Curtido (page 213), at room temperature

Simple Salsa (page 185), Tomatillo Salsa (page 180), or Chipotle Salsa (page 186), at room temperature

1 To prepare the fish, combine the oil and lime juice in a large shallow glass baking dish. Add the fish and turn to coat in the marinade. Set aside and let marinate for 15 minutes.

2 To prepare the sour cream sauce, combine all the ingredients in a small bowl and stir until well combined. Set aside.

3 Preheat a large heavy skillet over medium-high heat. Remove the fish from the marinade and place in the hot pan, skin side down. Cook the fish for 4 minutes on the first side and then flip and drizzle with the marinade. Cook on the second side for 3 to 5 minutes, depending on the thickness of the fish. Let rest for a few minutes, then flake the fish with a fork.

4 To warm the tortillas, stack them between damp paper towels and microwave for about 60 seconds.

5 Serve the warm tortillas, fish, sour cream sauce, corn relish, and salsa in separate bowls and allow the diners to assemble their own tacos.

Cranberry Chicken Salad

Serves 4 to 6

Chicken noodle soup is my go-to recipe for curing whatever ails me, my friends, or my family. After making the stock and setting aside a couple of cups of chicken, I am inevitably left with additional chicken, much of which ends up as chicken salad. With the Savory Cranberry-Apple Relish on hand, this chicken salad is anything but boring — sweet, crunchy, tangy, delicious.

Ingredients

- 2 **cups cooked chopped chicken or turkey**
- 2 **celery stalks, finely chopped**
- 1 **carrot, shredded**
- ½ **cup mayonnaise**
- ½ **cup Savory Cranberry-Apple Relish (page 166)**
- **salt and freshly ground black pepper**

Combine the chicken, celery, carrot, mayonnaise, and relish in a medium bowl and mix well. Season with salt and black pepper and serve.

Kitchen Notes

- The chicken salad may not need any salt, but be generous with the pepper.
- For a change of pace, substitute any fruit chutney (see chapter 5) for the cranberry relish.

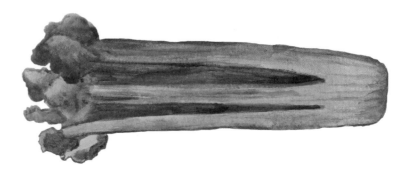

Pulled Chicken Barbecue

Serves 4 to 6

With homemade barbecue sauce already in the pantry, this dish couldn't be simpler to make. Slowly bake the chicken in the sauce until it is fork-tender and deeply infused with barbecue flavor. While the chicken bakes, you are free to be busy elsewhere. Serve with sandwich buns, coleslaw, pickles, potato chips, and plenty of napkins. Cold beer and lemonade wouldn't go amiss.

Ingredients

- **10 bone-in chicken thighs, skin and excess fat removed**
- **2 cups Barbecue Sauce (page 187)**
- **8–12 sandwich buns**
- **Dilled Dog Relish (page 152)**
- **Dilly Mustard Coleslaw (page 250)**

1 Preheat the oven to 300°F.

2 Arrange the chicken in a single layer in a 9- by 13-inch glass or ceramic baking dish. Pour the barbecue sauce over the chicken. Cover the baking dish with aluminum foil.

3 Bake for about 2½ hours, until the chicken is fork-tender and pulls apart easily. Remove from the oven and let cool slightly.

4 When the chicken is cool enough to handle, pull the meat off the bones and put it in a saucepan. Pour the cooking sauce from the baking dish into a tall container to allow the fat to rise to the surface. Skim off the fat and pour the remaining liquid over the chicken.

5 Reheat the chicken over low heat, stirring frequently. The chicken will break apart into shreds.

6 Serve hot, spooned over the buns and topped with the pickle relish. Serve with coleslaw.

Kitchen Notes

- If you prefer, omit the pickle relish and top the buns with coleslaw.
- This is a perfect dish for making ahead. You can bake the chicken, let cool, then refrigerate the chicken and juices separately. When you are ready to serve, skim off the fat from the juices and pour into a saucepan. Remove the chicken from the bones. Reheat over low heat, stirring occasionally.
- If you don't have time to refrigerate the juices, use a gravy separator. Pour the cooking liquids into the gravy separator and pour off the juices, leaving behind the fat.

Kimchi Chicken Stir-Fry

Serves 4

I worked my way through college, part of the time doing prep work at a Chinese restaurant run by a nuclear physicist whose post-doc had ended. His cooking was fantastic, and I learned a great deal from him. This dish is my own invention, but it leans heavily on the lessons learned on my first cooking job.

Ingredients

CHICKEN AND MARINADE

- 1 pound boneless skinless chicken thighs, cut into matchsticks
- 4 garlic cloves, minced
- 1 (1-inch) piece fresh ginger, peeled and minced, or 1-inch stack Pickled Ginger (page 229), minced
- 2 tablespoons Chinese rice wine or dry sherry
- 2 tablespoons soy sauce
- 2 teaspoons toasted sesame oil
- 1 tablespoon sugar

STIR-FRY

- 2 tablespoons peanut or other vegetable oil
- 2 cups Kimchi (page 58), Napa Cabbage and Carrot Kimchi (page 60), or Mild Kimchi (page 61)
- 1 cup bean sprouts, rinsed and drained
- 4 large scallions, white and tender green parts, sliced
- ½ cup roasted salted cashews or peanuts
- hot cooked white rice

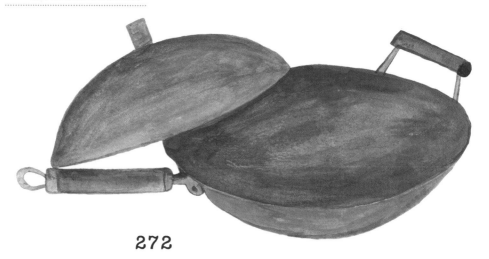

1 To prepare the chicken, combine the chicken, garlic, ginger, rice wine, soy sauce, sesame oil, and sugar in a medium bowl. Set aside to marinate for about 30 minutes.

2 Heat a large wok over high heat. Add 1 tablespoon of the peanut oil and swirl to coat the sides of the pan. Add the chicken and marinade and stir-fry for 4 to 6 minutes, until the chicken pieces are cooked through. Use a heatproof rubber spatula to scrape the chicken and sauce out of the wok into a medium bowl and keep warm.

3 Heat the remaining 1 tablespoon oil in the wok over high heat. Add the kimchi and stir-fry until the kimchi has crisped slightly and heated through, 3 to 4 minutes. Add the bean sprouts and scallions and stir-fry for 1 minute.

4 Return the chicken to the wok, add the cashews, and stir-fry for 1 minute to heat through.

5 Serve hot over the rice.

Kitchen Notes

- Whenever you cook with kimchi, you might want to open all your windows and run the exhaust fan on high. Airborne kimchi can be pretty irritating to the lungs.
- This is a good recipe to use with aging kimchi.

Roasted and Braised Duck
with Sauerkraut and Root Vegetables

Serves 4

This recipe is reason enough for making sauerkraut, which cuts the rich flavor of the duck meat. It appears in my book *Recipes from the Root Cellar*, and is too good not to repeat. The duck meat remains moist while still producing crisp skin and imbuing the vegetables with great flavor.

Ingredients

- 1 **duck (4–5 pounds)**
- **salt and freshly ground black pepper**
- 3 **potatoes, peeled and cubed**
- 3–4 **cups peeled and cubed root vegetables (carrots, celery root, parsnips, rutabagas, and/or turnips)**
- 4 **shallots, peeled and halved**
- 1 **quart Sauerkraut (page 56), rinsed and drained**
- ½ **cup dry white wine**
- 2 **bay leaves**

1 Preheat the oven to 375°F.

2 Place the duck in a large roasting pan. Prick the duck all over with a fork (very important) and sprinkle it with salt and pepper. Roast for 45 minutes.

3 Scatter the potatoes, root vegetables, and shallots around the duck. Turn the potatoes and vegetables so they are well coated with the rendered duck fat. Roast for another 45 minutes, checking occasionally to make sure the duck is browning. (If the duck is barely browning, increase the heat by 50 degrees; if it seems to be browning too quickly, decrease the heat slightly.)

4 Decrease the oven temperature to 300°F. Pour off all but a few tablespoons of the fat from the roasting pan (reserve for your next batch of roasted root vegetables). Scatter the sauerkraut around the duck, moisten it with the wine, and tuck the bay leaves in. Roast for another 30 minutes, until the duck is tender.

5 Let the duck rest, loosely covered with aluminum foil, for 10 minutes. Carve and serve with the sauerkraut and vegetables.

Spice-Crusted Pork Tenderloin with Chutney

Serves 6

This tasty, moist pork requires no pan sauce. Any chutney can be used here. I particularly like the Sweet-Tart Rhubarb Chutney on page 177.

Ingredients

- 2 teaspoons salt
- 1 teaspoon Chinese five-spice powder
- ½ teaspoon freshly ground black pepper
- ½ teaspoon ground allspice
- 2 garlic cloves, minced
- 2 (¾–1¼-pound) pork tenderloins, trimmed of silverskin and fat
- 1 tablespoon olive or canola oil
- 1 cup any chutney from chapter 5

1 Preheat the oven to 425°F.

2 Combine the salt, five-spice powder, pepper, allspice, and garlic in a small bowl. Rub all over the surface of the pork.

3 Heat the oil in a large ovenproof skillet over medium-high heat. Add the tenderloins and brown all over, 8 to 10 minutes. Spoon about one-third of the chutney over the meat.

4 Transfer to the oven and roast, basting with another one-third of the chutney, for 30 to 35 minutes, until the meat registers 150° to 155°F on an instant-read thermometer.

5 Let the meat stand, loosely covered with aluminum foil, for about 10 minutes. Carve the meat into slices about ½ inch thick and serve with the remaining chutney.

Szechuan Green Beans

Serves 4 to 6

Pickled Mustard Greens (page 68) replaces the traditional Tian-jian preserved greens in this recipe. It is a delicious way to enjoy green beans. All of the Chinese ingredients, except the Szechuan peppercorns, which are optional, can be found at a well-stocked supermarket. You'll need a large wok for this recipe. If you don't have a large wok, consider roasting the green beans instead of stir-frying (see Kitchen Notes, page 277). You could also deep-fry the green beans, as is traditional, but I do not see any advantage to frying over roasting.

Ingredients

MEAT AND MARINADE

½ pound ground pork

2 tablespoons soy sauce

1 tablespoon black bean sauce

1 tablespoon Chinese rice wine or dry sherry

1 tablespoon sugar

2 teaspoons Chinese chili paste with garlic

2 teaspoons toasted sesame oil

1 (½-inch) piece fresh ginger, peeled and minced, or ½-inch stack Pickled Ginger (page 229), minced

2 garlic cloves, minced

SAUCE

2 tablespoons soy sauce

1 tablespoon rice wine or sherry

1 tablespoon water

1 teaspoon sugar

TO FINISH

2 tablespoons peanut or other vegetable oil

2 pounds green beans, trimmed

½ cup well-drained Pickled Mustard Greens (page 68), finely chopped

1 teaspoon Szechuan peppercorns (optional)

hot cooked rice

1   To prepare the meat, combine the pork, soy sauce, black bean sauce, rice wine, sugar, chili paste, sesame oil, ginger, and garlic in a medium bowl. Mix well and set aside to marinate.

2   To make the sauce, in a small bowl, combine the soy sauce, rice wine, water, and sugar. Set aside.

3   To finish the dish, heat 1 tablespoon of the oil in a large wok over high heat. Add the pork and marinade and stir-fry until the meat browns, about 5 minutes. Using a heatproof rubber spatula, transfer the meat and juices to a clean bowl, scraping the wok clean.

4   Heat the remaining 1 tablespoon oil in the wok over high heat. Add the green beans and stir-fry until tender, 6 to 8 minutes.

5   Add the meat and marinade, sauce mixture, pickled mustard greens, and Szechuan peppercorns to the wok and stir everything together to coat the green beans with the sauce. Stir-fry for 1 minute to allow the flavors to blend. Serve hot over rice.

Kitchen Notes

- If you don't have a large wok, roast the beans. Preheat the oven to 450°F. Oil a large sheet pan. Toss the green beans with 2 tablespoons peanut or other vegetable oil. Arrange the beans in a single layer on the sheet pan. Roast on the bottom rack of the oven for 10 minutes, shaking the pan occasionally for even cooking. Cook the meat in a large skillet. Add the roasted green beans to the meat in the skillet, along with the sauce, pickled mustard greens, and Szechuan peppercorns.
- To make a good stir-fry, you really need a large wok and a high flame. For this recipe, be sure you have your kitchen exhaust fan running on high.

Pork Chops with Red Cabbage and Apple Relish

Serves 4

Smothering the pork chops in the relish while they finish cooking ensures that the meat remains moist. This is a very quick, very easy supper dish. Serve with mashed potatoes and a good German rye bread.

Ingredients

- **4 ounces thick-cut bacon, chopped**
- **1 onion, sliced**
- **4 (1-inch-thick) bone-in pork chops**
- **salt and freshly ground black pepper**
- **1 quart Red Cabbage and Apple Relish (page 162)**

1 Put the bacon in a large skillet over medium heat. When the bacon has given up some of its fat, add the onion. Cook, stirring, until the bacon is crisp and the onion tender, about 8 minutes. Remove the bacon and onion with a slotted spoon. Pour off all but a light coating of fat.

2 Meanwhile, pat dry the chops. Sprinkle both sides with salt and pepper. Return the skillet with the bacon fat to high heat and add the chops.

3 Cook the chops for 5 to 6 minutes on one side, until well browned. Turn the chops over and dump the jar of relish over them, distributing the relish so it smothers each chop. Cook on the second side for another 5 to 6 minutes, until the chops are well browned and the relish is heated through.

4 Transfer the chops to a heated platter and serve.

Kitchen Note

Try this recipe with chicken or turkey cutlets instead of pork.

Roast Pork with Sauerkraut

Serves 6

This classic delivers a flavorful, moist pork roast and plenty of yummy sauerkraut and vegetables. Serve with mashed potatoes.

Ingredients

- 8 cups Sauerkraut (page 56), drained
- 3 carrots, thickly sliced
- 2 apples, peeled, cored, and thickly sliced
- 1 large onion, halved and sliced
- 1 teaspoon crushed rosemary
- 1 tablespoon canola oil
- 1 (3- to 5-pound) bone-in pork loin roast
- 1 cup chicken broth
- freshly ground black pepper

1 Preheat the oven to 325°F.

2 Mix together the sauerkraut, carrots, apples, onion, and rosemary in a large roasting pan. Make a well in the center.

3 Heat the oil in a large skillet over medium-high heat. Add the pork and brown on all sides, about 15 minutes. Remove the pork and set in the large roasting pan so it is surrounded by the sauerkraut mixture.

4 Pour off all the fat from the skillet and discard. Place the skillet over medium heat, add the broth, and deglaze, scraping up any browned bits. Pour over the sauerkraut. Season generously with pepper. Tightly cover the pan with aluminum foil.

5 Roast for about 2 hours, until the roast registers 145° to 150°F on an instant-read thermometer.

6 Remove the meat to a warm platter and let rest for 15 minutes. Keep the sauerkraut mixture warm. Carve the meat and serve with the sauerkraut.

Kitchen Note

If the sauerkraut tastes too salty, rinse it under warm tap water before using.

Oven-Baked Barbecued Ribs

Serves 4

When your pantry is stocked with barbecue sauce, but the weather is too cold for grilling outdoors, consider oven-baked ribs. The smoked spices in the dry rub give a whisper of smoke flavor to the meat, and the sauce brings all the flavors together.

Ingredients

¼ cup firmly packed brown sugar

2 tablespoons chili powder

2 tablespoons minced garlic

2 tablespoons pimentón (smoked paprika)

2 tablespoons pickling or fine sea salt

1 tablespoon ground cumin

1 teaspoon ground chipotle

1 teaspoon dried oregano

1 teaspoon freshly ground black pepper

2 (2½- to 3-pound) slabs of spareribs or 3 (1–1½-pound) slabs baby back ribs

2 cups Barbecue Sauce (page 187)

1   Combine the brown sugar, chili powder, garlic, pimentón, salt, cumin, chipotle, oregano, and pepper in a small bowl and mix well. Rub the spice mixture all over both sides of the ribs. Place the ribs in a baking dish and refrigerate them overnight, loosely covered. If you haven't planned ahead, let the rubbed ribs sit for 1 hour before cooking.

2   Preheat the oven to 275°F. Lay out two overlapping lengths of heavy-duty aluminum foil for each rack. Each length of foil should be approximately twice the length of the racks to allow you to roll up the foil and seal it. Lay the ribs meat side up on the foil. Fold up the foil and seal completely. Place on baking sheets.

3   Bake for 2½ hours. Remove the ribs from the oven and increase the oven temperature to 450°F.

4   Carefully open the foil packages; there will be lots of steam. Let the ribs cool slightly, then drain the juices and reserve. Set the ribs in a large baking pan. If you want to reduce cleanup, line the baking pan with aluminum foil first. Skim the fat from the top of the drained juices and combine the juices with the barbecue sauce. Pour about half the sauce over the ribs.

5   Return the ribs to the oven and bake until the sauce is caramelized, about 30 minutes. Pour the remaining sauce over the ribs and serve immediately.

Kitchen Note

If you like spice, use more ground chipotle and less chili powder. Pimentón is smoked paprika; it adds smoke without heat. If you don't have any pimentón, you can omit it, but the dish will lack the flavor of smoke unless you go heavy with the ground chipotle.

Choucroute Garnie

Serves 6

French and German cuisine mingle in Alsace, where choucroute garnie developed as a perfect example of winter peasant food, complexly flavored and deeply satisfying. It is made of sauerkraut braised in white wine and served with an assortment of sausages and pork. Boiled potatoes and strong mustard accompany the dish. The dish is served in restaurants and bistros throughout France. We can't necessarily find the "classic" sausages here, but the dish is perfect with almost any sausage you might think to use. A slightly fruity Riesling is a good choice for the wine, but any white wine will work. Serve with lots of good bread, preferably French or German rye.

Ingredients

4	ounces salt pork or bacon, diced
2	onions, halved and sliced
2–3	carrots, cut into 1-inch chunks
1	large garlic clove, minced
10	cups Sauerkraut (page 56), rinsed and drained
1½	cups chicken broth
1	cup white wine
1	bay leaf
6	whole peppercorns
8	juniper berries
1½	pounds assorted smoked and fully cooked sausages
1	pound smoked boneless pork loin (Canadian bacon) or smoked boneless pork chops, cut into 6 slices
	salt and freshly ground black pepper
6	thin-skinned potatoes, peeled (optional) and quartered
	Homemade Mustard (page 169) or Dijon mustard, smooth or coarse-grained

282

1 Preheat the oven to 325°F.

2 Cook the bacon in a large Dutch oven over medium heat until lightly browned, about 7 minutes. Remove with a slotted spoon and set aside. Add the onions and carrots and sauté until soft, about 3 minutes. Stir in the garlic and sauté for 1 minute. Add the cooked bacon, sauerkraut, broth, white wine, bay leaf, peppercorns, and juniper berries. Bring to a simmer and cover.

3 Bake in the oven for 1 hour.

4 Add the sausages and pork, tossing the mixture to bury the meat in the sauerkraut. Taste the sauerkraut and add salt and pepper if needed. Cover, return to the oven, and bake for another 30 minutes.

5 Meanwhile, put the potatoes in a medium saucepan, cover with salted water, and bring to a boil. Decrease the heat and simmer for 15 to 20 minutes, until the potatoes are just tender. Drain the potatoes and add to the Dutch oven.

6 Serve the choucroute directly from the Dutch oven, or arrange it on a platter, the sauerkraut on the bottom and the meats on top and the potatoes around. Serve the mustard on the side.

Kitchen Notes

- Before cooking, rinse the sauerkraut until it no longer tastes salty.
- To stretch this to serve a bigger crowd, add more potatoes.

Korean Bulgogi Tacos with Kimchi

Serves 4 to 6

The Korean taco truck was born in L.A. as a felicitous combination of Korean and Mexican cuisine. The combinations of ingredients are seemingly infinite, and there are no rules. This taco is filled with Korean barbecued beef (*bulgogi* literally means fire meat) plus kimchi. If you like, you can make a more traditional Mexican or Tex-Mex meat and top it with kimchi. Figure out pleasing combinations for your kimchi and have at it. Summer barbecues will never be the same.

Ingredients

½ cup soy sauce

¼ cup Chinese rice wine or dry sherry

¼ cup honey

1 tablespoon Korean chili paste, sambal oelek (Indonesian chili paste), or Chinese chili paste with garlic

2 teaspoons toasted sesame oil

3 garlic cloves, minced

1 (1-inch) piece fresh ginger, peeled and minced, or 1-inch stack Pickled Ginger (page 229), minced

1½ pounds boneless beef short ribs, sliced about ½ inch thick

TO SERVE

12 soft corn tortillas

about 3 cups Kimchi (page 58), Napa Cabbage and Carrot Kimchi (page 60), or Mild Kimchi (page 61), drained

4 scallions, white and tender green parts, chopped

chopped fresh cilantro

lime wedges

Classic Hot Pepper Sauce (page 69) or Sriracha sauce

1   Combine the soy sauce, rice wine, honey, chili paste, sesame oil, garlic, and ginger in a shallow bowl or large zippered plastic bag. Mix well, add the beef, and toss gently to coat. Marinate for at least 4 hours, and up to 8 hours, in the refrigerator.

2   Wrap the tortillas in aluminum foil.

3   Prepare a medium-hot fire in a gas or charcoal grill. Lift the meat out of the marinade and place on the grill. Place the wrapped tortillas on the side of the grill, away from the direct heat. Cover the grill and cook the meat for about 2 minutes, until browned and grill-marked. Turn the meat over, replace the cover, and grill for 1 minute on the second side for rare meat. Remove the meat from the grill and place on a cutting board.

4   Slice the beef into short strips. Serve with the tortillas, kimchi, scallions, cilantro, lime, and hot sauce. Let the diners assemble their own tacos.

Kitchen Notes

- My ideal taco: First the meat, then the kimchi. Top with a sprinkle of scallion and chopped cilantro. Squeeze lime juice over. "It makes my mouth happy," said one of my guests.
- Be sure to drain the kimchi, otherwise it will make a soggy taco.
- If you can't wrap your mind around a Korean taco, serve the filling wrapped in lettuce leaves. It's a winner any way you do it.

German Chocolate Sauerkraut Cake

Serves 12 to 15

Coconut and sauerkraut mingle in the cake, fooling the tongue with their identical texture. No one will suspect sauerkraut.

Ingredients

CAKE

- 1 cup drained Sauerkraut (page 56)
- 2 cups unbleached all-purpose flour
- 2 cups sugar
- 1½ teaspoons baking soda
- ¼ teaspoon salt
- 1 cup brewed coffee
- ¾ cup (1½ sticks) unsalted butter
- 4 ounces unsweetened chocolate, cut into small pieces
- ¾ cup sour cream
- 4 eggs
- 1 teaspoon vanilla extract
- 1 cup lightly packed flaked sweetened coconut

COCONUT PECAN FROSTING

- 3 large egg yolks
- 1 cup evaporated milk
- ¾ cup firmly packed brown sugar
- ½ cup (1 stick) butter
- 1 teaspoon vanilla extract
- 1¼ cups lightly packed flaked sweetened coconut
- 1 cup chopped pecans

1   Preheat the oven to 350°F. Lightly grease a 9- by 13-inch baking pan.

2   Put the sauerkraut in a large bowl, cover with cold water, and let sit for a few minutes. Taste. If it is still salty and sour, change the water and repeat until the flavor has almost disappeared. Drain well. If necessary, chop the sauerkraut until it has the same size shreds as the coconut.

3   Stir together the flour, sugar, baking soda, and salt in a large mixing bowl.

4   Combine the coffee, butter, and chocolate in a saucepan over low heat. Stir occasionally until the butter and chocolate have melted. Remove from the heat.

5   Beat together the sour cream, eggs, and vanilla.

6   Make a well in the center of the flour mixture. Pour in the coffee mixture and sour cream mixture and whisk everything together until combined and smooth. Fold in the sauerkraut and coconut. Transfer the batter into the prepared pan.

7   Bake for about 50 minutes, until a cake tester inserted in the center of the cake comes out clean. Cool on a wire rack.

8   To make the frosting, in a heavy-bottomed saucepan, lightly beat the egg yolks with a wire whisk. Add the evaporated milk, brown sugar, and butter. Cook over low heat, stirring, until the mixture thickens, 8 to 10 minutes. Do not boil.

9   Remove the saucepan from the heat. Stir in the vanilla. Cool, stirring frequently. Add the coconut and pecans and beat until the frosting is of spreading consistency.

10 Frost the cake.

Kitchen Note

This cake is so moist and delicious, it doesn't really need the frosting. To dress up an unfrosted cake, sprinkle with confectioners' sugar and a little toasted coconut.

Peanut Butter-Chocolate Chip Sauerkraut Cake

Serves 12 to 15

A giant Reese's peanut butter cup, with the unexpected ingredient of sauerkraut, this cake has layers of irony baked into it. Bottom line? It tastes great. The cake is a great way to finish off that last cup in a quart jar of kraut that has been lingering in the refrigerator.

Ingredients

CAKE

- 1 cup Sauerkraut (page 56), well drained
- 2 cups all-purpose flour
- 1 tablespoon baking powder
- 1 teaspoon baking soda
- 1 teaspoon pickling or fine sea salt
- ¼ teaspoon ground cinnamon
- ½ cup butter, at room temperature
- ½ cup natural peanut butter
- 1¼ cups firmly packed brown sugar
- 4 eggs
- 1 teaspoon vanilla extract
- ½ cup mini chocolate chips, plus more for sprinkling on top

FUDGE FROSTING AND TOPPINGS

- 4 ounces dark chocolate
- ¼ cup (½ stick) butter
- 4 cups (1 pound) confectioners' sugar, sifted
- ½ cup milk, or more as needed
- 1 teaspoon vanilla extract
- ⅛ teaspoon pickling or fine sea salt
- 1 cup mini chocolate chips (optional)
- 1 cup chopped roasted salted peanuts (optional)

1. Preheat the oven to 350°F. Grease a 9- by 13-inch baking dish.

2. To wash the sauerkraut, put it in a large bowl, cover with cold water, and let it sit for a few minutes. Then taste. If it is still salty and sour, change the water and repeat. Drain and finely chop.

3. Sift together the flour, baking powder, baking soda, salt, and cinnamon.

4. Combine the butter, peanut butter, and brown sugar in the bowl of a stand mixer. Beat until light and fluffy. Add the eggs, one at a time, beating well after each addition. Beat in the vanilla. Add the flour mixture and beat until well blended. Fold in the sauerkraut and chocolate chips. Spread the batter in the prepared baking dish.

5. Bake for about 35 minutes, or until a wooden toothpick inserted in the center comes out clean. Cool completely before frosting.

6. To make the frosting, combine the chocolate and butter in a small saucepan. Melt over very low heat, stirring constantly.

7. Combine the confectioners' sugar, milk, vanilla, and salt in a mixing bowl. Beat until well combined. Add the chocolate mixture and beat until smooth. If the frosting is too thick to spread, thin with a little more milk added a teaspoon at a time. If the frosting is too thin, allow it to stand for a few minutes, stirring occasionally. Once it is the right consistency, work quickly because the frosting becomes hard upon standing. Frost the cake. If you like, sprinkle with the mini chocolate chips and peanuts.

Kitchen Note

Since Reese's cups are pretty salty, and I like the salty-sweet flavor combination, I use salted peanut butter, but you can use whichever one you normally stock.

Acknowledgments

Many people go into the making of a cookbook — editors, designers, sales people, publicists, illustrators — and my thanks go to all. But that's just the beginning.

This book is special to me because it is based on my very first cookbook. Many years ago, I was working as a cookbook editor for Garden Way Publishing, and I was looking for an author to write a book on making pickles. I couldn't find anyone to take on the project, so I was given permission to write it myself. Many friends and Garden Way authors contributed to that project, and many of their recipes remain in this edition. My thanks go to all those who worked on that first book.

In the intervening years I have written many more cookbooks, always with the support of friends and family, who have tested recipes and tasted recipes, who have walked with me to keep my spirits up and listened to my woes when recipes went awry. I thank them all, especially Alison Joseph.

To the farmers and gardeners who have kept me supplied with fresh vegetables and fruit when my own garden wasn't enough: my sincere gratitude.

Finally, my thanks go to my son, Sam Chesman, who was always willing to lend an ear. We spent hours together — in the garden and in the kitchen — talking cucumbers and pickles, vinegars and seasonings, salt and spice. His enthusiasm for pickling kept me going, even when things went a little sour.

Index

Other Storey Titles You Will Enjoy

. . . .

By the same author

Recipes from the Root Cellar, by Andrea Chesman.

A collection of more than 250 recipes for winter kitchen produce — jewel-toned root vegetables, hardy greens, sweet winter squashes, and potatoes of every kind.
400 pages. Paper. ISBN 978-1-60342-545-2.

Serving Up the Harvest, by Andrea Chesman.

A collection of 175 recipes to bring out the best in garden-fresh vegetables, with 14 master recipes that can accommodate whatever happens to be in your produce basket.
512 pages. Paper. ISBN 978-1-58017-663-7.

. . . .

The Beginner's Guide to Preserving Food at Home, by Janet Chadwick.

The best and quickest methods for preserving every common vegetable and fruit, with easy instructions to encourage even first-timers.
240 pages. Paper. ISBN 978-1-60342-145-4.

Fix, Freeze, Feast, by Kati Neville and Lindsay Tkacsik.

Great recipes that start with a warehouse club tray pack of meat and end with a freezer full of delicious meals, ready for thawing anytime.
256 pages. Paper. ISBN 978-1-60342-726-5.

Put 'em Up, by Sherri Brooks Vinton.

A comprehensive guide to creative preserving: bright flavors, flexible batch sizes, modern methods.
304 pages. Paper. ISBN 978-1-60342-546-9.

Root Cellaring, by Mike and Nancy Bubel.

Suitable for city and country folks, with information on harvesting and creating cold storage anywhere — even closets! — plus 50 recipes.
320 pages. Paper. ISBN 978-0-88266-703-4.

. . . .

These and other books from Storey Publishing are available
wherever quality books are sold or by calling 1-800-441-5700.
Visit us at www.storey.com.